JENNIFER BARCLAY

An Octopus in my Ouzo

*Loving Life on a
Greek Island*

summersdale

'But isn't it a bit dull at times?'
the Mole ventured to ask.

Kenneth Grahame, *The Wind in the Willows*

To go among the Greeks you
must be just a little mad.

Gwendolyn MacEwen, *Mermaids
and Ikons: A Greek Summer*

About the Author

Jennifer Barclay grew up in the north of England in a village on the edge of the Pennines; she left for Greece after university, lived in Canada and France and the south coast of England before moving to a Greek island. She works with books as an editor and agent and writes occasionally for newspapers and magazines. She has previously written *Meeting Mr Kim* and *Falling in Honey*, and her blog about daily life is at: **www.octopus-in-my-ouzo.blogspot.com**.

Note

It's difficult to find a perfect system of spelling Greek words in English letters, but in general I've spelled words pretty much as they sound, except where it would look too unusual. So for example, Yorgos, because that's how it's pronounced, not Georgos.

Male Greek names usually end in -s when they are the subject of a sentence (Yiannis) but drop the -s when you are addressing the person (Yianni!) or they are the object of the sentence (talking about Yianni). For simplicity, when I'm writing in English, I've used the -s form throughout, except in speech. I have added an 'h' to the endings of some words just to make it clear that the final syllable should be pronounced.

Contents

Prologue

Not so very long ago, I fell in love with a tiny Greek island. I had often dreamed about Greek islands, and wanted to see if I could find a way to live there – and I did. It was a bumpy journey but I ended up in a little house surrounded by fields and mountains and sea, next door to a place called the Honey Factory. I had my dream life. This book is about what happened when I started to live the dream.

It is tricky to write about your neighbours on an island that's a few miles long by a few miles wide. I don't want to get into trouble or cause people problems. Let's say that some of the details are made up and some of them are true, and you can judge for yourself. In my previous book, *Falling in Honey*, I changed the name of my friend Dimitris to Manolis and a few details of his life for privacy's sake, but he later said he wished I'd used his real name. So here, he's Dimitris.

Various anecdotes have appeared in different form on my blog, which I named An Octopus in my Ouzo because it sounded funny and Greek. This is a book about breaking the normal rules of life, and muddling along in a culture you half-understand. Putting an octopus in ouzo would be taking that to a colourful extreme, and I'm not necessarily endorsing the practice (unless the octopus so chooses) any more than I would recommend falling in honey.

I've tried to give a taste of the people, the culture and the flavours of a Mediterranean island all year round. This book is also about what it was like for me to reach out for everything I wanted. It's about real life, and really living. And how I began to learn to live small and think big.

Escape with me to the sun and the heat, light and colour, hills scented with herbs, the blue seas and blue skies of a wild island in the South Aegean.

Chapter 1

A Place Unlike
Anywhere Else

The midsummer sun seeps into the stone walls of my little house over the course of the day. The house looks grand from across the valley, but half of it is unfinished. The part I live in is one tall room with a wooden platform for the upstairs. When I arrived two months ago in April the nights were cool, but now in late June the bedroom is stifling. I move downstairs, where the window at the back of the house catches a breeze across fields from the Skafi valley, and another window faces the village clinging to the middle and lower reaches of the mountain. Lying on the couch, I fall asleep looking at the lights of the village and the stars above.

I wake up in the early morning rested and content, and am gathering up the sheet and pillow when I see a pale yellow scorpion on the armrest. More amused than alarmed since any danger has passed, I take a picture for fun to show friends, then wrap the scorpion in a blanket and remove it to the garden. Dimitris responds with a message:

....

'Be careful about scorpions, because you are used to walk barefooted. If by mistake to step on one, the influence of the poison lasts about 24 hours. Also, turn the cups in the wrong side if you do not like to find one of them inside and drink it. Sometimes the scorpions like to hide in to the cups. They like the humidity and there is the danger to boil with the tea.'

....

I do walk barefooted as often as possible; I don't tell him it was actually right by my pillow. I probably had a lucky escape.

I've known Dimitris, the high school headmaster, since I came to spend a month on this island two years ago. He loves to give advice, some of it very useful, but I try to figure out how a scorpion would hide in a cup. If the cup was empty, you'd see it – and if it wasn't empty, surely the scorpion would drown? There must be some truth in it, but I'm the ultimate sceptic when it comes to received wisdom. Still, I thank him for his warning in the afternoon when I run into him at Eristos beach. He picks up his wetsuit and *psarondoufeko*, spear gun, and slowly makes his way to the sea to go fishing for octopus.

This kilometre-long stretch of pebbles and sand that I had to myself in spring is now dotted with tents in the shade of the tamarisks, but the beach is still mostly empty. I spend an hour diving into blue water and lying on the sand in the sun, letting the warmth sink into my bones and clear any aches from sitting at the desk, then walk back through the valley to my house. It's next door to a storeroom and workshop filled with equipment for extracting honey. Back when I was in England and arranging to rent it, the owners referred to it as the 'honey factory'; I liked the idea of living at a honey factory, and told people that was my address. When I arrived, I was pleased to confirm that life was sweet living next door to the honey factory. It took me a couple of months of living here to realise that lots of people on the island make honey and the name on its own is meaningless – the family in reality just call it their *apothiki*, meaning outbuilding or workshop. The man who came to deliver a truckload of my belongings – boxes marked carefully with 'The Honey Factory, Megalo Horio' – simply rang a few people to find out who I was and where I lived. But by then the name had stuck.

Megalo Horio, while its name means 'big village', is a small settlement of white houses with blue shutters and doors, none quite the same, each facing a slightly different angle, hemmed in by a cluster of pine trees on the otherwise rocky slopes of a steep hill. Above are strewn the remnants of stone walls from earlier centuries. The ruined castle set into the sheer rock summit was mostly built by medieval knights during the crusades, but the entrance is from the ancient acropolis when a temple of Zeus and Athena was here. That's the view I look at when I wake up in the morning and go to sleep at night.

I approach my house along a dirt track in an old riverbed; the valley is known as Potamia. A fence all around the property keeps the goats out, and the gate is a haphazard buy garden supplies, I have an idea to protect the melons using kitchen scouring pads, opened out into silver netting. Improvisation is necessary here.

The drone of a *michanaki*, a motorbike, signals that Pavlos is on his way up the hill. He comes from the village every day to potter around the workshop and his own vegetable garden in the field below. He's a retired electrician, compact and wiry, with a slightly sad and bemused expression permanently on his face, and eyes that light up and gleam when he sees you. He switches off the engine and walks up the steps to the house with a handful of dark plums.

'I'd have brought more,' he says, 'but I didn't have a bag with me.' I thank him profusely, and he lights a cigarette, then asks, *'To kouneli irtheh?'* Did the rabbit come?

I say I haven't seen it today.

'Ercheteh ti nichta,' he says – it comes in the night. I imagine the rabbit stealthily tiptoeing into the garden wearing a black mask and a swag bag. Pavlos has been threatening for a while to shoot the pest and stew it into a hearty *stifado*. He finishes his cigarette then heads down to his garden, where I can hear him breaking up soil as I eat a couple of just-picked plums.

In T-shirt and shorts, I make some coffee and open my laptop, log on to the office server and go through my emails. The important thing for me is that this rural outpost comes with an internet connection so I can work. This is the plan, one that makes my situation a little different: I'm working full-time from home but I get to take extraordinary lunch breaks.

In the evening, the wind has dropped and it's hot even downstairs in the house. I pile quilts and blankets and pillows outside on the rough terrace, grateful to have no neighbours to witness my unconventional approach. I fall asleep in the fresh air, under the stars, listening to the high-pitched call of the Scops owl as well as the intermittent drone of the refrigerator in the *apothiki*. I wake in the early hours to see the moon straight ahead, so full and dazzlingly bright that it illuminates the sky and bathes the garden in silver light. I'd never have noticed this if I'd stayed in the house. Eventually I turn over and fall asleep again until the bees are buzzing around the basil and courgette flowers, the cicadas are revving up and sun lights the mountaintops all around.

Like many people who come to Greece on holiday, I often wondered if I could live on a Greek island. After university, I taught English in Athens for a year, and spent weekends and vacations on Crete and Santorini, Mykonos and Hydra and other islands. But the pull to find a career, to have the freedom to do more with my life, drove me farther afield. I've loved to travel and live in other countries; but at times when I've been without my own home for a long while, I've felt a need to settle and a longing to be back in Greece. Now I have years of experience working with books – as a literary agent in Canada, a freelance editor in France and a publisher in England – and I decided it was time to try working from home on a Greek island. It took me a long time to be comfortable saying: I can do the job, but I don't fit into the box.

My boss in England offered me a freelance contract, and a colleague found me tenants to cover the mortgage for the little flat I'd bought: a reasonably solid base with which to make this risky move. I love freedom and adventure, but also need some stability. I earn far less money than I used to, but my rent is low and it's not possible to spend lots of money here. My needs are simple.

I count my blessings that I've got myself into a situation where I can be outdoors more, and the countryside is on my doorstep. When did I start to notice, I wonder, that exercise outdoors in nature grounded me and made me happier? Over the last few years when I lived near the south coast of England, if I needed a pick-me-up I would always cycle a few miles north of town and then walk up a hill in the South Downs topped by the outline of a prehistoric fort. But it was usually only on weekends, or on rare summer evenings when the weather was good and I still had the energy after work. Here in Tilos, I can sleep under the stars, and be at my desk (barefoot, but who's to know?) first thing in the morning, ticking off items in my diary. And both work and life feel better than ever. That's the idea: to live a better life in lots of ways; eat local food; spend more time in nature.

Often I ascend the stone steps to the flat roof just to look at the fields stretching away in three directions, and the steep limestone hills, empty except for tiny chapels hiding faded frescoes, and the blue of the sea. Sometimes I look up to see eagles circling high overhead. I can walk to a cave where the bones of the last elephants in Europe were found, buried in volcanic ash. This is a wild, rugged and colourful place with few people, where roads don't have names or numbers, beaches aren't cluttered with signs and entertainments. Lacking many of the things that can make life noisy and complicated, it's unlike anywhere else I've found and I love it. Still, I grew up in a village surrounded by hills in the north of England, so in some ways I've come full circle but to a better climate.

The sky is a deep blue, the temperature reaches up towards 40°C and there's a strong sense that we're tiny specks on a baking hot rock in the Mediterranean. The dominant smell as I walk up the dirt track towards Skafi is of sage burning to a crisp in the sun. Then there's the rich, sweet aroma of a fig tree by Menelaos' farm, which looks at first sight like a junkyard, but every bit of junk is something that is being put to good use, and the space in between is filled with goats and sheep. Menelaos, a strong, sturdily built man with tousled grey hair and a smiling face, is often working in his fields there, digging or planting, and he'll stand up and wave, and ask *'Pou pas?'*, where are you going? *Banio?* Swimming?

Another twenty minutes down a footpath takes me to a green valley opening out into a natural stretch of pebbles flashing white against a deep sapphire sea, with patches of sand the pink of the inside of a ripe fig. In late spring, I had it to myself. Now a few hardy summer visitors make it here and build little shelters out of bamboo cane as there are no trees for shade. At the end of the afternoon, it's deserted again, and peaceful. There's a cove to the right, over the rocks, where the sea gets deep quickly. I love to strip off and dive naked into the blue, lie on the shore in the warm sun, then swim back towards the shallower, rockier stretches with my snorkel to watch the fish. When I'm ready to leave, I gather some wood and cane to take home for rigging up nets in the garden.

Occasionally, I'm invited to a gathering at someone's house in the village: a good excuse to swap the dusty shorts and T-shirt for a strappy dress. Several outsiders have bought and restored old homes here, dropping in for a few weeks' holiday a year. These impromptu invitations of summer are a change from quiet evenings at home and an easy way to make new friends. One evening it's the house of an Italian man who has friends and family staying with him; most of the group except me speaks Italian, so I simply soak up the pleasures of eating and drinking in the warm evening air, my body feeling alive from the swimming and walking and summer sun. When I walk home down the dusty track later, I switch off the torch and let my eyes adjust to the darkness so I can see the jagged mountaintops silhouetted around me. The clear sky is full of piercingly bright stars and the pale arc of the Milky Way.

People ask how long I plan to stay here. I don't know. I can't know what life will really be like here over the months and maybe years to come. This is an experiment in an alternative way of living. I walk, climb hills, swim, feel the warm sun on my skin every day and speak the beautiful language, and enjoy life. In some ways, I'm able to enjoy life more because of the strange twist that happened in the journey here. I was with someone, and we were going to move here together, but it didn't work out that way. I think I was always meant to come here alone and to see what life brings.

Chapter 2

You'll Go Crazy

I'm early for the bus so I go to wait on the bench in the shade. An old man comes down the lane and joins me on the bench and we start to talk. He says I speak good Greek.

'I don't think so! I want to say so much and I don't know how.'

'Ah, don't worry, slowly you'll learn. You can't know it automatically!'

Having studied Ancient Greek at school, come to Greece on holiday as a teenager, lived in Greece for a year after university and taken several holiday trips, I have the basics of the language. But I've become lazy about opening the grammar books. No: not lazy, but when I finish my work, I want to relax and make the most of the summer.

'I'm going to Ay'Antoni for a swim,' announces the old man, and I realise he's carrying swimming trunks in a little plastic bag. 'It gets hot up here in the village in the middle of the day. It's a lovely little beach down there.'

Pantelis, father of Pavlos, joins us at the bus stop, swiftly followed by Irini, who has the tiny mini-market with the pretty, hand-painted sign up the narrow alleyway opposite. Just below the village *kafeneion*, or traditional cafe, Irini's shop has unfathomable opening hours that fit around her goat-tending duties. Irini is a bulky and warm-hearted lady, often leaning on a tall stick, and you would have to work hard to remain a stranger to her. The shop doesn't sell much that I need but I try to visit from time to time and find something to buy because otherwise Irini asks me, as she does now:

'*Pou eiseh?*'

This is a tricky one to answer, as it literally means 'Where are you?', which seems an odd question to ask someone standing in front of you. I think it really means 'Where've you been?'

'At home,' I say, and hedge my bets by adding, 'But now I'm heading to Livadia to take the *Diagoras* to Rhodes.'

'Oh, the *Diagoras* is late! Still in Kalymnos.' The big ferry, the Blue Star *Diagoras*, comes from Athens and stops at several islands before Tilos. Irini must have been on the phone to someone, maybe waiting for a shipment to arrive.

'Oh no! So I'll have to wait a couple of hours in Livadia?'

The village of Megalo Horio is seen as *pano*, 'upstairs' as local people sometimes translate it. It has its feet in the fertile Eristos valley, and around the other side of the mountain is the northern harbour of Ayios Antonis. Livadia, built on the edge of the large bay to the south of the island where the ferries come and go, is *kahto*, 'downstairs'. Being by the sea, it has hotels and rooms to rent, and several shops and cafes in the square – though most of them close in the middle of the day, siesta time.

'Longer,' says the young woman with a little son who's joined us at the bench also. 'How long does it take from Kalymnos?' she asks the old man, who isn't sure, but they all offer an opinion. Suffice to say, it will be a while.

'I could take the other boat at four,' I say – unusually today, there are two ferries – 'but it costs more, *pio poli...*'

'*Pio polla,*' corrects the old man with a smile. 'See, I've taught you one thing today!'

It's true; little conversations like this will gradually improve my Greek, as well as bringing me closer to the community, something that's important to me as an outsider who'd like to stay. I probably spend too much time alone at my house.

Down the hill comes Nikos, the retired, somewhat rotund travelling barber with thick round glasses. When I stayed in Livadia for a month two years ago, trying to determine if I could live here, I watched him zipping around the island on his scooter, and one day I looked down from the terrace of my apartment to see the baker sitting on a chair in the alleyway wearing a cape while Nikos leaned over him with his scissors. He's the husband of Vicky, long-time curator of the diminutive museum in the village. Carrying a shoulder bag and looking frazzled, Nikos launches into a speech to Irini so rapid that I've no idea what he's talking about, though I think he mentions music and lots of people.

Eventually the bus comes and I'm wished *kalo taxithi*, a good journey, and some of us leave and some stay. The bus winds its route to Ayios Andonis, where the little harbour and shady beach look lovely and I think I must go there for lunch or dinner this summer sometime. Someone from the taverna meets the bus and takes their delivery of sacks of bread from the bakery. As we set off again and loop around to Eristos beach, the driver drops Nikos as close as possible to En Plo, where he is going to pick up his *michanaki* – it seems he left his scooter there last night after going to hear the live music at the taverna.

If I had a car, it would be so much more convenient, but I'd miss all of this. And I wouldn't want to miss it for the world.

When you live in a place with a permanent population of roughly five hundred, every now and then you have to go to a bigger place to visit a doctor or a dentist, or to buy hardware or underwear, or to get to an airport. For Tilos residents, that bigger place is usually the island of Rhodes, and on Friday when the ferry schedule allows for a trip there and back in one day, islanders will often be seen around Mandraki, the old port area in Rhodes town, running their city errands. This time, I'm leaving for a quick trip to England in early July, but spending a couple of days in Rhodes first.

Rhodes is one of the larger Greek islands and in the summer is busy with people and cars, a different world from Tilos. The waterfront is lined with boats offering excursions, and stands selling fresh orange juice and corn on the cob cooked on the griddle; beyond the car park is Elli Beach, covered with bodies on sunbeds, but sometimes I like to sit in one of the trendy cafes there and listen to music.

Walking around the flamboyant dome of the New Market in the early evening, my eye is caught by some shoes in the window of a shop and I decide to go inside. I am deliberating if I can justify acquiring them – living, as I do, up a dusty dirt track in the middle of nowhere – when one of the men in the shop who have been talking amongst themselves asks:

'*Eiseh Italitha?*' Are you Italian?

I smile. I love being asked if I'm Italian; even if it is just a very slick sales pitch. It seems surprising at first that so many Italians visit these islands when there is plenty of sunshine in Italy, but the country's connections with the Dodecanese go back a long way. The wide boulevard that stretches from the New Market to the old casino at the tip of the island, passing the gates of the old harbour which the Colossus once bestrode, according to legend, is lined with grand edifices from when the Italians ruled the island from 1912 until World War Two, as well as some from the earlier Ottoman rule.

I reply in Greek that, no, I'm from England (not bothering to mention the blend of Hungarian and Scots blood on my father's side).

'What? No! Impossible! You don't look English. Look at your colour. Father Greek? Mother Greek?' I suppose many of the English they see at this time of year are lobster-red from lying on sunbeds for two weeks in blistering heat.

'No! But thank you. I live on Tilos.'

There is general hilarity. 'What?! You can't live on Tilos! You'll go crazy! No, it's just... it's very small. I know people from Tilos, my wife's family. *Katse, re...*' Sit down, he says, using the *'re'* word, often tagged on to a phrase among friends, suggesting matey familiarity. 'Sit down, it's a family shop, this!'

And so I do. We chat, and I leave buying shoes for another time.

The next day, my friend Hari drives us down the coast to Kalathos for an afternoon at the beach. I met him one evening here in late spring, when I was reading a newspaper at a bar and he started reading over my shoulder. He's a heavy-built Greek man who was born in Alexandria, Egypt; he has a deep, husky voice, a subtle smile and twinkling eyes. He's kind and funny and extravagant in his public persona; can tell the same joke a hundred times without flinching; yet is shy and reserved in private, and a creature of habit. When he can afford to stop work, he'll escape to his little house on the small island of Leros and go fishing, or maybe set up a taverna. But for now, with the Greek economy in crisis, he spends his days chasing payments from restaurants he supplies with food. And when I come to Rhodes, he looks after me very well, buying me little treats and teaching me to cook Greek dishes. I am actually smitten with him, though everyone says he's too old for me.

We stop to pick up frappé coffees for the road, a frozen bottle of water for the beach, and as we continue south past the monastery of Zambika high on its pointed hill above the sea, he puts his hand out of the window and declares it is burning. He knows the road very well and drives with purpose, continually overtaking. As we descend towards the beautiful plain of Malona, a goat runs out in front of the car and he brakes fast. 'Reflexes!' he says, smiling and shaking his head.

When we get to the beach, the sand is like hot coals, and Hari stands in the sea and declares he's not getting out.

He later tells me off quite seriously for swimming after eating because I could get stomach cramp; when I protest that it was only a sandwich, he says, 'I'm not going to rescue you if you're drowning, then.' Not swimming for hours after lunch is another piece of received wisdom I'm somewhat sceptical about. Greeks swear by it, but the Greek summer habit is to eat a heavy lunch, then sleep during the heat of the day. The rest of us may survive because we eat lighter meals. Driving back to town, he puts on his reading glasses to compose a text to his son while speeding through the traffic. We clearly have different ideas about what is dangerous behaviour.

In the evening, we dress up and go to a restaurant with live music. I drink wine and Hari drinks clear liquor called *tsipouro*, loading our glasses with masses of ice, and we eat sea urchin roe and salt-cured anchovies and marinated octopus.

Only towards midnight is it reasonable to head into the Old Town. Of course, the narrow, winding, cobbled, ancient streets are pedestrian-only but, 'We Greeks like to be unlegal,' says Hari, so we drive, careering around corners and frightening tourists heading back to their rooms. Every five minutes he gets a call with some work problem. In a loud music bar, we watch the weekend fashion show, and dance to silly, sexy, summer party pop. I don't want to go to England tomorrow.

'Eh, is nothing. Four, five days we will sit here again. Don't you worry about nothing. The life is too short,' says Hari. 'You must enjoy while you can! Because who knows what is around the corner? We could leave here and get hit by a train. OK, we don't have trains here in *Rhodos*, but anyway...'

Arriving in England, I stand on the train station platform and look up. Where is the sun? What is that strange white stuff entirely covering the sky?

England looks very green and flat and a little strange to me, having grown accustomed to a South Aegean summer. There's a drizzly sort of rain, something I haven't seen in months, and the ground of the train station is dotted with the ugly black spots of old chewing gum. On the train, nobody's talking.

There are some sunny days, and I go out without an umbrella then get drenched when it suddenly turns to rainstorms. I've already forgotten what an English summer is like, and the world of commuting and traffic feels equally odd.

The main reason for the trip is for work and it's fun to see colleagues; in between work meetings, it's also good to spend time with family and friends. People want to know I'm doing OK on my own; my plans for moving to Greece changed quite dramatically at the eleventh hour, and I had no time to see people to reassure them I was fine. In fact, I am full of energy and beaming with happiness after these first few months of Mediterranean life, and this new adventure has given me confidence in myself. Nothing can shake the euphoria.

Chapter 3

Finding My Island Feet

As a child, coming to Greece on family holidays, I was spellbound by the traditional dancing: the dramatic men's dances, shows of strength and agility and passion. Living on the island for a few months has given me the opportunity to learn my first steps of traditional dance, a long-held ambition, at the weekly class in Livadia, which – appropriately enough for me – takes place in the primary school. Although I could catch the bus, during my first week back in Tilos I decide to enjoy the hour-long walk there across one of the emptier sections of the island.

Turning on to the road, I pass the helipad. On the occasions when a helicopter thunders in, the throbbing power that beats the air as it touches down just a little way from my house gives me a thrill; yet unless it's a military helicopter, it's usually arriving for a medical emergency, to take someone to hospital in Rhodes. It stops just long enough to pick someone up then pulls away, leaving peace behind, just the birds crying out and the gentle sound of crickets. There's a path from there up the mountain to the Italian observatory, dating from the time of the occupation.

To the right is Harkadio Cave, where the elephant bones were found, and above it are the ruins of another castle of the Knights of St John. As the road gains height and reaches a disused quarry, goats lounge nonchalantly at the roadside on mounds of gravel or in the shade of an old piece of machinery, or sometimes across the road, struggling to their feet awkwardly if a car needs to pass. The route sweeps downhill again to '*porselanes*', where building materials are extracted by the islanders for making houses, and ochre and white cliffs of a porous stone provide little caves for goats to shelter from the midday sun. Falcons usually circle high above here at the end of the afternoon. Running parallel to the road is the old footpath that used to join the settlements of Megalo Horio and Mikro Horio.

At the crest of the hill is a chapel, then the *venzinadiko* or petrol station, where Nikos Ikonomou sits outside on a couch until 2 p.m. when he closes up for the day. Mikro Horio can be seen on the slopes above: once a thriving village of about two and a half thousand people, now deserted, its stone houses blending into the hillside. After occupation by the German army during World War Two, when the livestock was plundered and curfews prevented people from tending their farms, many residents of Mikro Horio emigrated to find a living elsewhere; the rest moved to the coast at Livadia, abandoning the old village in the 1960s. I first learned about this from Vangelis, who became my neighbour and friend during my month in Livadia, and who wrote an account of his experiences growing up there.

To the left is a path to the beach of Lethra. There are a couple more houses and then the edge of the plateau where the road zigzags down to Livadia, and the magnificent, smooth curve of the bay reveals itself, fringed by white pebbles. All around, the hills sweep up to sharp outcrops of rock and on a summit stands the stone wall of the ruined castle of Agriosykia. There are faint outlines of old farming terraces improbably high up.

Kalos tin! is the welcome that each member of the dance class gets as we gather on the steps of the school. Only women attend, and it's another chance to get to know more people: locals who like to practise and improve, and a few *xeni*, foreign women who live here. Instruction is in Greek, as is the general chatter, gossip and clowning around.

The traditional dances for women are performed in circles all together, with small steps that at first seem far less interesting than the men's dances. But I've started to realise there's more to them than meets the eye. The teacher likes to warm us up – while stragglers arrive – with the local *sousta*. There are so many variations on Greek dances, depending on the region they come from. The sousta was the first dance I tried at a festival, and like many foreigners I got confused. Seeing a line of dancers with arms criss-crossed, the natural instinct is to cross your arms. Instead – as I learned very quickly from fellow dancers – you open your arms, reaching over the people on either side of you to hold the hand of their neighbour, binding the line together tightly. I now learn from others at the dance class how to hold my hands: the leading hand palm up, to be led, the other palm down, to lead. The steps are simple: two tiny steps to the right, one step forward, with a slight bounce. While I'm practising the basics at the back of the line, the teacher demonstrates a more complex move to the women at the front.

Midsummer nights on Greek islands are full of traditional festivals and music, which is why some knowledge of the dances is important. The biggest festival, on 27 July, is that of the island's patron saint, Saint Panteleimon, and a good number of men on the island are named Pantelis after the saint. Panteleimon the 'all-merciful' is depicted on icons with what looks like a box of watercolour paints, but is in fact the medicine he used to heal the sick. The main monastery on the island is dedicated to him, a fifteenth-century building amid a spring-fed oasis high up on remote grey cliffs overlooking the sea, where there was once a temple to the ancient god Poseidon. It's no longer a working monastery but is looked after by the priest of Megalo Horio.

The celebration lasts for three days. The day before the eve is a time of 'lying in wait' called *proparamoni*, and pilgrims stay up on the mountain, sleeping on mattresses in the leafy compound of the monastery. The eve of the saint's day is the festival's main celebration and feast, known as a *paniyiri*. Souvlaki sizzle on the grill and goat is cooked in tomato sauce in huge pots, to be served with roasted potatoes. Hundreds of people drive by car or motorbike, or take a packed bus as I do up the road cut into the cliffs for a night of music and dancing.

The road seems perfectly innocuous by day, with my feet solidly planted on the ground, and it's a spectacular walk. By night, I consider it terrifying. Locals think it's absurd to be scared of the road to the monastery, but on one side is the mountain, down which rocks regularly tumble aided by roaming goats, while on the other side is a stomach-churning sheer drop of hundreds of metres. When half the vehicles on the island are driving up and down it, maybe after a drink or two, a little tired in the early hours... it's not the most relaxing end to the evening, even if the locals do say that the saint protects and there has never been an accident since the road was built.

A night or two after the festival of Ayios (Saint) Panteleimon, an easy walk home for me in Megalo Horio, is an event called the *Koupa* or Cup, so called after the most important dance of the evening, where the woman at the front of the line holds aloft a large cup or bowl. When a man wants to praise the dancing skills of a woman – perhaps his wife or daughter – he puts money in the cup and leads her to the front of the line. Usually each woman will only get a few minutes of leading before she's replaced, and the cup is filled with notes.

The *Koupa* takes place in the tiny square next to the church, overlooked by the *kafeneion*. The proximity of church and cafe is no coincidence: both are at the heart of Greek village life. Musicians sit on the stone bench underneath the church's twin arches, its walls smooth with whitewashed plaster except for the exposed stonework around the doorway. The ground is a sea of round grey pebbles on a zigzag design denoting waves.

I buy a can of beer from Sofia at the *kafeneion* and wander down the steps. People crowd around the square, everyone in good spirits. A local man I've never met before, about my age and dressed in flip-flops and board shorts, starts chatting to me and offers me a plastic cup of a clear spirit called *souma*. It's very strong, and probably quite good for getting you in the mood for dancing. He introduces himself as Apostolis and soon drags me up to join the circle for the *sousta*. I'm now confident enough to join in, and with his encouragement I have fun. The *sousta* is an inclusive, meandering dance that can go on for as long as people keep joining the line, and the musicians keep playing.

I meet Apostolis' friends: a lively and spirited woman from Athens, a quiet man from northern Greece who's stationed with the army on the nearby island of Kos, and a dark-eyed fisherman from Tilos whose profile reminds me of artwork on ancient Attic vases. Around 2 a.m., Apostolis suggests we all decamp to Mikro Horio. Stelios the fisherman says he's not coming as he has to be up for work in a few hours. The others take a motorbike and I opt to go in Apostolis' truck. This seems like a bad idea when I see the truck.

'On second thoughts, I think I'm feeling a little tired. I'll walk home. Have a good time!'

'Why?' he asks.

'Um... When did you crash the truck?' The entire front of it is crumpled and parts are missing.

'What, that? Oh, that's because I lent my truck to Stelios to drive. I'm a good driver, I'm just too nice!'

'Really?' It's almost certainly a lie, but it's a convincing lie, as Stelios does have scars from a road accident or two. Well, you only live once. I get in. We're not going very far.

Mikro Horio remained deserted for decades after the 1960s. Then some enterprising types came up with the idea of a summer-only music bar, opening around midnight. A narrow dirt track leads off the main road and twists uphill into darkness. The bar is in an old stone house, with a dance floor covered only by moonlight and a sky full of stars. A few empty houses in the abandoned village are dimly lit as if by candles, and the only other lights are on the Turkish coast in the distance. We drink, we dance, we laugh... And sometime in the early hours of the morning, conveyed home by a bashed-up truck, I happily collapse into my bed.

While the terrace is still cool and in shadow, I sit working in the peace and quiet of the early morning at the big, heavy pine table I shipped with other belongings when I moved.

'We have tables here!' Maria said, laughing, when I admitted I'd brought it from England. Maria is Pavlos' wife and always insists I can have whatever I need. She's cheerful and kind. But acquiring a solid wooden table in Tilos wouldn't be easy, and this gives me a lot more pleasure than a wobbly white plastic one. I love the way the sun has bleached the wood. I rub oil into it to keep it from drying out too much. Perhaps wooden tables remind people here of the tough old days, and plastic seems clean and modern. When I tell her my father gave me the table, she understands – family trumps everything.

A peaceful home office is conducive to concentration. I don't have any problem finding the discipline to work; if I don't work, I don't get paid and can't afford to live here. The only noise is of Pavlos and a friend throwing rubbish into the back of a truck, preparing for the honey-making that's coming soon. When I need a break, I potter around the garden to stretch. For the first time, having always lived in apartments as an adult, I have my own garden.

After my ten days away in England, the garden became a small forest and I've been spending hours cutting things back, mostly the bush of *horta*. *Horta* is the word for any sort of grass – hence our word horticulture – and in a culinary sense, edible *horta* tends to mean any kind of wild-growing, leafy greens, boiled and served with olive oil and lemon. Unfortunately, this one plant had grown almost into a tree. The courgettes had ballooned into weighty marrows, which I stuffed with a mixture of rice and tomatoes and herbs and baked in the oven. The bees are enjoying the flowers on the rocket.

I've been wondering why there are so many green tomatoes on my plants but they never seem to ripen. There were a handful of reddening ones last night, but none when I went to water them this morning, and finally I get it. The birds are taking them all for breakfast. The early bird here doesn't need to catch the worm. It has a ready supply of tomatoes. Using a handful of bamboo stakes from Skafi beach, I string up CDs over the plants to dangle and sparkle in the wind, selecting those least likely to be missed. It's a technique I've seen others use; a form of Tilos improvisation. We shall see how much the birds like *Ibiza: The Sunset Sessions* (Disc Three) and *Learn to Speak Korean in 60 Minutes.*

I'm not convinced this will be enough to protect my little crops from avian thieves, but a careful scouring of the village supermarket shelves doesn't yield anything that might serve as netting. I rummage around in my cupboards and then, in a stroke of inspiration, I remember my portable string hammock – unlikely to be used now that the summer campers are taking up every tree on Eristos beach – and drape it over the lot. Fingers crossed it works. Pavlos appears confident about the efficacy of my tomato cage, though on a day like today with no breath of wind, the CDs hang like Christmas decorations.

The melon plant has become a bit clingy, throwing out tendrils like there's no tomorrow and wrapping them deftly and securely around the stalks of the sunflowers. The sunflowers are being stoic about it but I think a conversation about needing space is on the cards. The melon plant also wrapped a tendril around what looks like a ball of tumbleweed. I wish it would wrap tendrils around the rabbit.

When the sun comes up over the terrace, I move inside to work at the kitchen table, and in the early afternoon I close the computer and cycle to Eristos beach. I stop at the far end then go for a long swim around the little headland to the empty cove on the other side. The cliffs are shades of rust-red and purple-brown with splashes of green caper bushes, the colour of the sand like watermelon. My shoulders have the nicest gentle ache afterwards from all the swimming. I must do that more often. This is what I came here to do.

Back home, I do a little more work then I write an email to my friend Steven in England, mentioning how nice it can be living on my own for a while: having the bed to myself, being able to eat *baklava* for lunch if I feel like it, reading a book while eating dinner rustled up from whatever's in the kitchen. It's good having a glass of wine while lying on the terrace and idly watching the sunset; observing how the little lizard comes along to his favourite piece of driftwood and clings to it; admiring my sunflowers. I always imagined sunflowers would take ages to grow, but these mighty, sturdy things have grown from tiny seeds in less than two months.

This is the good, calm life that I wanted for myself, and also the one I thought would be perfect to raise a child in – surrounded by nature and the sea, a Gerald Durrell-type, old-fashioned kind of childhood in the fresh air. It's only come to me recently, this maternal urge. I was trying to conceive with Matt, the boyfriend I planned to move here with, envisioning a home and a family here. According to the doctor I saw in England a few months ago, there's no physical obstacle to my becoming pregnant. But am I likely to get to the necessary place in a relationship in time for another attempt?

I have discussed with my family the idea of raising a child alone. They would be supportive and help as much as possible. It would be challenging, but at least I work from home now. Afterwards, I'd have time to find the right father for my child. Of course it wouldn't be perfect, but I've tried. And life just doesn't always fall that way.

I've talked to Steven about this often over the past few years. He already knew he wanted children even when we met at university – back when I had no interest in children whatsoever – and he now has teenaged kids he's very proud of, even though he had a bit of a mid-life crisis while raising them. He emails back that everyone feels inept as a parent, but children are quite resilient and manage to do well even in imperfect circumstances. I can't help thinking of another friend who I saw when I was in England in July; I originally met him when he was walking his boys to school, and he always seemed to have a perfect life, the kind of life that made me feel a little shabby, but now his wife is filing for divorce.

Life isn't perfect and we can only do our best. I feel that Tilos is, for now, the right place for me. And if there's an opportunity to add a child to my world, then I will do my best.

Chapter 4

Black Ribbons and Driftwood

There's a strange commotion in the garden. By the angry sound of Pavlos' voice, I think maybe the rabbit has returned. Then I hear hooves. I go out to see.

A couple of goats have got in and are hungrily eyeing all the well-watered flowers and plants. Pavlos emerges from the honey factory in his red football T-shirt and baseball cap and shorts, shouting at the goats for sneaking in – though to be fair to the goats, the gate is wide open, and this is the time of year they are hungriest, as all the wild plants are parched.

However, they know an angry gardener when they see one, and in response to his hue and cry, they race back across the garden and leap over the wall – not realising there's a fence on the other side. One makes it; the other is trapped between the wall and the fence.

Most Tilos goats are beautiful, noble-looking creatures with chestnut or jet-black glossy hair, twisting wide horns and long beards; some are pretty, pale faun-coloured ones. This one is your Average Joe goat, black and white, short haired with stumpy horns and a big belly, and a slightly scared look in its eye as Pavlos grabs its horns and pulls it over the wall. I notice it isn't wearing a tag. Some do, some don't, and though most belong to someone, they wander at will around the hillsides.

'Bring me a knife!' He's yanking the goat up by the horns. 'Bring me a knife! We'll put it on the spit...'

I laugh nervously. Is he joking – gentle Pavlos, the guy who won't use pesticides, *farmaka*, on his vegetables in case the birds eat them? He has a determined look on his face, winding rope around the goat's horns to keep hold of it. He's been working hard on his garden; plus he wasn't able to go to the festival of Ayios Panteleimon, as Maria is in mourning after the death of a cousin, so he didn't get to eat the goat cooked in huge pots on the coals at the *paniyiri*, the celebratory feast with music and dancing. There's no meat Tilians like better.

Muttering, he drags the goat out of the gate and around the corner of the house, where he ties it to a tree. Then I hear him drive off on his motorbike.

Is he off to get a knife? From inside, I hear the goat scrabbling around for a while; then it stops. Curious, I go to take a look. It seems to have got the rope twisted around itself in a panic, and is lying upside down with its head at an awkward angle. The rope tightens around its neck and it's panting heavily, its tongue hanging out. Then it stops moving, seems to stop breathing. It looks like it's about to die a nasty death in the glaring sun: surely Pavlos didn't intend that? Reaching out, I manage to untangle it somehow, pulling this way and that until the rope is no longer strangling it. Still it doesn't move. Then suddenly the breath comes again.

Somehow, pulling the rope away, I get the goat on to its feet.

Is it the right thing to do, interfering? It's probably best to respect the way people do things here; their relationship with animals. I decide to get out of the way before Pavlos comes back. I don't want to get into trouble. I have to go up to the village shop anyway.

I take the overgrown shortcut through the field, a path that emerges halfway up the road into the village. Just then the bus is coming round the corner. I stand to one side to let it pass but it slows down.

'It's OK!' I say, but the driver, also called Pavlos, insists on stopping just to give me a ride the few minutes' walk up the hill.

'Eh, it's difficult in this heat!' he says.

With a smile on my face, I arrive at the shop to find Eleftheria juggling two mobile phones and a landline. She manages to stop talking for long enough to sort me out with cheese, eggs, green peppers and *retsina*. Two ladies in the shop, Greek but not local, tell me they like the colour of my hair; it's gone very fair in the sun. I follow the road to the KEP office; the KEP fulfils all sorts of functions to help out local citizens, and is where the post is left for the village. I'm inordinately pleased to be given the key to my very own post box – a marker that I am a resident of Tilos. Stepping outside, I stop to look at the deep magenta bougainvillaea and lush green trees and beyond, the view across the valley to my stone house on the brush-covered hillside. What a place to live.

Wine bottles clinking in my bag as I amble along the footpath home, I pick a couple of ripe, sun-warm figs from the tree as I walk past, breaking open their soft green skin to check they are moist inside. They ripen only in August, a short season; the trees must belong to someone but if no one else is picking them, I assume no one will mind. Prickly pear fruit, *fragosika*, are also ripening now and delicious, but require more care when removing the skin with its fine, hair-like spines.

Starting up the hill, I see the red splash of Pavlos' T-shirt as he bends down over the goat. My heart sinks.

Then the goat comes tearing down the track and leaps away up the hill and out of sight.

'I freed it,' says Pavlos.

My bet is that he asked Maria for a knife and she said no.

There's another *Koupa* in the village just after the late August festival of Panayia Kamariani. It would be a perfect opportunity for me to get together with my new English friend Anna. I met her at the Greek dance class, and we said we must get together for a drink sometime. We don our best dresses and fancy shoes, she arrives on the bus from Livadia and we head up the steps of the whitewashed alley to the *kafeneion* – only to find out we've got the wrong night.

Amid jibes from Sofia, the not-to-be-messed-with proprietress, we grab a bottle of retsina anyway and a table on the terrace, and we exchange stories of our Greek adventures.

Slim with boyishly short hair, Anna fell in love with Greece and the backwater charms of Tilos twenty years ago. She works as a legal assistant in London, though a few years ago after a serious health scare she decided to spend as much time here as possible. She'd love to find a sufficiently progressive employer in order to work from home. This year she's here for the whole summer before she has to go back and find a contract.

It's soon clear that we've had so many similar experiences we're almost finishing one another's sentences, and find much to laugh about. For both of us, too, sitting on the *kafeneion* terrace on a summer's evening beside locals discussing the issues of their day is something special. Every now and then we're interrupted by someone who asks if we really thought it was the *Koupa* tonight. Who cares? It's an excuse for another night out; I love having a friend to gossip with.

'Jennifer!' barks Sofia in her deep voice as I delicately descend the steps from the terrace to ask for another bottle of retsina. 'You'd better not wear those shoes tomorrow. You won't be able to dance in them!' Her joke sets her off laughing. My shoes are high wedge heels held on by black ribbons, bought in Rhodes on my way back from England for not very much money; I love them, even though they're a little small for me, and I'm sure I can dance in them if I want to badly enough. 'And you'd better not drink too much either!'

Grinning, I grab a can of soda water to splash into the retsina, making the simple resinated wine bubbly – Greek champagne.

Next to us is a table of village men including Pantelis. He walks with a stick and has a weathered, lined face which always lights up when he sees me, and invariably asks about my mother and her friend Hermi who came to visit a few months ago. He rather enjoyed a surprise shoulder massage Hermi gave him over the stuffed goat lunch Maria cooked for us all. Sitting with him, in dress trousers and a shirt, is Nikitas, thin as a rake, leaning back in his chair with a cigarette held casually between his fingers, his eyes half-closed by droopy lids. He insists on handing us a plate of salted tuna from their meze.

It's a wonderful evening with my new friend. Sometimes it pays to get the day wrong.

Next night is a little like déjà vu; I'm wearing my favourite outfit all over again. It's not as if I have a vast array to choose from, and this sparkly, figure-hugging number is actually the easiest thing to throw on. I bought it at a vastly reduced price, even though at the time it was two sizes too small, figuring I might lose weight during a summer of walking, swimming and sunshine in Tilos. I did. I'm not sure the same will happen with the shoes.

Anna arrives on the bus and we find a table overlooking the square, where older ladies, having bagged the best spots, sit in a row – arms crossed, not drinking, not talking, just waiting. Meanwhile, the older men and the young musicians are warming up with a few drinks in the *kafeneion*. It sounds like they might have been warming up for a while. The sky is a darkening blue. Above us on the wild, steep hillside, a delicate string of lights leads up to the honey-coloured walls of the ruined castle, lit up at night throughout the summer.

The singing gets louder and the ladies down below remain stoically in their seats, biding their time, in the light from the open church windows. Then there's a stirring inside the *kafeneion*, and suddenly the procession is on.

'I'm not sure if they'll actually make it down the steps,' says Anna.

The men are merrily swaying, singing in deep voices, shoulder to shoulder as they emerge through the archway, down the steps and into the square, where they finish the song standing in a tight circle, arms around one another. There's some back-slapping and everyone disperses to the tables, the musicians taking their place on the bench by the church.

We snag a table that appears to be free – a white plastic table, of course – though we worry it was reserved for someone important, like the priest. Never mind – we'll be up dancing for most of the night, I hope.

I spot the fisherman, Stelios, dressed in black jeans and T-shirt, and ask if he wants to join us.

He sits down and announces, 'I have *souma*. Nectar!'

The priest, Papa Manolis, with his long grey beard and black robes, dances alongside holidaymakers and toddlers. Local men in their twenties and thirties show off some frenetic footwork. Villagers in their sixties and seventies with creaky legs are some of the most enthusiastic dancers; for them, this is still, I imagine, one of the highlights of their social calendar. We join in a few dances, and watch the others with admiration. The musicians are tireless, playing the traditional instruments of lute and lyra long into the night.

By the early hours, the old folks are still going strong, but we're beginning to flag. Anna looks around for someone who might be driving to Livadia, and it doesn't take long to be offered a lift.

I'm about to walk home when Stelios suggests taking a spin to Eristos for a quiet drink at the makeshift bar of driftwood and bamboo that is set up on the sand every summer. He doesn't have his own place in Tilos as he usually works in Athens or Rhodes during the winter and, as is the traditional way, his home is with his parents in the village; but in the summer, he mostly camps on Eristos beach among friends he's known for years. He persuades me to get on the back of his motorbike. I try not to worry as we vroom off down the dark road.

As we arrive, I hear a message come through on my phone – it's from Anna: 'I think he likes you!' I smile – she is wicked. I don't believe for a minute that this lovely young man would be interested in me that way; he's just enjoying the company. But it feels like another good Greek island night, and I kick off my shoes as we walk down the cool sand under the stars, the waves sweeping in to shore.

Chapter 5

Dancing Through Doorways

It's early morning. The sun has crept up the hillsides on both sides of the wide bay, highlighting the reds and blues and yellows of the rock. The sea is calm and blue, the long stretch of beach deserted. Back among the feathery trees at the top of the beach there are scraps of bright colour: tents, the occasional hammock, wraps tied on branches for shade. Inside the tents, everyone seems to be sleeping. A zip opens, and two figures crawl out and on to the sand, scamper down to the end of the beach, and dive into the sea.

When they emerge, the woman pulls her tight, sparkly dress back on rather sheepishly, considering how inappropriate it looks in the early morning on a hippie beach, hoping no one will see.

It went like this. We were sitting at the wooden beach bar with glasses of *souma*. We started chatting and I asked him where he lived in the village. It turned out his mother was Vicky the museum curator, and his father Nikos the barber. I laughed, saying I knew his parents. Then he suddenly grabbed me with those strong fisherman arms and silenced my laugh with a passionate kiss. It was all a bit of a shock, but I was hardly going to say no to the gorgeous young man with huge dark eyes, long eyelashes, Dennis the Menace hair, broad shoulders and caramel skin. And then, well, there was the choice of riding the motorbike back to the village, or sleeping in the tent.

He drives me home in the morning after our wake-up swim. When he calls me on the phone later in the day, I can't understand a word – it's easier to talk *apo konda* – 'from close', or face to face. He comes by the house in the early afternoon and says, with Greek bluntness, 'Make me a coffee.' We laugh and hold one another a lot. He scratches me with his stubble and I learn the Greek word for hedgehog. Leaving for work, he kisses me goodbye and lifts me off my feet; he's used to hauling in nets full of fish. I watch him drive off down the dirt track on his motorbike, his eyes squinting, a roll-up in his mouth.

There is a language barrier, since Stelios' English and my Greek are both limited. But actions speak louder than words to me, since my last boyfriend lied to me spectacularly. This feels simple and genuine. I'm fairly sure it isn't serious, especially given that he's younger than me, not even thirty; but every day Stelios comes to my house, or I meet him at Eristos.

Someone once asked me, rather rudely I thought, whether I shouldn't try staying single. I've tried, believe me, and I like spending time on my own, but love is just too nice to give up. (Didn't Robert Palmer write a song about that?) If at first you don't succeed, try, try again: this maxim I apply avidly, it seems, to relationships. It used to be embarrassing when friends – happy couples with bouncy children – would ask, 'And are you still with... what's his name again?' And very often, I wasn't. I've had a lot of relationships and must have been responsible for the break-up of at least half of them. People sometimes say I've been unlucky with men, but another way of looking at it is that men have been unlucky with me. I decide to go dancing through an unexpected doorway, to see what I find (to paraphrase Dire Straits).

It's closing in on the end of August and the people who set up elaborate camp for the summer are beginning to dismantle it all for another year. One week all the spaces under the trees are taken, the nearby restaurants full, and the next week there's no one. Stelios takes me along to meet a group of his friends who've been coming here every summer for twenty years. They're packing up to take the ferry back to Athens and he's thinking of taking the weekend ferry to see a rock concert with them.

'Why don't you come to Athens?' he asks.

I laugh it off. Then I wonder: why not? I can take a long weekend off. He may have to leave the island to find work soon; why shouldn't we enjoy ourselves first? When he adds that he really wants to see the new Acropolis Museum, I decide to go. Since I studied Ancient Greek at school, the ancient history holds a fascination for me.

The year I finished university, I lived in Athens in the neighbourhood of Galatsi and taught English in a language school or *frontistirio*. From the top of my apartment building I had hazy views across the dirty-white city, then covered in clouds of smog, to the surrounding mountains and the gleaming silver sea. I loved wandering the streets, lingering over statues in museums. I spent Sunday afternoons at a cafe in Monastiraki, the old market area, where they played *rembetika*, an Eastern style of blues music that originated in the urban 'underground' in the early twentieth century; and many an evening at a hard-to-find backstreet taverna run by the parents of a friend, a favourite haunt of actors which only got going after the theatres closed; or wandering the streets of Exarchia looking for somewhere to dance. Although the city was polished up a few years ago for the Olympics and the air no longer gives you nosebleeds, at heart it still feels a 'dirty old town' to me, full of history and memories and a lingering grittiness that's part of its appeal.

On the long journey to Athens, I pass time by reading and I sneak glances at Stelios with his nose buried in a book. Promising, I think. On paper, it may seem a ridiculous relationship: so many years between us, and only the basics of language in common. Yet we were both born in cities (he in Athens, I in Manchester) and grew up in villages surrounded by hills before going away to further our education. We have similar outlooks on life: cheerful, optimistic, hard-working, determined; we're both people who want to find our own routes to happiness, not necessarily via the standard model. I've had just as much success with apparently unsuitable relationships as with apparently suitable ones.

The closest we get to the Acropolis on the first day is a distant view of it as we sit for 2 hours with his best friend Stratos drinking coffee in Thissio. I'd forgotten that Athens with Greek friends would mean spending many hours at a time drinking coffee with *parea*, company, and the rest of the time waiting for other friends or finding a good place to eat.

That evening, we drive on motorbikes for miles across the outer suburbs of the city to the concert venue in Petroupoli where the singer friend they came to see is performing as warm-up act for legendary Greek rocker Vassilis Papakonstantinou. So much time is spent eating souvlaki – sticks of grilled meat – while chatting and waiting outside the gates for the rest of the *parea* that we actually miss their friend's performance.

Next day, Stelios wants to go shopping; Tilos has just one clothes shop, for women only, and he needs new jeans and T-shirts. I find some new gear for myself and am rewarded by being called a *koukla*, a doll. We have coffee in Monastiraki and discuss going to the Acropolis Museum.

'But first we should eat,' says Stratos, and a debate ensues about where.

We set off on the motorbikes down Piraeus Street, the wide road that stretches from Omonia Square down to the port, and I am enthralled by the colourful, large-scale street art that covers the grimy buildings. We drive a fair way and then, because I've been looking carefully at the art, I notice we've circled back again.

'Isn't this the street we drove down before?' I ask after twenty minutes.

It turns out no one remembers exactly how to get to the restaurant. But just as I am wondering how important it is to find this particular restaurant, we take an unpromising side street and find ourselves in Gazi, a cool neighbourhood of understated little eateries. In a shady courtyard we eat a very good meal of fried anchovies, fried cheese, falafel with tahini and boiled beetroot, its stems and leaves glistening with olive oil. The nearby walls are covered in clever, beautifully drawn street art. Opposite us is a wall painted with lines and lines of ornate writing, phrases running into phrases that take some deciphering, and some English words catch my eye and strike me: '... one hope one quest enjoy every minute unstoppable open your eyes and you will see have as much fun as possible...'

We drink ouzo, and afterwards no one is really in the mood for the museum. In the evening, there is a plan for the *parea* to drive across the city again to a park where the singer friend will perform privately for her friends who missed the concert. After another motorbike ride into the suburbs, which leaves me feeling somewhat cheated of an evening in the Athens I love, by 1 a.m. I am sitting in the dark next to a shopping mall and cinema complex, by a duck pond, while half the friends go off to buy souvlaki. No wonder everyone smokes – to pass the time. I am not exactly thrilled with this. The waiting around feels pointless and, somewhat disenchanted by the whole idea of the singer and wanting to be awake enough to enjoy my last day, I ask Stelios if we can leave. He agrees.

On the last day, after stopping for food and coffee, we do finally make it to the Acropolis Museum. The upper floor is dedicated to all the marble frescoes that were 'violently plundered', according to the signage, by Lord Elgin and are in the British Museum, leaving only replicas here. I fall in love again with a *kore* statue, a young female probably dedicated to the goddess Athena. I used to visit museums on weekends here and was entranced by *kore* and *kouros* statues, ancient marble figures of women and men. In archaic times they had been stylised and resembled Egyptian statues, but they became more Greek as the centuries passed, each one unique. This *kore*, an enigmatic half-smile on her face, one of those semi-destroyed during ancient raids on the temple, is perhaps the same one whose photograph – torn out of the guidebook – I had pinned on my bedroom wall.

On motorbikes, Stelios and Stratos take me to the port. I have to leave to meet my friend Claire in Kos, then in two days we'll join Stelios on the next ferry back to Tilos.

'Take care of each other,' I say.

'We always do,' they reply. It tugs at my heart.

They wait and wave goodbye as the big boat pulls away.

Claire and I used to go to classes at the gym together before I moved here, and now she's coming to Tilos for a holiday, flying to the larger Dodecanese island of

Kos. I meet her in Kos town and take her to spend a day swimming at the hot springs of Therma. We catch up on the news of our lives over some good Greek food before we meet up with Stelios on the *Diagoras* ferry for the few hours' journey to Tilos. I offer her my bedroom in the house for a couple of weeks while she explores the island – I'm happy to sleep downstairs on the couch or outside on the terrace, as I'm up early in the mornings at my desk.

One evening, Claire and I go out to dinner at Kastro in Megalo Horio, which has good, home-grown food: Dina and her husband keep their own goats and pigs, grow many of their own vegetables and make their own olive oil. Stelios joins us a little later when he's finished work. Bringing another plate of food, Dina asks Claire how she's enjoying Tilos; then jokes that we should find her a nice local boy so she can come and live here. Since Stelios is about Claire's age, Dina starts teasing him, asking him when he's going to get married.

'I'm too young for that!' he says.

'How old are you now?' she asks him.

'Twenty-seven.'

I choke on a sip of wine.

When Dina leaves, I say under my breath, 'I thought you said you were twenty-eight?'

'Next birthday,' he says.

One day he comes over with a huge batch of red mullet and *skaros*, extremely tasty little fish, so I invite Anna to join us for dinner at my house. While Stelios is out with the fishing boat in the evening, putting out the nets,

I make salad from the garden, and mix yoghurt, garlic, grated cucumber and olive oil for tzatziki, squeezing the juice out of the cucumber so the tzatziki is thick and creamy. I lay food out on the wooden table on the terrace along with drinks, and leave Anna and Claire to chat while I gut the fish. Stelios is late so I start frying them. He arrives as it's getting dark, takes one look at the frying pan and says far more olive oil is needed. He takes over. Much later, after dinner, we have an idea to go dancing at Mikro Horio bar, as it may be closing soon for the season. We debate how we might get there. Claire begs off, ready for sleep, so that solves the problem: Anna and I will both ride on the back of Stelios' motorbike, he insists. No problem. He's not had much to drink as he was busy cooking. I think Claire is still a little shocked and relieved to be staying at home as we laughingly roar off down the dirt track in the dark, three of us on the bike without a crash helmet between us. Welcome to life on a tiny Greek island.

Although it's mid-September, locals joke that it's the 47th August – because midsummer weather continues, blissfully unaware that autumn should be on its way. While night sometimes brings a cool breeze, swimming and cold showers are still essential during the hot days. So when Claire and I drop in to see Maria and her daughter Evgenia one afternoon at their house halfway up the hill to the village, we're grateful for glasses of cool *soumada*, almond cordial. Pavlos and Maria were in Athens at the same time I was, for a wedding. '*Zougla!*' Pavlos called it – jungle. Now we learn from Maria, as she's shooing away a cat that's determined to get in the house, that someone has been stealing the eggs from their hens.

'What,' I ask, 'an animal?'

'No, people have been stealing them!'

Goodness. I'm surprised.

Maria says it's not the first time. 'In Athens they rob banks – in Tilos it's just eggs!'

It's also a reminder of what Pantelis was saying the other night when he treated us to a bottle of retsina in the *kafeneion*. Life is hard in Greece at the moment, with people losing their livelihood, the prices of everything going up and no way to pay for it all. A new property tax is being imposed via electricity bills, which means people who don't pay up have their power cut off. Which makes it doubly kind when a pensioner like him insists on buying us retsina.

All summer, people have talked about whether Greece will leave the eurozone. On the islands, many say they'd prefer to return to the nation's former currency, the drachma, as the cheaper prices would attract tourists; others say those benefits would be short-lived. Tilos, like many islands, has been less affected by the crisis than cities on the mainland. The public workers are the worst hit, those who work for the local council or phone service or schools; salaries in the public sector have been cut by over a quarter. There's very little other work except tourism and farming, which remain steady year after year. At least if you're hungry, there's always the option of growing something, gathering wild food or catching a fish.

When Claire leaves, I suggest to Stelios that he stay at my house whenever he wants to, rather than driving back up to his parents' place. He always leaves at dawn, when the owner of the fishing boat rings him; cigarette smoke drifts up towards the bedroom as he makes coffee. I expect that once the summer is really over, he'll drift away to a job elsewhere, using his training as a plumber to find work in construction, even though work is now scarce and his last employer on Rhodes still owes him seven months' worth of pay and says he's broke.

'Maybe you'll take me to England so I can find work there?' he says, half-joking.

'Make no mistake,' I say, 'I'm not going back to England for a while, not even for you.'

Chapter 6

The Seahorse

'In the evening we put out nets, *richnoumeh dichtia*, and in the morning we take out fish, *vgazoumeh psaria*.'

The fishermen go out when the sun's coming up, as that's when the fish come out. In summer that could be 5 a.m., but this late September Sunday it's 7 a.m., and I've been invited along because soon they'll be switching to a different kind of net, the *trata*, when the season opens for that type of fishing. We stop at the bakery for breakfast of warm *spanakopita*, spinach pie.

Nikos Haralambakis is the owner of the boat, appropriately named as Saint Nicholas is the patron saint of fishermen. He's in his early forties and has been fishing for thirty years, since he was a boy, in all seasons. Nikos is one of seven brothers, including Yorgos who has the *kafeneion* in Livadia, and another Stelios who works with him on the boat. The fishermen change into orange rubber overalls and rubber boots. Someone sits at the back to steer. I'm given a seat in the middle where I can see everything and keep out of the way.

It's a calm morning, cool as we set out, a few wisps of cloud on the hilltops. Along the headland to the south of the bay, the water is still a pale grey. At the first net, Nikos' brother uses a wooden pole to hook the float out of the water and reels in the rope; then a motor takes over, winching it over a series of wheels; he pulls out the fish and tosses them into a bucket of seawater, and winds the net into a neat heap.

Nikos leans over the side, watching to see what's coming in; shouts, 'Good skaros, take it!' and instructions to the rudder to keep the boat where he needs it. *'Bros!'* Forward. *'Anichta!'* Away from land. *'Isia!'* Straight.

The first fish to come over the side include spiky orange *skorpio* or scorpion fish, and *yermani*, Germans, with poisonous spines that can give a nasty sting; all these are extracted expertly from the nets with bare hands. For a while there's nothing, and then about six good-sized fish, followed by a *karavitha*, a type of reddish-brown lobster with no pincers but a powerful tail that curls and snaps back. The lobster's a good find; it can fetch up to €40 a kilo. Then there's a *sinagritha*, 2 kilos at least, the 'king of fish', silvery blue. When eventually there's nothing more coming up but weeds, it's time to move on.

Feegeh! Go! *Valeh gazi...* Give it some gas.

Crossing the bay to the north side allows a brief break for a cigarette and fresh coffees. A sudden panic: no more coffees! Searches are conducted for the disposable plastic frappé cups. A brief despondent lull, knowing there's no more coffee this morning. The disposable cups come with their own coffee and sugar so you just add water and shake, and they're probably very useful to busy fishermen; but having seen the empty plastic cups being disposed of over the side of the boat, the part of me that cares about the environment thinks maybe the fish will be happier.

The island looks different from here, outside; the sun is coming up now over the side of a mountain and brightening the colours. We skirt the shore where the cliffs and the coves are a rich red, reflecting in the still water, pass Gaidouronisi, Donkey Island, then stop at the next net. Tiny fish have to be extricated and thrown back, but soon the bucket starts filling up. There's a flurry of excitement when a strange-looking fish appears, blue-green spots on top, bright white bloated belly: *lagokefalos*.

'If you eat this, you die!' Nikos stabs the poisonous fish, an invasive species, in the head with a knife before throwing it overboard.

Then someone finds a seahorse in the net, an *alogaki tis thalassas* – little horse of the sea – otherwise known as *ippocampos*. They put it in my hand. It's beautiful, a tiny, perfect, grey, dragon-like creature. 'Take this home. It's beautiful for the house!'

But it's alive, and it doesn't want to die. I don't want it dead in my house. Its mouth forms an 'o' as it gasps for air and it flexes its body and curls its tail in and out. I keep it in my hand and try to ignore it. I'm a guest and don't want to be rude by throwing it overboard. It could even be bad luck to throw it back, and I'm trying not to be a pest while the men do their work – I'm grateful to be here. They celebrate the arrival of a nice catch of reddish-white *barbounia*, red mullet, a good fish to sell. Nikos' brother starts singing a popular Greek folk song that has a chorus about a black horse and a white horse. I laugh; I seem to remember it's a song about a man with two girlfriends. *'To allo alogo, eineh aspro...'*

It's horrible watching a seahorse die, its little body stretching out in what looks like agony. I look at the sad thing in my hand, wrapping its tail around the pen I'm holding.

Stelios assures me, 'There are lots of them.' Of course all the fish we're catching today are meeting the same fate, so why do I feel this way about the damn seahorse? Because we have a sentimental attachment to seahorses, the way they faintly resemble an embryo curled up inside its mother... Or because nobody needs to eat this, so it's dying to be beautiful in my house; dying, in fact, for no reason, as I can't imagine decorating my house with a dead seahorse. It's a cultural difference. I put it to one side.

The fish is packed in a box, sluiced down with fresh seawater and covered with wet hessian in the shade. We continue past the pretty beach of Lethra, then another little island, Prasouda, and mineral-blue rocks that drop sheer into the sea until we reach turquoise water, where on a sliver of pale beach a couple of goats are picking their way down the rocks to drink.

'How can the goats here drink salt water?' I ask Stelios.

'There's nothing else in the summer. It's evolution!'

We stop, and the men gather in the net, unsnagging knots, pulling off rocks and plants, sometimes singing a little to pass the time. There are no fish for a while, and they all look a little edgy. Then suddenly, we know why.

A big grey seal emerges from the sea nearby, flips over and disappears again.

'This, the *fokia*, is why we take no fish here.'

The seals eat the fish from the nets. They eat through the nets to get at the fish – Stelios shows me the holes. It's an easy feast. The seal surfaces again on the other side of the boat. Monk seals are an endangered species but they thrive on the fish around the shores of Tilos, which is a protected conservation area.

'That's a small one,' says Nikos. 'They get bigger.'

This net is empty and we continue in a more sombre mood. Two cormorants stand on some low, jagged rocks silhouetted black and grey against a silver-blue sea in the early morning light. The seal comes up again, eating a fish.

Next time, we're farther out, deeper. The winch winds up rope, then net, and soon up over the side is a lobster, an *astako* with pincers and feelers, purple with orange markings. There's also a cuttlefish, *soupia*. And because we're fishing deep, there are clumps of compacted earth and weeds that get caught in the nets and have to be stamped out flamenco-style, leaving a big mess in the boat. Stamping out the chunks of dirt, winding nets into piles, standing for hours to extricate fins and feelers, leaning over to pull out the fish, it's got to be exhausting. Occasionally a fish caught in the net has been eaten away by something else, and they still have to extricate the remains and throw it overboard as the net has to be cleaned. They wind the nets twice over a wooden pole to remove all the dirt, and then sweep and sluice the deck.

All the rope and net and spiny fish and salt water every day – no wonder Stelios has rough hands.

Nikos places several live lobsters carefully under the wet hessian sack as if he's tucking them up in bed, and they stop moving. '*Ipno!*' he says. 'Sleep. That was a good net.' Seals don't eat lobsters.

No sooner has the deck been cleaned than we're preparing to pull in another deep net. This one's coming from 140 metres, outside the mouth of Livadia harbour. It brings in a *smerna*, a moray eel, glistening brown and yellow. Nikos gives it a swift blow to the head with his boot to kill it quickly, as if it smells blood or food (the other fish) it can be dangerous. Then small sharks or dogfish, *galeos*, start to come in, one after another, five or six of them; they do look like miniature sharks, with smooth, silky, dark-grey skin and bright-blue glassy marbles for eyes. Stelios opens a shell and hands me a fresh scallop to eat.

As it gets closer to midday, the sun is hot overhead and since the boat is continually moving around, they have to keep moving the boxes of fish into the shade and wetting the hessian. As we chug back to port, Nikos gets on the phone. In the summer, he sells direct to the island's restaurants; in winter, when they're closed, a small catch might be sold locally and the rest put on ice and shipped to Rhodes or Athens. There aren't as many fish as there used to be, and the water has warmed up so there are more fish from Africa like the poisonous *lagokefalos*, and no more mackerel.

There's a little more singing while the hard work of winding and cleaning and sorting progresses. I've never seen three Greek men smoke so few cigarettes: there's no time. I'd never have imagined so much shaking out of nets, sweeping and washing, day in, day out. They continue winding nets into piles ready for the evening, selling and filleting fish, as I step off the boat, still awkwardly holding the seahorse.

I've never been interested in watching sport, but this morning a text came through from Anna asking if I'd like to go to the football, and seeing the Tilos team play at the start of the season seems an important step in getting to know my new home.

The football ground is a ten-minute walk from my house; I set off along the dirt track surrounded by sage bushes and cypress trees and roaming goats, pass the entrance to the village, the high school and the army base, and reach the ground just before kick-off, wandering in past cars parked haphazardly, saying hello to people in the half-full stand as I make my way to a seat beside my friend. And the view makes me think it really might be a beautiful game after all. Trees surround the pitch, and beyond are the rugged, empty hills, with a deep blue sky above. To the left are the first few houses of the village and the church belfry.

The team line up alongside the boys from the neighbouring island of Symi, then all shake hands and move into position. At the outset, it looks as if our boys in red and blue might be out of practice, having spent their summer working in bars, rooms, restaurants, shops or driving the bus. But soon they're passing gracefully and pushing forward confidently. Within the first fifteen minutes, Tilos has scored. Gooooooaal! Two local ladies lead a round of 'Ti-los, Ti-los!' We're in a very vocal part of the crowd.

Both teams are an assortment of shapes and sizes but they do appear to be playing their hearts out. After Symi equalises, the yellow cards start to mount up. Anna says Tilos matches have been known to get a little heated, with the odd fight. There's a bit of rolling around the pitch, and Yorgos the nurse makes an appearance.

At *imichrono*, half-time, a couple of little boys come out on to the pitch with refreshments for the players, and their mum follows to take a photo. The score is 3–1 to Tilos, and Anna and I celebrate by buying cold drinks and juicy pork souvlaki, which have been sizzling on the grill. There's no queue, as the crowd is pretty small, just the half-full stand of those of us who've paid €5 for a seat, and half a dozen men leaning on the railings at the other side. After school finishes, a few teenage girls saunter in to join the crowd.

Symi scores again early in the second half. For the rest of the match, the ladies next to us shout themselves hoarse. They know all the Tilos team and are somehow related to most of them, and they direct the match play-by-play. A lady supporter uses choice language that makes the army boys grin. A few balls shoot over the fence into the eucalyptus trees, both teams get more yellow cards, and at one point an injury is ignored as a fight nearly breaks out at the other end of the pitch. It isn't a dull game. And the Tilos team hangs on to its win.

It occurs to me that the population of Tilos is a lot smaller than Symi, meaning that they are the underdogs. I check with Stelios, who has joined us.

'Yes, Symi is two thousand people. We are three hundred. And we drink and smoke a lot.'

The official number of Tilos residents is about seven hundred, but others say it's as low as three hundred in winter; I estimate around five hundred, depending on the time of year. Some work or study elsewhere, and even many who run summer businesses on the island leave when the season ends. It's a sad reality that the money they have made during the summer leaves with them. Not everyone can live on the island all year round. Anna will leave soon too for work back in England.

Later, I'm picking ripe tomatoes when Pavlos shouts hello. '*Yeia sou*, Jennifer!'

I tell him I went to the football. 'Usually I don't watch football,' I say, 'but it was nice as I knew so many people.'

'Everyone knows you now... As winter comes, it's more like that,' says Pavlos. '*Emeis kai emeis!*' It's an expression that means literally 'we and we', something like 'just us'. October is almost here, and it will just be the permanent residents left.

'When the rain comes, we'll plant onions, potatoes, carrots,' says Pavlos. 'Have you still got honey? I'll bring you some more.'

'Thank you, but this time I want to *buy* it!'

'No! We'll give it to you. If you want to buy it, we won't give you any!'

While I'm watering the plants, Stelios arrives and, since he doesn't have fishing tonight, potters around looking at courgette flowers. Back indoors, I see he's looking up recipes online. While Greeks tend to be strict about what goes into a particular dish, Stelios also improvises sometimes. At first when he cooked something and said, 'You'll never have tasted anything like this!' I thought he was bragging, but he actually meant it was his own recipe.

'Gather some mint from the garden,' he says now. 'And grate some graviera.'

He cuts eight courgette flowers and then chops a tiny courgette into thin slices. I mix the grated, salty, firm cheese with the chopped mint *(diosmo)* and an egg. We find half an onion in the fridge to add, a few cherry tomatoes from the garden, and grind in some pepper.

I put the oil in the frying pan, while he instructs, *'Valeh, valeh!'* – keep going!

He realises there are still ants in the courgette flowers and we have to put them in deep water to get them out – 'Let's see if they know how to swim...' Then he fills the yellow flowers with the mix and we douse them in flour. He puts them all in the hot oil to cook, and takes them out when they start to brown. Soon they're on the table, smelling delicious. We taste them. They're good. I had been sceptical about the point of stuffing courgette flowers but it's really just an excuse to eat soft and sticky fried cheese.

'Something missing?' he asks.

'Maybe more herbs?' I suggest.

'Or salt,' he says.

But they're very moreish. A successful experiment.

He's brought home a crab claw and an orange *mataki* or eye of the sea – part of a shell – which he found in the fishing nets and thought would look good on a necklace. He's still undecided as to whether he'll leave; there isn't much work anywhere in Greece this year, so although it's tough, he's also lucky that he could continue fishing on the island through the winter.

Which is why, one afternoon not long after, I find myself scrambling down a rough, slippery track on the back of a motorbike.

Chapter 7

Forces of Nature

There's a large and unwieldy bag of potatoes sitting on the handlebars of the motorbike and a sack of goat manure balanced precariously on the seat in front. I am terrified as we skid around in the rocks and sand. Stelios shouts at me in Greek – but what he is telling me to do, I have no idea.

We are on our way back from Menelaos' farm on the way to Skafi. Now that Stelios may be staying here over the winter, he is taking more of an interest in the garden. Menelaos owns hundreds if not thousands of goats and sheep, and the garden needs fertiliser. While we were there, Stelios asked for a bag of potatoes as well, and will repay him with some fish or a beer at a later date. Usually when I'm on the back of the motorbike and bouncing around down an uneven track, he says '*Min fovaseh*', don't be afraid, but this time he's shouting and I wish I could get off the bike.

Eventually, I discover that he wants me to grab hold of the sack of manure to stop it sliding off the seat – linguistically a little beyond me, and physically not so easy either. Of course I am grateful, however, for the help with acquiring what I want for the garden. We eventually make it home.

Now that there's fertiliser, I can plant the beetroot seeds. Pavlos takes over, mixing them with some earth in a bucket before scattering them on ground that's freshly dug with manure. I wanted to do the digging myself, but if I try digging the garden in front of Pavlos and Stelios, they will laugh at my feebleness and tell me I'm doing it wrong. How could an English woman know how to dig a garden? How difficult can it be though, I wonder…?

I don't really know why I feel the need for blisters on my hands. I like experimenting with my very first garden. I want the exercise, to feel strong; already I'm physically stronger as my new life here involves so much walking and swimming. And moving to Tilos alone, relying on myself, has worked so far; I don't want to become dependent on anyone else. If I'd been dependent, I might not have got here in the first place. Anyway, it's just a beetroot patch… I give in, let the men do the work, and will sneak in some gardening when no one's around.

'What's that,' said Pavlos, pointing at my new plant, '*dendrolivano*?'

'Yes.' I admit it's rosemary. I know exactly what he's going to say next.

'Why did you buy that? Where, in Rhodes? We have lots of it here in Tilos! How much did you pay?'

Stelios had said exactly the same. I find myself lying again about the price, just to defend myself: I say two euros, when it was actually three.

'Oh. Well, that's OK.'

It's my garden, and my money, and I just wanted it. Sometimes paying a couple of euros is a lot easier than procuring things the Tilos way.

My dad visits for a few days in early October. It's supposed to be five days, but almost on arrival he learns that Greek air traffic controllers are planning to strike on the day he's due to fly home – so he's somewhat stressed by the likelihood that he'll have to change his flight and leave early in order to make it back in time for work. He loves staying by the beach in Livadia, where he can lie on a sunbed and read a book, but one day I meet him and we drive his rental car to Eristos Beach Hotel for lunch. I want it to be a relaxing experience, but after we've waited a while at a table on the empty terrace I can tell he's wondering what's going on, so I head for the kitchen. I return to explain that I've ordered Greek salad and a couple of beers but they've run out of tomatoes – it's the end of the season – and are going to get some from the farm.

Dad looks incredulous. 'It's a Greek taverna and they don't have any tomatoes?'

He and Mum introduced me to Greece when I was little and I can see his point, but the ones they get freshly picked from the farm up the road will be even better, and to me it's the quirks of Tilos that make it special. There again, perhaps I'd be just as exasperated if it were my holiday. Living here, I'm protective of my relationship with the local people in whose community I'm trying to live a peaceful life. I get defensive because I want everyone to love Tilos the way I do.

After a very good Greek salad, Dad snoozes in the sunshine for the afternoon while I work, then we go into Megalo Horio, stopping at Pavlos and Maria's so I can introduce them. Maria is delighted to meet my father, even though she doesn't speak English and he doesn't speak Greek. She sits us down and offers us a spoon sweet. Greek women often keep fruit preserved in sugary syrup, and offer a spoonful to guests.

Dad has a dread of Greek sweets, however. I once gave him the name and address of a lovely lady in Lipsi who had treated me like a long-lost daughter when I stayed with her for a few weeks. Dad, on holiday in Lipsi, felt compelled to go along to see her, and recalls with horror how he and his girlfriend were forced to sit down on the balcony, drink coffee and eat sweets while Eleni insisted on making conversation with them in Greek, of which they didn't understand a word.

So now, as Maria is offering a *glyko*, Dad whispers to me, 'Can you tell her I've got diabetes?'

I do.

'Oh, that's sad,' she says, putting away her jar of candied fruit and patting his hand. 'Well, I hope you'll come and visit again, and we can cook stuffed goat for you!'

Afraid that Dad will concoct another illness, I usher him out the door and up the road to the *kafeneion*, where he drinks a beer and feeds peanuts to the ants on the terrace; Sofia seems to realise that eccentricity runs in the family.

Back to my quiet routine a few days later after Dad leaves, I walk up to the supermarket. Megalo Horio has two shops, Irini's mini-mini-market up the alley towards the *kafeneion*, and the 'supermarket' – which is two rooms of sometimes unbridled chaos, spilling out on to the road where the bus squeezes past, amid flowerpots painted blue. The place is stuffed full of the most eclectic mix of what a villager might need, although the sign out front merely advertises 'Cigarettes', which are kept on a very high shelf and need to be knocked down by whatever comes to hand, a mop handle or Menelaos' stick. This supermarket, a centre of village life, is owned by Eleftheria's mother Rena – another form of the name Irini. You don't have to be called Irini to have a shop in Megalo Horio, but it helps.

Yorgos the nurse, thin and bespectacled with a sly sense of humour, is in the supermarket, too, searching for something up and down one aisle. I'm searching for something up and down the other aisle. When we reach the end, we swap and do the same as if it's a sitcom.

'What are you looking for?'

'*Chlorini*, bleach.'

'Me too! Where is it?'

We swap aisles again and look in vain. When we give up, Rena comes and points it out, hidden behind something else.

'Here we are,' says Yorgos, handing me a bottle, grinning. 'Good for the hair.'

Walking back through the village I run into old Pantelis, who looks happy to see me and stops to talk.

'Where's your father? He's gone already? Just three days in Tilos?'

'Unfortunately yes – he had to go home for work. But I'm sure he'll be back.'

'And your mother, when is she coming?'

'Oh, as soon as she can! She has a husband and a dog back in England...'

Once you've visited Tilos, you're part of the family.

Since the weather has cooled down, for exercise I decide to walk up to the castle. I haven't been up there since late spring and neither have many other people, by the looks of the overgrown path. There are a few flies about and one keeps coming back to my arm. A moment later, there are hornets buzzing around my head and in my hair. I feel a sting on my back as I start to run down the path, trying to shield my head somehow without losing my footing. Eventually they leave me alone. I've had hornets buzzing around my house before and they've been harmless: I must have kicked a hornets' nest. The sting is quite painful but doesn't look bad. I shower and make myself a cup of tea and look after myself for the afternoon.

And then, the next day, it comes.

I've heard of it, but never experienced it before: the wonderful smell of the countryside when the first rain falls on the oregano, thyme and sage plants after they've been scorched by the sun for five or six months.

The day starts when we are awoken by violent winds. The canopy in the garden flaps around crazily. Stelios dashes outside to untie it and stop it from tearing. Chairs and my shoes are scattered everywhere. Delos tells me the beehives he took down to Ayios Andonis last night have blown over.

At lunchtime, the wind has died down and I walk up to the village, warm in jeans and flip-flops and vest top, the sky turning blue. It doesn't look like rain is coming. But dark clouds cover the sky during the afternoon as I sit and work, my hornet sting still itching but no longer hurting. Then the rain falls and falls...

I'm used to rain in England; frequent rain, inappropriate summer rain; not deluges of sky-falling-down rain.

As the torrential downpour softens to a gentle pattering, I set off down the muddy track and it's like walking through a church filled with incense, so intense is the fragrance of the herbs. It's also very still, and so clear I can hear the waves crashing on the shore at Eristos a few kilometres away. A cockerel crows as the rain dies away. White wispy clouds play over the tops of the mountains. Everything is fresh and the rain brings it all into bright, high definition – the stones of ruined buildings, the trees, the mountainsides.

There is a Greek word for autumn, *fthinoporo*, but I hardly ever hear it. People mostly say it's winter when the rain starts, when the summer businesses close and it's only permanent residents on the island. Autumn means a decline, a waning, but although the days are growing shorter, the seasons are different here. When the rains start to fall after the long, dry summer, the forces of nature bring everything to life.

Stelios, while still joking that he's only hanging around so I'll take him to England, makes the decision not to go away for work but to stay in Tilos with me. He works long hours on the fishing boat, leaving me with plenty of time alone, which is important to me, and I'm even happy when he messes up my kitchen-office with his tobacco and cooking and sugary coffee cups. So, given that we're moving on to a more serious stage of the relationship, there's something we need to talk about.

I think he'll probably run away when I tell him I want to see if it's possible to have a child.

'All women do,' he says, matter-of-factly.

'No, they don't,' I say. 'I didn't for a long time.'

A woman doesn't get past her early forties without ever being pregnant just because she didn't get around to it. Friends remember me as someone who had no interest at all in kids. Even into my thirties, I wasn't sure. I thought if it was ever supposed to happen, then I would know. It was only in my mid-thirties that my body's forces of nature kicked in; only as I turned forty, single, that I realised how strongly I wanted to try, if it were still possible. Stelios already knows about my last relationship. I explain as well as I can in my basic Greek.

'I understand if this changes things for you. This is just something I have to do now. If you don't want to stay, it's OK. I want to try to be a mother, but I don't need to have a husband, not immediately. I know it's strange. But I'm in a difficult situation. I've thought it all through a lot. You don't have to stay and be a father if you don't want to.'

But Stelios loves kids and his eyes have lit up. He says, 'It's OK. I understand. We will see what happens.'

We decide to take it one step at a time.

After a few days of rain, the sunshine returns and in the early afternoon I walk down the road to Eristos beach. Near the sea, I encounter Dimitris the fruit and vegetable seller, just outside his family's tiny taverna, now closed of course for the winter. He's carrying a towel.

'Number eighty-six!' he shouts: eighty-six swims this year. When he reaches a hundred swims, he'll stop. He's usually the only other person I see at the beach, though occasionally I'll see my teacher friend Dimitris with his wetsuit and harpoon, off to find fish or octopus.

Halfway back home is the other farm where I buy vegetables. Michalis is no longer sitting in the shade of the tree, and his crates and scales have been packed away for winter, but his son Yorgos is in the field nearby planting cabbages and cauliflowers. He gives me a bag of seedlings and instructs me to plant them that day, 60 cm apart. I get home and start preparing the ground for them, while Stelios makes bread and chaos in the kitchen.

'Jennifer!' he shouts.

I run inside.

'Can you add some flour?' His hands are sticky with dough.

I add flour to the bowl and go back to my garden.

'Jennifer!'

I drop the trowel again and go inside.

'Can you plug in my mobile?' He needs it charged for the evening. He never knows exactly what time Nikos will call him for fishing.

'Jennifer!'

I dig a little more and then, more slowly this time, go inside. The oven door is open, the bread under a towel.

'OK, we leave it now to get big. Have you finished in the garden yet?'

Er, no, not yet – there have been a few interruptions. Gradually, the smell of baking bread fills the house.

Chapter 8

Normal Service Will Be Resumed

For a week or so now, the sole Tilos ATM on the outside wall of what may be the tiniest bank in the world has not been working. 'Use another branch nearest you,' said the message on the screen. The nearest branch is on Rhodes – a bank withdrawal could take a day or more, depending on ferries. Perhaps someone pointed this out, as a few days later the technician has still not arrived, but the message has been changed: 'Normal service will be resumed in a few minutes.'

I've started to feel like that myself: always on the brink of normal service, but not quite getting there. Life seems more hectic, busier than it was before.

'Miss! Hello, miss!' Grinning 8-year-olds are waving at me across the square in Livadia. Which ones are they? Kyriakos, perhaps, and Yorgos? For now their names are a bit of a blur – entertaining a dozen noisy children is something I haven't done for quite a while.

It all started when I got a message from Dimitris the headmaster that Irini, who works in the doctor's office in Megalo Horio, wanted to talk to me about something. I figured I'd see her when I went up to the village, but before that happened, Stelios said, 'Oh, something I had to tell you...' and it was that Irini wanted to speak to me. Then I got a Facebook message from Evgenia, saying Maria wanted to see me.

I went to see Maria – and of course she wanted to tell me that Irini needed to talk to me. It was good to see Maria anyway, and as a side benefit I got some fried aubergines and delicious local cheese marinated in red wine – the kind of thing you can only get if you happen to know someone who makes it.

So I went to see Irini the next day in the medical centre, a couple of tiny rooms half-hidden behind the mass of bougainvillaea covering the pergola over the road through the village. It turned out a group of parents, Irini included, were looking for someone to help the kids with their English for the winter, and since I used to teach in a language school in Athens, Dimitris recommended me.

Now more than ever, youngsters need to learn English; in the economic crisis, unemployment has skyrocketed and during this period thousands of Greeks have left for Australia and other countries to find work. But running an English school, like so many other things, is difficult on an island with a tiny population, and beyond the normal school curriculum there's no English tuition available. The economies of scale possible in big schools in big places go out the window here with only about twenty-five schoolchildren, all of different ages; there's no dedicated premises; the cost of licences and insurance doesn't bear thinking about; and in the winter there's no afternoon bus to bring children from the outlying settlements for extracurricular activities. Course books cost a whopping €25 each and would have to be bought in Rhodes along with supplies like photocopy paper.

So in the absence of a language school, the idea is to hold informal English sessions. I arrange a preliminary discussion at the junior school, and there I meet parents who care a lot about their children's education – mostly Greeks but also those from other countries such as Bulgaria or Ukraine who have settled here, whose children have had to learn Greek as well as English. They say they'll leave it up to me to decide what's needed and how to organise things, which is even more nerve-wracking. I take names and notes, and leave with my head spinning and a date to meet the kids.

I decide to give it my best shot. It will be a challenge, a way to get to know people, to get out of the house and be more involved with the community; most of my days are spent working at a desk remotely with people abroad. My work contract with my company in England is for four days a week, the fifth reserved for freelancing, so technically I have time to do a half-day of English sessions twice a week. I have just agreed to take on an additional freelance contract, but I'll squeeze it in over the weekends. Since I can only spare two half-days, I have to divide all the kids aged eight to eighteen into just two groups, meaning each group will vary enormously in ability; but that's the best I can offer. I'll do a session with each group, one after the other, two afternoons a week from four until seven.

So much for my quiet life. It makes me nervous signing a form saying I take full responsibility for any damage to the school property or anything that goes missing. Many of the children I've seen around but I have no idea who they're related to, what their names are or how they are likely to behave.

My first meeting with the children is a few days later. The teenagers are kind and polite and surprise me with their excellent English. I think I'm going to enjoy getting to know them, and if we can keep up their progress it will be a good thing. I bring biscuits to my meeting with the younger ones – bribe them to be good by promising treats. It's funny how smaller children produce much more sound, even before you feed them sugar. They start well, and my Greek is good enough to communicate. It's easy to spot the problem areas; the main problem will be my propensity to laugh at their jokes, which will only encourage their naughtiness – but it's hard not to, as even the little terrors are adorable.

'Any questions?' I ask in Greek at the end.

One hand flies up. 'Yes, miss. When can we eat the biscuits?'

I'm grateful to my friend Dimitris for recommending me.

Back when Dimitris and I first met, when I came for a month to try out living here, we spent afternoons at beaches together, snorkelling around rocks. Now that I'm seeing Stelios, he's told me he'd prefer to keep his distance, and since he lives in Livadia our paths don't cross very much. But he invites me to the celebration of his name day in the last week of October.

Most Greek people are named after a saint, and the celebration, or *yortee*, that you have on the saint's day is more important than a birthday. Greek calendars and diaries are usefully marked with all the name days, but I haven't yet got around to buying a Greek calendar, so I still forget everyone's name day unless I'm invited to celebrate.

Most of Dimitris' friends are teachers and live in Livadia, but one who lives in Megalo Horio offers to pick me up along the way, since there's no evening bus at this time of year. She and I buy him a gift from the shop near where we park. The nights feel even darker now that many restaurants have shut down for the winter. Dimitris has invited us to Mikro Kafe on the waterfront, one of the few places still open, where I imagine I'd spend more evenings if I lived in this village. The stone walls and dark woodwork feel cosy when it's dark and cold outside, and there's music. I wish my friend, who still looks very young for someone who's nearing 50, *khronia polla*, many years, or many happy returns.

It's a strange life being a teacher in Greece, and I learn more about it this evening. The government decides where to send teachers to fill its needs across the country, and informs them at the end of each summer where they'll be posted for the year. One of the women is from Athens and has a son in school; she's had to leave him with his father. Of course she can go to see him but only when ferry schedules permit, mainly during holidays; and the cost of travel is high on a teacher's salary – especially when that salary has been cut because of what's simply become known as the *krisi*, the crisis. The cost of living on a small, remote island can be high compared with a city – there are no cheap markets because of the small population and shipping costs add to the prices – so even ordinary household goods or petrol for a car can be expensive. The teachers have mostly trained and worked their first years in a big city such as Athens, so they don't have friends and family nearby to help out. It can be lonely and a strain; since the staff changes from year to year, it's hard to have permanent friends.

It's a convivial evening and I enjoy the company. But I'm worried about staying late, as I have a piece of work to start the next morning and my time now is tighter than it used to be. I also feel a little awkward, thinking they're speaking English or slow Greek for my benefit; and I find it difficult making conversation in noisy places. If I mention that I'm leaving, the teacher who gave me a lift here will feel pressured to cut short her night to take me home, so I slip out quietly without saying anything. I pay for my glass of wine at the bar, have a quick chat with a couple of English friends, and happily set off walking. It's a mild night with lots of stars, and I enjoy the hour-long walk in the dark on the quiet road. Young Saeed passes me on a scooter, stops and tries to insist on giving me a ride.

'No thanks – I'm almost home!'

'*Ela re,* come on!' he shouts, but I grin and wave until he drives on.

I send Dimitris a message before I go to bed, thanking him for the invitation and explaining why I left early, and I receive one back from him the next day.

Thank you for your company last night, now there is the explanation for your sudden departure without say anything.

I do not like your action to pay for your drink, the Greek custom is paying the human which invites people. I will owe a drink.

All best Dimitris

I realise I've made a faux pas, a cultural gaffe, and I write back at once saying I hope he realises I didn't mean to offend him. I was only trying to do the right thing and not break up the party.

I have never felt the need for a car. Though I passed my driving test while at university, I subsequently felt no need or desire to drive. Living in cities in Greece, Canada, France and England, I cycled, walked, took buses and trains and taxis (still so much cheaper than owning a car). People always claimed there was too much traffic on the roads, but no one bothered to do anything about it. Not having a car was good for the planet and good for me.

A couple of years ago, I decided that being able to drive once in a while might be useful, such as at Christmas when public transport in England grinds to a halt and I have to rely on my parents to deliver me from one house to the other. So I took refresher lessons, but then life got turned upside down and I never got around to driving. When my mum visited Tilos this summer, she encouraged me to drive the hire car around the quiet roads. My dad let me drive his hire car, too, when he came, although being given unwanted advice by him and Stelios simultaneously in two languages nearly made me give up again.

So I know how to drive, but I think that even if the weather turns wintry, walking to Livadia and back to do the English sessions will be good for me. Stelios laughs and tells me I might change my mind when there's a huge electrical storm and rain lashing down. Walking 4 miles for fun is one thing; walking it loaded down with books, papers and my laptop, spending 3 hours with demanding children and walking back again, twice a week, is quite another. And then there's Leo from Megalo Horio, whose family doesn't have a car. He can't join in if someone doesn't take him home.

Ironically, after surviving all my life so far without a car, now I might need one on an island that's about 7 miles long by 3 wide. Naturally, I'm hesitant. Apart from anything else, it could be the beginning of the end for the strong leg muscles I've been building.

My first thought is to rent a car for the winter: presumably the hire cars aren't used in the winter and a deal for several months might be good for everyone. But when I enquire, I learn the cars aren't insured during the winter. When they factor in the extra cost for getting insurance, the amount for six months would be half the price of buying a used car outright and getting it insured and road-tested. So I start to consider buying one.

The question is causing a little stress, which is funny as the editing job I have just started is a book about managing stress. I made a conscious decision to cut back on stress a couple of years ago, especially when I decided to try to get pregnant. I seem to have most of the book's recommendations covered – from eating healthy fats and low GI foods, walking and swimming, to appreciating what you have and living in the moment.

'Take control of your spending', says the book. Spending large amounts of money makes me nervous, and it's early in my life in Tilos to be making big investments. Plus it doesn't quite fit with my plan to reduce my needs. Legally, I can't own a car without a Greek driving licence, so I have to give the money to Stelios – a man I've been with for just two months – so he can buy it and let me use it. If I had any issues with trust after the end of my last relationship, they're certainly being put to the test.

A week later, fit but exhausted having walked to Livadia and back three times in one week, I hear reports that the parents and kids are happy with their English sessions. So if I'm going to continue, it's time to bite the bullet. A car is for sale in Tilos but it seems a lot of money for a fairly rusty thing, so we decide to go to Rhodes to see one of Stelios' cousins, whose girlfriend is selling hers.

We can take the big ship *Diagoras* on Friday morning and return that evening, and now I know about the online 'marine tracker' which you can use to find its position and know if it's arriving on time at 6 a.m. We drive to Livadia on the motorbike, and a golden sun is rising over the harbour; we're treated to a spectacular view of Symi harbour 2 hours later, and arrive in Rhodes around mid-morning.

The car is a bright-red Citröen Saxo. It's not too big, not too expensive, and old enough that I won't mind bashing it occasionally – but it seems to run well. I sense that it's the car for me. We sit around drinking coffee for a while, and the sale is agreed. Stelios knows a good mechanic who can service it for us, so we leave it with him in the afternoon. In the couple of hours we have left, I buy some English language materials; Stelios pays a visit to a fish merchant who owes the fishing boat thousands of euros but professes to be too broke to pay.

The quay where the *Diagoras* docks in Rhodes again after its long round trip to Kastellorizo is full of people from various small islands, loaded with shopping. It's dark and cold, exposed to the elements, but people wait patiently for the lights of the ship to appear. We arrive back in Tilos close to midnight. On nights like this in the winter, with bags to carry, it will be good to have a car to drive home. For now, we have had to leave the car with the mechanic, and he promises to put it on the ferry in a few days; in yet another leap of faith, I've had to leave behind the car I've just paid all that money for.

Chapter 9

The Austerity Diet

A few days later, the big ship docks at the harbour and amidst all the frenzy of people and trucks coming and going as quickly as possible, Stelios dashes on to the boat, finds the car and drives it down the ramp and off the boat. I most certainly could not have done that.

'*Kalo riziko!*' exclaims Delos when he sees our new red car outside the honey factory the next morning. When you acquire something new in Greece, people wish you good roots for your new purchase, or *me yeia!*, may you enjoy it with health.

I drive to Ayios Andonis just because I can, to see the waves dashing in to shore. In the distance is the humped back of Kos, with Kalymnos rising up behind it, and a Turkish peninsula – no signs of man visible, just layers of land.

Twice a week, I must think up activities to do with the kids. I've learned that a few hours of concentrated preparation to ensure that I can keep the group entertained non-stop is the only way to keep a semblance of control. We can't just follow a course in a book, because some of the kids have already completed them, so I gather exercises from different books as well as resources I find online, and I create some myself. I don't yet have a photocopier so I have to go to the *dimos*, the council office opposite the church, and ask *Kyria* Vicky, the museum curator – it's more polite for me to use 'Mrs' in front of a name in a situation like this, I've learned – to photocopy everything I need twelve times while I stand and wait. I'm not sure she's figured out that I'm practically living with her son, or what she thinks about it, but her manner is very friendly if somewhat formal.

In the next English session, the little kids are giving me a big headache. They're good as gold for the first half of the class, but after break they're endlessly distracted. I know that some are bored while others are completely lost. The big kids just tell the little kids the answers, which is very endearing but doesn't really get us anywhere. Just as I'm saying goodbye to them, feeling utterly drained, a man I don't know strides into the room and shouts at me for holding a class on an important public holiday: Ochi Day, the anniversary of the famous day in 1940 when the Greek prime minister, Metaxas, rejected the ultimatum made by Mussolini that Axis forces should be allowed to enter Greece and occupy strategic locations.

I knew it was 28 October but assumed I'd have been told if the English session wasn't supposed to happen – and the kids all showed up. As he rants at me, I only understand about half of what he says, but I think I've made another big mistake.

This is all too complex, I think as he leaves. I've taken on too much. It's beyond me. All I'm trying to do is help the children keep up with their English, as their parents asked. The last thing I want is to offend anyone. Surely everyone knows I'm new here and not familiar with how things should be done. No one else has said anything.

I'm crying as two of the diligent teenage girls arrive, and I apologise, tell them what happened. They tell me not to worry – clearly they think the issue is debatable. I ask if they want to do the English session and they do. The older class behaves well, apart from one kid who's been adorable recently but doesn't want to do anything today. It's as if they take it in turns to be naughty, but it's natural: they're just teenagers, going through good days and bad.

By the end of the 3 hours, I'm frazzled. Leo's not where we arranged I'd pick him up, but playing football in the square, maybe because I'm late. Grumpily, I drive down and he runs up to the car. I'd usually turn around at the ferry dock, but the big ship is coming into port so there are cars everywhere. I panic, not being very used to driving around other cars. Best to do a three-point-turn, I think. But in my haste, I back the car into the building behind me. Which is the police station.

There's a gruesome sound, and the word that comes out of my mouth is not the most polite. I apologise to Leo, and get out to see the damage. Mercifully, there is none – either to the car, or the police station. And there's no one around watching. So I get back in, and drive off.

As we drive up the hill, I explain to 12-year-old Leo why it's been a hard day, and just talking to him cheers me up. He's Albanian but has mostly grown up on Tilos, and in addition to speaking Greek, he's on his way to speaking excellent English. I started him off with the younger kids, the eight to twelves, but I think he's going to have to move up to be with the older kids soon, he's doing so well. He seems very clever – maybe something to do with having hard-working parents who had the resourcefulness to move here for a better life. I ask him what other subjects he likes at school and he says maths and physics.

'Difficult!' I comment.

'Yes, that's why I like them.'

For this week, he gives me a reason to be putting myself through all the stress. In spite of Greece going to hell in a handbasket economically, I am becoming more rooted in island life, committed to staying through the winter, and have planted my winter vegetables. I've received my permanent resident card for Tilos: it's not an essential item – and it happened in a very hurried way, with Stelios ringing me and telling me to come to the KEP office in ten minutes to get it done because he'd told them his girlfriend needed one – but it gets me a discount on certain ferries, a barely comprehensible lesson from Vicky about the voting system in Greece, and most of all it makes me feel good. The weather is still sunny and warm in the daytime, and I'm looking forward to a quiet winter of blankets and books.

It rains. And then it rains some more. I start off thinking it's good for the garden, then worry that the newly planted seeds have drowned or been washed away. But the half-drowned beetroot seeds, I notice, are beginning to grow little green shoots. I now eye flocks of birds warily. I must find some nets.

And the rain brings something far more fearsome: *saligaria*.

On the island, snails are a treat, a delicacy which people love to gather from the hillsides. I should try them. I am, after all, open to trying new things, unlike Stelios. Once, when he bought 5 kilos of broccoli, I pureed broccoli soup and left him some for supper.

'I can't eat that,' he said, simply.

I told him he was being rude and he said he was only being honest. We've got beyond that, but even so my haphazard throwing-together of whatever ingredients I can rustle up is anathema to him. Stelios will ask what I'm cooking, and I'll say, 'Food! It doesn't have a name.' He's Greek, and although he's sometimes open to improvising, feels you should have a name for what you're cooking. There are only two types of soup: fish soup and soup. Not broccoli soup. Broccoli is eaten with lemon and oil. For a nation that likes to be unlegal when it comes to authority, they do have a lot of other rules.

I've tasted snails twice before: once at a taverna in Athens a long time ago; another time at a bistro in the south of France, when they were so caked in garlic butter that they were unrecognisable. Neither occasion would make me excited about the idea of snails. This time, I am assured that the local recipe makes all the difference, and I can learn how to cook them.

Stelios goes out one day and comes back with two ominously bulging plastic bags. First, we must leave the snails with some food for a couple of days, which will clean out anything poisonous they might have been eating. I'm already thinking this may be a bad idea. We put them in two big pans with sacks tied over the top so they can breathe, place them on chairs and leave them with wild sage to eat in the hope it will give them good flavour. The empty building next door comes in useful at times like this. I check on them the next day and find one of the sacks has come loose, and the snails are slowly making their way down the side of the pot and the chair legs, trying to escape. I feel sorry as I drop them all back in the pot... Sorry for them, and perhaps a little bit for me, too.

After two days, the new food should have gone through their system and they're ready for cleaning. And just in case I'm being too subtle here, we're talking about cleaning up snail excrement. I suddenly become very busy with an urgent work deadline and unfortunately have to leave this part to Stelios. But my desk is approximately 2 metres from the kitchen sink, and however I try to ignore it, there's an unmistakeable clicking of shells in the sink as the snails try to escape again up the sides of the sink. Snails can move surprisingly fast when they want to.

Then we get to the really lovely part, I learn. We must boil them, and scoop off the slime that comes out. It just gets better, doesn't it? I can't believe I've never tried this before.

'But you'll like them afterwards!' insists Stelios.

After the slime-scooping part, he takes another big pot and heats olive oil, bay leaf, roughly chopped onion and garlic, adds salt and pepper... um, snails... water and a tin of tomatoes, then brings it to the boil and leaves it to simmer. The season for good fresh tomatoes has passed, and locals would rather use tinned tomatoes than flavourless ones in the winter. The smell becomes rich and hearty as they cook. It's beginning to seem more like actual food.

And the big moment is here: they're on the table, two bowls, looking lovely.

The sauce is good, especially with warm, fresh-from-the-oven, home-made bread. I'm just not terribly keen on the snails. I can't say cooking them ourselves has added to the pleasure, in this case. I can understand that in the old days when fresh meat was harder to acquire, finding snails on the side of the mountain would be a huge treat. But I don't see the urgent need to eat them now – unless austerity measures make life profoundly tough here. I think in the future I will leave the snails to those who appreciate their finer qualities. Gamely, I eat a fair few. Even Stelios decides he doesn't like the bigger snails much. We end up throwing quite a lot away.

Thankfully, there are plenty of other things to gather and eat on the island. I now get lemons fresh from Pavlos' *horafaki* or little field; not perfect on the outside but when you cut them open the smell and taste are delicious. 'Why did you buy lemons? Always ask first if we have any!'

Also in season are *gavafes*, guava. I've had guava that are red inside but these are a type of apple guava, green fruits with a white flesh inside, a little like pears but with a distinctive aroma which makes the kitchen smell heavenly. Trees in the village yield huge red pomegranates that start to ripen from late summer on. I never understood the point of pomegranates – they seemed too much work for little reward – until now. As I pull the fruit apart, sections of it fall away from the skin and in my mouth the pockets of flesh burst, releasing sweet juice.

Pavlos shows me his new carob tree. Carob seedpods were the closest thing they could get to chocolate during the war and in the 1950s and 1960s. Now, he says, maybe we're going back to that time, with the financial crisis – maybe soon, the children will eat carob again.

In any case, we have to be more self-sufficient now that most of the restaurants on the island have closed – if I have a craving for pizza, I'd better learn to make it myself. There are fewer deliveries of fresh food to the shops. The farm trucks sell produce from time to time in the villages, but never at a time when I happen to be there. I forage in the garden daily for a few last tomatoes and courgettes, rocket and basil.

Last week we bought 4 kilos of locally raised pork. Stupidly, I expected it to come as steaks. Stelios stomped in with his fishing clothes on and produced from a bloody plastic bag a large lump of dead pig, which he proceeded to tear into with a knife, leaving the kitchen smeared with bone and blood. The whole issue of buying the pork was a little fraught, as it turned out to be surprisingly expensive and I don't usually eat much meat. I asked if we could buy less, but he explained: when someone kills a pig, you buy a section of it, chop it up and freeze it. They don't just kill pigs whenever you feel like eating pork, and then sell you a kilo. So another thing I've never really used before, but have to get accustomed to, is a freezer.

I was wrong, however, to question buying the meat. It tastes extraordinary, worth every penny; nothing like pork that comes in packages in big supermarkets but dark, savoury and juicy simply chopped into bite-sized pieces and fried in olive oil and wine. I soon learn, also, my new favourite winter meal: pieces of pork oven-roasted in a baking tray filled with potatoes, garlic, lemon juice, oregano and olive oil. On a cool rainy day, the oven heats the house, spreading delicious aromas.

Chapter 10

Sunshine After Rain

In the wonderfully chaotic Megalo Horio supermarket, I ask Eleftheria to help me locate some coloured pencils in the stationery section, which looks like several teenagers' school lockers that have not been tidied all year. She cheerily rummages around for a while and says her little boy Kyriakos has probably taken them. Kyriakos has huge, dark eyes and thick jet-black hair, just like Eleftheria's. She hunts a little longer under random stacks of paper and I hear things falling off the back of the shelf, but eventually she produces exactly what I was looking for. I take my pack of pencils to the English sessions – and on opening the packet, find a red pencil missing and another broken. A little boy has been in there, after all.

There were no further repercussions about my holding English groups on 28 October, and the sessions gradually become something of a joy. For the younger group, the girls arrive early and write the date on the board; usually little Maria tells me with great fervour about something she's been doing, so fast that I can hardly understand a word and must interpret what she means from the actions that accompany the monologue, though last week it seemed rather improbably to be dancing on ice. I mention to Leo that we'll have to split them up if they're naughty; he spreads the word and everyone is on their best behaviour for at least ten minutes. If the younger group gets overly chaotic, I get them all to draw seahorses and give everyone gold stars. Little faces become very serious over the question of stars, and they also have an inordinate love of photocopies. The rumour runs around the room: *Fototipiehs!!!*

At some point in the session there is always some outraged shouting about someone making fun of someone else, and who started it, and who said what, and it is hilarious to watch their angry faces and their tiny hands calling for justice. I open my eyes dramatically wide, suck in my breath and ask, '*Keh pios pethaneh?*' Who died? And they grin sheepishly, say, 'No one...' and we get back to work. Having to speak Greek with these youngsters is good practice for me. I constantly have a dictionary to hand.

One day I hide toy animals around the classroom for a treasure hunt, a cunning exercise to get them to practise the question 'Where?' and the words *in*, *on* and *under*. To my dismay, the kids spot all the animals within seconds of arrival, yet they are still thrilled by the game. The toy animals were gifts from my ex-boyfriend, shipped over to Tilos along with all our other belongings before it was revealed that he wasn't coming with me after all, and I'm glad I've found a good use for them. Nothing is wasted here.

I tell Leo we'll be moving him up to the older group now that I've had a month or so to assess his level.

The young kids say they are sad that he won't be with them any longer, and ask if he can just sit in the room with them for company. The older kids are wonderful also. I give them an exercise that involves writing about 'your best friend'. 'Miss?' asks Chris. 'Can I write about more than one best friend? Because I have five best friends and I don't want any of them to feel bad.'

I had been hoping that with my twice-weekly trips to Livadia and a car, there would be more opportunities for going out at night, but I have to drive Leo home afterwards. In any case, things are quiet even in the bigger village of Livadia; Yorgos the *kafeneion* owner has gone away to Thailand for a holiday, leaving a strange emptiness in the square. My progress at dance class has fallen by the wayside for now as I don't have time, and I no longer get social evenings out with my pal Anna as she has returned to England. She spends her evenings after work recovering on the sofa, she writes in her email, missing Tilos and cheering herself up by listening to Greek songs on her computer. The new contract position requires her to learn all about aircraft financing. I reckon that may come in handy. When a vast pleasure cruiser docked in Livadia harbour in the summer there were rumours that it belonged to the owner of an airline – if he comes back next year, they'll have something to talk about.

One evening, I leave Leo to play football in the square with his friends for a while and I stroll down to the ferry dock to relax. I love the excitement of the big ferry coming in. One family is reunited; someone else's grandmother is going away and being wished *Kalo himona!* (Have a good winter!). Yorgos the nurse is receiving a shipment of medicine, and asks me to watch one box while he cycles with the other to the pharmacy. Yorgos Orfanos, the man with the big truck who delivered my belongings this spring, is bringing in a big batch of young olive and fruit trees. The fishermen are sending fish to Athens. And someone is unloading a... a car that's been in an accident? It's red, but thankfully it's not mine. Andreas from the younger English group rushes up to me to tell me he can count to ten in Italian. The affection of these young kids makes the stress of a busy week worthwhile, and I'm glad I took it all on.

As I drive home, the colours of the sky over Eristos are so beautiful I have to stop and look. The lights of Megalo Horio are like gold and silver glinting in a dark cave. A little owl is standing at the side of the road on the way up to the village. Sometimes I have to pinch myself.

I hear birds, and the distant heavy crash of waves. The quiet morning is interrupted only by the arrival of a truck with a delivery. I thought I might have dreamed the crunched-up red car being offloaded from the ferry, but no, as I'm doing the washing-up and admiring the view outside the window, the honey factory compound takes delivery of a demolished red car in a skip. It's surreal, but such things almost seem normal now. Later Pavlos explains he just wants it for spare parts.

By lunchtime, last night's rainclouds have cleared away leaving a blue sky, and the heavy rain overnight has washed everything clean so that every rock and tree stands out as if newly made. The fields are covered in a soft blanket of new grass. There's nothing as beautiful as the sunshine that comes after rain. I walk to the beach and have the bay to myself; take my shoes off, feel the sand under my feet. The sea is colder now, but still irresistible, beautiful for swimming once you brave the first chill. The rippling water glistens, and there's a fishing boat out; the land looks majestic, calm, bathed in hazy light. Walking home again, I look up and see an eagle circling in the sky. I see the eagles more in this season.

A rather insistent cat arrives while I'm sitting at the kitchen table doing my work and sinks its claws into my legs; it bites my feet and sits next to the fridge looking pointedly at the door, then tries to get inside when I open it. In spite of its bullying methods, it's nice having an animal around, and the cat is naturally keen on the fish scraps that appear from time to time, and licking out empty yoghurt pots. One evening, there's a loud bang, which frightens the life out of me – it's spooky enough sometimes being in a house in the dark in the middle of nowhere – but when I look up I see it's the cat hurling itself at the window, and I burst out laughing. It becomes known as Psycho Cat, and starts to turn into a permanent resident.

On my birthday morning in late November, I'm awake early at fisherman o'clock, and drive up just past Ayios Andonis to park the car at the monastery of Kamariani. The sun has not yet risen over the ridge, this side still a muted grey as I make my way up the hill on the footpath.

Golden sunlight tinged with pink starts to spill over the ragged top of the ridge. Soon the limestone outcrops of rocks are bathed in pale yellow light, and the slopes are green, the sky a pale blue streaked with thin white clouds. The sea below is silent and still. I reach a little chapel with ancient marble built into the dry stone walls, and cross over to the other side of the mountain. The path continues along a sheer slope of grey and red rockslides above the road, from where austere cliffs drop away into nothing. When I reach the monastery of Ayios Panteleimon it is quiet, its door still closed as it's not yet ten o'clock, the leaves on the trees now turned to yellow and brown. Over the door is a painted icon on a gold background; the young, thin saint with dark olive skin and green and red robes is dipping a long spoon into his box of medicine. Water gushes from the spring in the courtyard, so I let it pool in my hands and drink my fill.

I feel compelled to walk out on to a high promontory, taking great care where I plant my feet. The light on this late-November morning is soft, the mood one of peace and utter solitude; inland, just the rocky curve of the island, and out to sea nothing but stillness, islands in the haze. Trees cling to the sheer sides of the mountain, goats clamber on precipitous ledges, as I walk back in warm sunlight. In the distance, the headland beyond Ayios Andonis casts reflections on the mirror-like blue-grey waters. I reach the car and drive back to Plaka, walk down the track and plunge into the cold water for a swim. The small finger of promontory that shelters the bay is like the submerged back of a sea creature.

For my birthday, I have invited a dozen friends to the *kafeneion* in Megalo Horio in the evening, and ordered an array of food from Sofia – food must be ordered in advance during the winter. Unfortunately, in the afternoon, Eleftheria calls to say it's unlikely she and her husband will be able to make it, and Yorgos the nurse makes his apologies, too, as do a few others. It's a little disappointing, but Stelios invites his parents, Vicky and Nikos, at the last minute – they live just above the *kafeneion* and call in there most evenings anyway. It seems they know that Stelios and I are together, and it's all been quietly accepted as a good thing, thankfully. Dimitris comes and even brings a gift; Vicky seems quite impressed that the head of the high school is a friend of mine.

Ian and Sibylle, who've lived in Ayios Andonis for years, said they'd come, but there's no sign of them. I sometimes see Ian walking alone towards Skafi and we say hello – he walks all over the island. I expect they've got better things to do, but they finally arrive on Greek time, by which time we've somehow managed to polish off all the food. They tell me not to take it personally that few local people have come along – it happens.

Khronia polla, many years, is the Greek wish for your birthday; and *oti epithimiseis*, whatever you wish for. I couldn't really wish for better days.

Chapter 11

Darkness and Light

It stays sunny for so long that I don't mind seeing clouds again in early December. When I've had enough of being tethered to my desk, staring at a computer, I lace up my hiking boots and start walking, not necessarily with a plan of where I'm going.

While people always tend to be friendly on Tilos, at this time of year everyone says hello or waves when you pass them on the road because there are no strangers. Winter in Tilos is reinforcing my love of solitude, however, and I gravitate towards lonelier places like Ayios Andonis. The settlement has only a few houses, some half-built, a disused petrol station, a little harbour. With clouds brooding over the craggy hilltops, and a lonely boat on the grey sea in the distant misting rain, it feels beautifully desolate; flotsam and jetsam on the empty beach make me imagine the beginning of a dark mystery novel.

I follow a road I've never tried before, uphill through dark-green trees along the side of a reddish crevasse. At the top, I find Nikos the goat farmer, with his black beard and unruly hair, just closing the gate on his animals. Yesterday, 6 December, was the day of Saint Nicholas and we were invited to celebrate his name day. At the end of a dark road, Nikos' house was warm and festive. His partner had been cooking for days, it seemed: *keftedes*, or meatballs, *revithokeftedes* or chickpea fritters, *dolmades* made of cabbage leaves stuffed with rice and meat, salads – the plates just kept coming. I couldn't bear to watch, though, when she ladled pure thyme honey into a jar and then mixed it with synthetic spicy ketchup out of a squeezy plastic bottle to make American-style chicken wings. I know it's just my being a food snob, preferring everything to be local and natural, but it was another seahorse moment.

During the evening, Nikos told me that one of the goats most prized for its ability to produce milk and young is an English breed, which has long ears and a spotted coat 'like a Dalmatian'. I nodded away as he talked, so pleased to be getting by in a conversation in Greek about goat breeds that I didn't stop to think until later that he might be winding me up. So now I ask if he was making fun. No, he says, he was totally serious. He keeps different breeds, he says, pointing out an alpine goat with wide twisted horns and distinctive markings that's clambering up the hillside.

'These goats here inside, they're just the bad goats,' he says. 'They like to go down to the village to find food instead of looking for it up here. It's good we're getting some rain. Without that, there's no grass and I have to buy maize.'

We admire the view over the sea and the valley. The light rain is wetting my clothes, but it's not at all cold.

I say goodbye, then descend to Ayios Andonis and follow the stone footpath around the mountainside to Megalo Horio, a bird of prey hovering above. Arriving at the village, I am struck by how beautiful the tiny whitewashed alleyways in that part of the village are, the bougainvillaea heavy with magenta flowers even in December, lemons ripe on the trees. This last month Tilos has been more beautiful than I've ever seen it, the light so clear, Eristos bay glowing silver with the afternoon sunshine.

It's been the gentlest of Decembers; warm enough to swim in the sea and do exercises in the sun on the beach, and yet cool enough to be perfect for walking – no need to carry water, and in hiking boots I can cut across country and head for the hills, spotting bright-yellow crocus and mauve colchicums. I feel very lucky to be here over the winter.

The views keep changing, depending on the weather and which way the wind is blowing. On a sunny afternoon at Ayios Andonis, the island of Nisyros appears more clearly than I have ever seen it before, every topographical feature of the distinctive volcanic dome clearly defined, sheer cliffs plunging into the sea – you could practically see what they were having for dinner up in the village of Nikia on the rim of the caldera. From my house, looking down the Eristos valley, the island of Karpathos is often visible on the horizon like a rock rising from mist. One day when the sea at Eristos is dark grey and almost navy blue, a gap in the clouds opens and a streak of silver spreads across the water.

Another afternoon I explore the old donkey track to the abandoned village of Mikro Horio, where I disturb a couple of families of sheep; the lambs are obliviously suckling their mothers, wagging their little tails, but the ewes look alarmed at the intruder. Back down in the valley, I see a few old goat carcasses. A Byzantine chapel near Harkadio Cave is now a home for goats, judging by the floor, but the altar is ancient carved marble.

Pavlos sees me returning to the honey factory. 'You've got a car and yet you're still walking?!' Yes, thankfully, I am. Exhausted but happy, I boil spinach-like *horta* and fry a couple of the fresh eggs Pavlos generously brought the other day. I eat them with leftover roasted peppers, tomatoes, onions and courgettes in lots of oil and herbs. No point in walking if there's no feast at the end of it.

At dusk I go out to the village to take pictures of the simple white stars strung over the road for Christmas, and white lights in the shape of a boat wishing everyone *khronia polla*, many years – a phrase that can be used for any happy celebration. Tall Yiannis who works for the telephone company OTE is walking his dogs; a couple of ladies sit on a terrace sorting vegetables; Eleftheria's brother Zafeiris is scaling a huge fish on the main road; a little boy is out walking alone. Low voices can be heard from the *kafeneion*, and it's quiet enough to hear conversations from houses in the tiny alleys with their old, curved walls, all whitewash and flowers.

Here, there is none of the fuss that often goes with Christmas, no spending frenzy, no sales – the shops are exactly the same as they are all year round, and mercifully without Christmas tunes. I would love a quiet Christmas in Tilos, but it will have to wait for another year. Soon I am leaving for England, for work and then celebrations with family, when Stelios will join me. I am fortunate to have people I love, who want to see me. And it's good to catch up with colleagues and clients face to face. Living permanently in Tilos doesn't have to mean spending every day, every week here. The important thing is that it's my base, my rock, my place to come home to. As an adult, I've never felt so strongly about the place I call home before. I want to keep calling this island home for a long time.

For my last swim of the year in mid-December, I walk to Skafi beach and little fish jump out of the sea as I wade in. By three in the afternoon the beach is getting covered in shadows; as I return home at four, the sun is just going behind the mountain. Pavlos arrives soon after on his little scooter, switches it off and lights up his cigarette.

'*Iremia,*' he says. Peace. 'I want to come and drink my coffee here.' He puts his hands in the pockets of his jacket and like a magician pulls out four eggs. '*Freska.*'

On Christmas Day in London, I meet my 10-year-old cousin Luisa for the first time. She's grown up on a farm, and I recognise that she's bored being stuck in the house all day surrounded by adults. So I walk with her down to the river where we watch the geese and the swans, and she can climb on railings and run down the muddy path, and I tell her about the magical island where I live.

Stelios arrives on Boxing Day. He's never travelled outside Greece before. I meet him at the airport and we walk into my dad's house to find a party in full swing. It certainly puts his English to the test, but he charms everyone.

The next day, we go to see the sights in central London. The train into the city slows down at a station where works are going on, and five men in high-visibility jackets and hard hats are standing around a hole, leaning on their spades, looking on while a sixth man digs.

'It's just like Greece!' says Stelios, grinning.

Buckingham Palace and Trafalgar Square look dreary and grey, and I wonder why people flock to see them. Stelios is much more impressed by a sports car dealership and other fancy shops in Kensington on our way to an absurdly expensive lunch with some visiting family of mine. We get on well and have fun, and the only thing he dislikes about England is being unable to sit inside and have a cigarette with his coffee. So on his second morning, I'm pleased to see the sun faintly shining. I take him to a French-style cafe and we sit outside so he can have a cigarette. His parents have been calling him every day, just as they do back home – this is normal for a Greek family – so it's no surprise when his phone rings. But it's suddenly clear from his expression that something is wrong.

His father has had a stroke. Thankfully the doctor was close by in the village and he was treated right away, and the helicopter was called to take him to Rhodes general hospital. We change our flights, cancel all our plans, dash to my mum's for the afternoon and then fly back to Greece.

By the time we arrive at the hospital, the doctors have given Nikos tests and say he'll be fine: the stroke was minor. If he'd lived on Rhodes he could have gone home, but they don't want him taking the ferry to Tilos until they're sure. Although I know Vicky and Nikos, it's suddenly very intimate arriving to see them in the hospital and it gives me a bit of a shock when Nikos refers to me as the *nifi*, meaning 'bride' or 'daughter-in-law'. But it's an enormous relief to everyone that Nikos is well. We stay at his cousin's flat in one of the villages and pass a low-key New Year's Eve, feeling that sweet relief of a terrible darkness averted.

When we return to Tilos, the hills and fields are bright green, and there are white almond blossoms. In the Eristos valley there's an abundance of yellow Bermuda buttercups with clover-like leaves, but when I reach the beach it's hardly recognisable: big waves are sweeping in under dark clouds, the wind is blustery and the beach is strewn with seaweed and wet driftwood right up to the treeline. As I walk back, though, the sun comes out and it's so hot I have to pull off my jacket and scarf and jumper.

January is full of colour. Around Livadia and on the pink path to Lethra beach, the hillsides are covered in wild cyclamen, dark-green leaves with white or pink flowers. More often than not when out walking, I see a large brown eagle hovering on majestic wings high above the fields, and one day I set out in the car down the dirt track and startle an eagle that has just caught a snake and is carrying it off. There are three pairs of rare Bonelli's eagles on the island, which is unusual as they tend to require a large territory for hunting. This powerful bird, known locally as *spitzaetos*, lives in southern Europe, north Africa and the Middle East as far as Asia, hunting for rabbits and partridges, mice and lizards, and searching up to 200 miles a day for food. The other major bird of prey here, the Eleonora's falcon, is more abundant, eating insects or small migrating birds. Together with the Mediterranean shag or cormorant, known as a *thalassokorakos* or sea-crow, which nests in crevices or caves near the sea, these endangered species are protected in Tilos. Unspoiled islands provide rare ecosystems for them.

It rains for three days straight. In what seems like a break in the rain, we drive to Plaka for a walk, but don't get much farther than the little church of St Nicholas. We wait in the abandoned house on the hillside, watching the rain on the trees where the peacocks are sheltering, and listen to the sea down below. I think what a beautiful place it would be to live – completely impractical, but beautiful. The island has so many empty houses, half-finished or half-dilapidated.

Rain often brings thunder and lightning, and being on a rock in the middle of the sea seems to intensify the storms. We unplug the power cable on computers and modem as soon as we hear thunder, but one evening at the first big flash of lightning, the modem makes a loud crack and a bright white spark and explodes into pieces. We hadn't thought of unplugging the phone line. The same happens to others in the village, even those with surge protectors. That lightning is powerful stuff, and this little house on its own in the Potamia valley is vulnerable. We need to keep a spare modem, as the nearest shop is in Rhodes. Yiannis the technician is kept busy by the storms.

Through January, I wake often in the early hours to lightning flashing through the windows, thunder very close, and have to run down and unplug everything. Sometimes I'm so cold afterwards I'm unable to get back to sleep, listening to the noise of the wind howling and the rain lashing the walls. I only have a couple of tiny electric heaters, and this is turning into a particularly cold winter. When I first agreed to rent the house, it was just for a few summer months, and there was no heating installed. I must speak to Delos about putting in a heating unit – here on the island people usually have air conditioners fixed to the wall for blowing hot air and cold, unless they have a wood-burning fireplace. For now, I decide to keep everything unplugged at night, and stay as warm as possible in bed. I pile on all the quilts and blankets.

Surrounded by farms and wild food, we are lucky here, and the winter is constantly relieved by spells of sunshine and the joys of nature. But winter has its challenges, and the austerity measures that have been imposed across the country make things tougher. People like Vicky who work for the local council have only been paid for one month out of the past six. Strikes affect the ferries the island relies on. When the ferries can't come because of strikes or storms, the shops start to run out of fresh vegetables and meat. There's nowhere now to pop out spontaneously for something different for dinner, although Kastro restaurant in Megalo Horio will always make food if we let Dina know in advance; otherwise, every meal has to be cooked.

During this winter, five older people have died on the island; one was in his eighties and still walked every day and loved dancing at the festivals. Another, Eleftheria's grandfather, was ninety-four and she says he seemed perfectly fine the evening before – he simply didn't wake up the next day. It's normal, and not a bad way to go, but when I see the abandoned ruins of houses in and around the village that blend in so beautifully with the landscape – stone walls, wooden roof beams, an olive press overgrown with a rambling prickly pear bush – I start to think about the old ways dying out with the old people of the island. Young people from Tilos, if they find a way to stay on the island, tend to prefer modern, more convenient houses.

There is something about being part of a very small community on a small island that intensifies the experience of life. I start to recognise the slow, off-key tolling of the church bell that signifies death.

Chapter 12

Death and Life

February starts out warm and bright; I turn off the heaters, open the doors, and dry the washing outside in the sun. When I walk towards Eristos I can hear the waves from far away across the silent valley. In the other direction towards Skafi, there's often the lovely jangling of bells as Menelaos herds his sheep down off the mountain.

All the rain has brought up beetroots in abundance, and a few are big enough to pick. I prepare them as we ate them at the restaurant in Athens: boiling until slightly soft when the skins peel off easily under the cold tap; cooking the green leaves and stalks quickly afterwards; chopping them all into fork-sized pieces and drenching them in olive oil, lemon and finely chopped garlic. On days when the sea's not too rough for fishing, we sometimes eat fish soup with homemade bread, or *palamitha*, a kind of tuna, baked in the oven with potatoes, olive oil, lemon and herbs. I make salad with lettuce from the garden, or *vrouves* – wild greens.

Back at my office in the UK before I moved here, I would often waste my lunchtime going to Marks & Spencer to do food shopping, then seeing the twenty-minute long queues at the checkout and abandoning the idea. Here there's no need: in winter the kitchen is constantly full of big bags of oranges, cabbages, cauliflower, broccoli and spicy *horta* leaves, which Stelios is now dutifully buying from the farm vans in Livadia when he's there with the car. During the winter, he drives the car to work, rather than take the motorbike; I wonder where all the coffee cups are disappearing to, then find them in the car.

And it's green as St Patrick's Day all over the island. Wherever I walk, I am constantly startling families of goats, the youngsters bounding about on stocky legs, play-fighting and making a beeline for their mother's milk. On the way up to the village I take the shortcut through the field with Rena's goats and sheep. One little goat is leaping up high in the air on all fours, trying to headbutt his friend. Another has discovered that a hay bale covered in plastic makes a great slide, and keeps climbing up and slithering down it. When they see me, they stop playing and act serious, pretending they were just munching grass all along.

Then a big storm rolls over again – thunder and lightning, wind and rain. The strength of the wind is measured on the Beaufort scale, which ranges from one to ten, and this one's at least a nine. While I'm in Livadia for an English meet-up with the children, the storm takes the power out. I expect the kids to pack up their books and go home, but they keep doing their exercises by the light of their mobile phones. They're used to it. I grope my way down the rain-slick school steps in the pitch black. At home at seven in the evening with the power still off, it's too dark to do anything except read in bed by torchlight. The wind howls like a banshee around the house, scooping up crates and old beehive frames from the honey factory and blowing them around the yard while rain and hail scratch at the door. Rain floods the road and wind whips up the sea; the walls of our house absorb the damp and I run out of jumpers and socks to pile on.

Once the storm dies down, I take the opportunity to go to Rhodes on the Dodekanisos Express. The sea hasn't completely calmed down but there are things I need to do and my schedule doesn't give me much leeway. Locally known as the Spanos after the owner, this ferry is a fast and reliable catamaran that goes up and down the Dodecanese islands twice a week, connecting Tilos with Rhodes and Kos – though it doesn't give you enough time to do your errands and come back on the same day.

When I get to the harbour, men are pulling wood out of the water: pieces of a ship that brought illegal immigrants a few years ago, including Saeed and a couple of other boys. They'd been through terrible experiences in the Middle East, lost family, and were abandoned by people traffickers who brought them from Turkey and left them on a remote part of Tilos. The boat's been sitting in the harbour ever since, but finally sank in the last big storm, and locals are carting off bits they can put to use.

I get a seat at the back of the ferry: the centre at the back is the best place to be in bad weather. Once on the open sea the catamaran bounces up and down, climbing and descending some very large waves. People groan and dash to the toilets to be sick. An army officer hurries down the stairs and to the bathroom with his hand over his mouth, looking decidedly green. I don't often get seasick, but I'm feeling so queasy with cold sweats and a nasty headache that I even consider getting off the boat when we stop at the island of Halki, though it would mean being stuck there for two days. But it's only another hour: I can handle it. An old lady in black embarks at Halki and sits next to me, commenting that the sea is calm, *bonantza*. I don't like to tell her that's only the harbour; before long she is closing her eyes and moaning. On arrival, I reward myself with a good hot chocolate in one of my favourite cafes.

Back home in Tilos, I am watching a nice American video online to learn how to cook squid. Although the chef is genuinely helpful with showing how to clean and prepare it, he annoys me when he smugly talks about the salad to go with it, the basil leaves and green beans. It's not his fault, of course, but it's best not to look at recipes for things we don't have and can't buy.

Lately the fishermen have been seeing big turtles in the sea, and catching lots of squid – this is the season for them. Stelios arrived home late yesterday and stomped in the door as usual, sweatpants tucked into his heavy white rubber boots, clutching a dirty looking plastic bag full of squid and cuttlefish. I'd made dinner, but as he fell asleep (he really does think about food when he's going to sleep) he said, 'You cook the *kalamaria* and the *soupia* tomorrow, however you like.'

I haven't had a lot of experience cooking squid and cuttlefish. I watch the video a couple of times and am bracing myself for the new experience when Stelios conveniently arrives home early and says he'll do the cooking. Phew.

There's not a lot of preamble when it comes to Stelios in the kitchen. True to form, within minutes he's standing over a kitchen sink full of dirty dishes in his fishing wellies and padded red rain jacket, removing cuttlefish bones with his hands.

'Can you get me a knife?'

I pass him a knife and soon notice this has little in common with the neat slicing work of the nice American video. Googly eyes are excised with precision so as not to waste a thing. Fishermen who pull squid out of the sea with their hands don't waste bits. People who live with fishermen tend to find unidentified globs of fishy stuff lurking in the washing-up. It's all a bit much since my head has been buried in the rarefied work of editing a book until moments ago. I skulk off outside to get some fresh air.

'You must watch so you know how to do it,' says Stelios, calling me back.

Unfortunately, as the ink sacs start ripping, everything gets very black and I can't make head nor tail, so to speak, of what's going on. But I do remember one bit from the video.

'Aren't you supposed to remove the stomach?'

'No, it's tasty, we cook all! And the ink.'

OK... I help by chopping an onion and heating oil, as instructed. Minutes later there's a shiny, thick, pitch-black soup of bodies and tentacles and ink bubbling and spitting away on the cooker. I survey the scene around us: it looks like we've invited Jackson Pollock over to do the cooking.

'We can add rice if you like,' says Stelios.

I like the idea of rice but am still unsure if I'll like the squid and cuttlefish. I suppose I'm just having snail flashbacks; it's all rather pungent and earthy. We slosh in some water and red wine from time to time. And then he scoops up a bit of shiny black risotto for me to taste.

'Oh – it's amazing!'

Stelios beams, relieved that I like it. It's sweet and savoury together, deeply flavoursome, strange but wonderful. Perfect with a light frisée salad with garlicky, mustardy dressing – luckily, as that's what happened to be in the fridge.

On a blissfully warm and sunny February afternoon, I walk through Eristos valley, the fields full of big white daisies and poppies, and stroll along the seashore with my feet in the sea, dreaming of spring. The storms have damaged some of the trees, and the beach is full of bits of plastic that get washed up. But it's very wild and beautiful.

The next morning, I drive to Livadia to pay the car insurance at the bank and am early enough to pop into the *zaharoplasteio* to buy a spanakopita. A *zaharoplasteio* usually specialises in sweets, but Roula makes savoury pastries, too, including some of the best spinach pie money can buy, and it sells out quickly. I go inside and ask her how she is, but immediately see she's not well at all – she's been crying.

She sighs. 'Ah, my cousin died...'

'Oh... I'm so sorry. Your cousin...?'

'Vangelis.'

No... My heart leaps in my chest.

I go to sit by the sea as the news sinks in.

Vangelis 'Zorba' Papadopoulos, loved by so many. We've all known he had cancer.

People say that when he ran his own restaurant he was generous to an extreme – customers always became friends. For the short time I knew him, he seemed to live every day doing what he loved – the simple things, being around friends and family. He was so full of humour, had such a good heart; he became friends with many visitors who loved the island as he did. He felt that the foreigners breathed new life into Tilos.

I remember the days when I'd be swimming in Livadia and he'd drive by on his scooter, tell me to come for dinner at eight. He'd talk with feeling about growing up in Mikro Horio; island traditions he wanted to preserve, like making charcoal on the mountain in the winter, and looking after goats and sheep. I helped him print up the short book he'd written about Tilos in the past, so he could sell it. He was thinking of writing a new one.

He went away for treatment. But then he was back to his usual joking self, and last summer he insisted on working in his son's meze restaurant, or *ouzeri*. He was always welcoming guests on to the busy terrace at

Gorgona. Ingrid, who translated his book for him, said in September that his voice was occasionally failing. When did I last see him? It was late in the year I think, when he was leaving on the big ferry to see a doctor. I asked how he was and he said he wasn't well. He looked tired.

The funeral is the following day; he died in Rhodes, but he will be buried in the cemetery in Livadia. The day is freezing cold, but there is bright sunshine. It seems most of the island gathers for his funeral in the courtyard of the stately white church by the sea. I recognise and say hello to a few; most look distraught; it is terrible to see his elderly mother who only recently saw another son die. The island doesn't have a hearse, so in Tilos style, Vangelis is taken to his final resting place in a flat-bed truck. The whole crowd walks behind the truck to the cemetery on the back road, where the priest says a few words, then everyone takes a handful of earth and throws it on the coffin.

There is no feeling of a celebration of Vangelis' life at the funeral; it is all raw pain. But privately I celebrate the man he was – someone who believed in enjoying every day. I go home and, amid intermittent internet connection because the rain and thunder are back, I find out that my mum and stepdad enjoyed their wedding anniversary the previous day, Valentine's Day, and my brother got engaged to his girlfriend: news to warm the heart. I'm also holding a happy secret inside me that won't allow me to grieve too much.

Chapter 13

Perfect

When I noticed my period was two weeks late, I was hopeful, and once I mentioned it to Stelios, he immediately rode his motorbike to the pharmacy in Livadia to buy a pregnancy test. I was hesitant as it's hard to have any secrets in a place where everyone knows everyone, but Stelios asked the pharmacist to keep quiet. We were both so excited – but the test said no. Then I started to worry, because if I wasn't pregnant, what was causing my period to be late? What was causing the hard pressure inside me – something bad? I woke in the night, tossing and turning as the wind howled around the house, feeling my way down the staircase to the icy bathroom.

Then I tried a second test a few days later, and it was positive. A blood test confirmed it. As if that weren't enough proof, I feel sick and tired all day.

One day I must drag myself out of the house to see the schoolkids, but the only thing I can face eating is half a smoked cheese, which I devour straight from the packet as I stand by the fridge. Other days I dream of comfort food, cheddar cheese and baked beans on white toast –

inconvenient since you can't buy cheddar or baked beans and we don't have a toaster.

As I've heard one Greek man say to another: 'There are three things you can never hide. Pregnancy, love, and a cough.'

Stelios arrives home with a massive 30-litre container of fresh olive oil, which he immediately starts decanting into bottles on the doorstep while a few feet away I'm trying to have a serious scheduled Skype chat with my boss in the UK. I have to laugh. Unfortunately the smell of home-made bread and thick green olive oil makes me nauseous; all I want to eat is tinned food. It's so wrong. One day I have a serious urge to eat spaghetti bolognese, and since the butcher doesn't have any fresh meat, Stelios has to beg and borrow from someone.

Pregnant isn't a pretty word in Greek: *egios*, it's easy to remember as it sounds like an egg with an oddly masculine ending. I've been hoping for this moment for years, but I am hopelessly uneducated in the matter of pregnancy; thankfully there are plenty of online resources, but all they tell me is that I can't buy any of the things I need to eat in Tilos.

I go to Rhodes to see the doctor – Stelios suggests I register with a private one recommended by his cousin – and the scan reveals a tiny, two-month-old creature with a steadily beating heart, although it's still not exactly clear to me which way is up. 'Perfect!' says the doctor. He sends me off for more tests and then I enjoy a sunny afternoon and a big pizza, and shop for kiwi fruit and red peppers. On the ferry back, late in the evening, I see Dimitris; we sit together on the way home, and I can't help telling him my news. He harrumphs, and says something about King Herod, and the unhappy couples he knows with children.

Two months is early to start telling people – anything could happen until the first three months are up. And yet it's very difficult to go about daily life without explaining why I can't drag open the cumbersome wood-and-wire gate to the honey factory, or why I have to go to Rhodes. So we tell people; we decide we need all the help and support and understanding we can get. I then have to deal with people telling me to take care all the time. It's bad enough with Stelios watching my every move – now I can't go to the shop without being told to be careful, that I shouldn't do this or that. Of course they mean well, but it makes me grumpy. It's as if I'm no longer the owner of my own body; I'm carrying something precious that belongs to someone else – to Stelios, to his family, to the whole island.

'How's the baby?' people ask.

How on earth do I know?

'I hope for the best,' I say.

Late February is the start of Lent, which brings the *Apokries* celebration; in Greek, it means the time you turn away from meat, and is celebrated something like Halloween, with people dressing up in funny or ghoulish costumes and masks. As with most Greek parties, it starts at midnight. It's probably my general exhaustion but I haven't yet grasped the appeal of going out at midnight when, in February, it's been cold and dark and silent around our isolated house for hours, and it's hard to imagine a party happening anywhere. I have a good excuse to miss it – I can't spend all night in boisterous company in a smoky bar. But thankfully I don't have to be a complete killjoy because, a couple of days later, Stelios and I are invited by his friend Yorgos to a lunch with a dozen friends to celebrate *Kathari Deftera*, Clean Monday. This is the first of the forty days of Lent – the time of cleansing of both body and spirit to prepare for Easter.

The original plan was to have a picnic lunch outside at the monastery of Ayios Panteleimon, but thanks to a morning rainstorm, we don't have to brave that treacherous road where I always have visions of a rockslide, a tiny slip of the steering wheel... Instead, we are gathering at En Plo, one of the tavernas set back from Eristos beach, owned by Yorgos' family. I always worry about being invited to occasions where I'm the only non-Greek. Will I fit in? Will it be embarrassing not being able to follow the conversation? But everyone's in a good mood, and they compliment me on my Greek, though I only understand about half of what is said. Apostolis is there, and we blame him for everything, as he introduced us... We joke that we'll send him the doctor's bill.

Stelios is enjoying himself, relaxing with a drink and talking to his friends about his baby. I am happy, too, but I know things can go wrong, and want to be cautious until we know for sure that it's OK. He keeps insisting that I joke to another couple, *'Seira sas,'* your turn next. I don't want to; there may be any number of reasons why they don't have children. In his cups, he keeps goading me,

'Go on, say it, go on... Hey, Jennifer has something to tell you...' I have to be obstinate and say no.

The long table is piled with barbecued squid and octopus, loads of taramasalata, cockles, prawns, bean salads and chickpea fritters, and halva for dessert. Anything with blood, or milk or eggs is forbidden. We bring beetroot with garlic dressing, which no one eats.

The tradition is to go out and fly kites afterwards, but everyone is collapsing after eating so much. It feels like Christmas Day, and it gives me a warm glow to have lived a little more of Tilos life, thanks to Stelios. Since I've not been drinking wine, I go home and work afterwards, while everyone else is snoozing.

I was looking forward to the solitary days of winter: evenings wrapped up in blankets, reading piles of books, a glass of red and a glowing fire.

The blankets are no problem. Unfortunately, by early March I've run out of books to read and because the ferries are affected by storms and strikes, the post doesn't bring my new order; I could buy ebooks but when I look at text on a screen for much of the day, I can't bear to do that for pleasure. As for that nice glass of red, Stelios will barely let me take a sniff of the glass in my current condition. We can't have a real fire in this house; Delos says he's ordered an air conditioner but because of the ferry problems, it hasn't arrived. The big storms that blow up to 10 Beaufort take out the power for hours – the rating of storms on the Beaufort scale quickly becomes part of your vocabulary when you live on a Greek island in the winter, and 10 is fearsome – so we can't even use the little heater. Mould creeps into the cupboards and wardrobes, coating belongings, and grey patches appear on the walls. I dream of a thick duvet, a hot water bottle, a day when we won't have to worry about losing another modem to lightning. I sleep for 12 hours straight.

One evening is brightened by the making of halva. I've always thought of halva as the very sweet sesame cake that you buy in packets or in slabs from the supermarket; so sweet that I like it best eaten with yoghurt. But I learn from Stelios there's another kind, made from semolina. As a child, I hated semolina: bland white gloop with a blob of red jam to make it tasty. I think I've changed my mind when I taste this. We tip half a kilo of honey into a pan with water and, as it heats up, add the zest of a fresh orange, some cinnamon and a few cloves. In another pan we heat olive oil, then stir in the dry semolina as if it were risotto, keeping it moving until all the oil is absorbed and the whole thing is cooking without burning. The two pans get mixed together with sultanas and crushed walnuts, and the mixture is pressed into bowls and left to cool into a delicious dessert.

When a freezing cold wind blows hard for two days, I can't go out while weak and groggy, nauseous and exhausted; an umbrella is useless and the rains wash away the dirt roads around our house. The only rubber boots I have are a second-hand pair of Stelios', with a hole in one of them. There's no indoor swimming pool or gym, cinema or library here.

'You'll have to learn to play cards, Jennifer,' said someone, laughing kindly. 'That's what everyone does here.'

I don't like cards but I try accompanying Stelios on a couple of his evenings at the *biriba* tournament. The game brings together a diverse group of people who seem to have one thing in common apart from their love of cards: chain-smoking. I sit there trying to be sociable while not actually breathing very much. Though I enjoy the atmosphere at Mikro Kafe, I soon get sick of drinking sweet hot chocolate. I drink so much mixed fruit juice from a box that I will never be able to tolerate the smell of it again.

When Stelios can't go fishing because the seas are rough, he sits at home, playing *biriba* on his computer and reading odd news items, talking to me from time to time. I'm sure he only wants to keep me company, but it's tricky when I'm trying to concentrate on work – which is often – in our tiny house where the kitchen/living room is also my office. I've had so much work this winter, which in some ways is good since we now need all the money we can get, but the deadlines seem endless and, along with English sessions and pregnancy, it's wearing me down. My tiredness exacerbates our communication problems.

'It says here in the news they've found a new constellation,' he says.

'Uh-huh,' I respond distractedly, looking up from what I'm reading. 'Sorry, what? I didn't understand.'

We speak only Greek together and there's a big word I'm not familiar with. But instead of figuring out that it's probably the word that we don't use very often, 'constellation', he repeats and translates the most obvious word in the sentence, 'new'. Surely he knows after all this time that I am familiar with the word 'new'? When I'm frustrated or angry, I tend to lapse into Anglo-Saxon.

Stelios wants me to give him English lessons but it feels too much like work and I have no energy. We try to keep up the romance in the relationship; though now with my heightened, odd sense of smell thanks to pregnancy, the beard he insists on growing smells bad to me. We used to joke that he was a *skantjokiros*, a hedgehog, when he had a few days' stubble. Bring back the hedgehog! He gives up smoking since I've given up caffeine and alcohol, which is very good of him, but it makes him stressed and he flies off the handle when I say something that upsets him.

He is making plans to build a house on a piece of land, a *horafi*, belonging to his father. His father started building a house there years ago but abandoned the project, and now wants to give Stelios the land. A friend has drawn up a plan of how the shell of the small house could be expanded and completed. At first it seemed a wonderful idea. But I'm not sure I'd want to spend winter months on Tilos with a young child, now I've seen the difficulties. I start feeling trapped, worry about losing my independence and am concerned about our compatibility; Stelios puts it all down to the hormones, but I want to explain it's more than that. It would be hard enough to explain in my own language what I'm going through; it's hard enough to understand it myself.

Still, summer visits for a day or two at a time – afternoons where I can sit outside with bare feet, listening to the sound of the birds and the bees, or walk along Eristos beach with my feet in the sea. I potter in the garden, pulling up weeds and beetroots. When I explain to Stelios I need some space, he goes out to find asparagus, *sparagia*, searching the fields for the spiky bushes that yield its thin shoots, and cooks up an omelette with it. The flavour is very intense. In the evening, he is still outside in the garden trying to plant potatoes and onions in almost total darkness; I hear him on the phone to his cousin, asking if the eyes go up or down.

Everyone says they've never seen Stelios so happy. People have been asking if we're getting married, and are surprised when I say no, I don't want to get married. Stelios and I have only known one another for six months, and from the beginning we discussed this. It takes years to know for sure if you're in a good relationship; but I didn't have years to get pregnant. Still, it's clear he'll be a devoted father. And every day when I get out of bed, I am incredibly happy, thrilled with the idea that we are having a child. Stelios reassures me that I shouldn't worry about feeling trapped; we'll do our best, and if in the long run we can't stay together, we'll work something out. It's not a perfect situation in a conventional sense, but life isn't always like that. Sometimes you have to break the rules to do what you want, what you need.

People say this has been the coldest, longest winter in memory; and it must be one of the saddest, too. The church bell starts to ring – a slow tolling, off-key.

At lunchtime on 10 March in Megalo Horio, hundreds of people stand in the square outside the church, around the *dimos*, the council office, and on the terrace of the *kafeneion* above in sombre silence, and the priests start chanting. Tasos Aliferis, the mayor, has died aged sixty-one after a battle with cancer. The tall, lanky doctor came to Tilos two decades ago from the Peloponnese and was a much revered and loved mayor, a visionary for the island and a friend to many. The island is officially in mourning; school is cancelled, the fishing boats rest for the day out of respect. Sadly, he didn't die in his adopted home; he was away seeking medical treatment in the US. On the night when his body is brought back here, lights are lit around Harkadio Cave and the football field and the helicopter pad.

Tasos will be remembered for many things, and I barely have an inkling of his influence. What I do know is he brought in the hunting ban that made Tilos a conservation area – a ban that went against the Greek constitution, as did the first same-sex wedding in Greece, which he allowed to take place on the island; and he allowed some of those first refugees from the Middle East to stay and integrate. Not all of his schemes were successful – the reservoir at Eristos was never used, nor was the recycling plant – but he was constantly fighting on the island's behalf, a strong force for the independent spirit of Tilos. In many ways, Tilos makes its own rules in order to thrive, and Tasos was part of that – what I like to think of as the People's Republic of Tilos.

In spite of the the sadness, every day I see something that reminds me how much I love this place. During breaks in the clouds I take gentle walks by the sea, drink in the smell of herbs after rain, notice leaves appearing on the trees, watch cormorants fishing off the dock, sit in the sunshine and listen to the waves. I love the wildness of this island – empty beaches, rugged hills, the changing, endless sea surrounding us.

Anna has escaped London to spend three weeks in Tilos, and I drive down to Livadia to see her. In late afternoon the bay is perfectly still, like a mirror, the shores of Turkey practically hidden by a haze. We sit in Mikro Kafe and catch up on news. At seven, as I'm leaving, a huge, bright full moon comes up over the headland.

Stelios spots what he thinks is my package of books in the post office – the order I've been waiting weeks for. It turns out the replacement postman, covering while the usual postmaster is on holiday, doesn't know who I am so he doesn't bother trying to deliver it. I ask Stelios to pick it up while he's in Livadia next day – and the post office is closed, for no apparent reason except that it's a Friday and most likely the postman has taken the ferry to Rhodes. Sometimes, sometimes the People's Republic of Tilos appears to take rule-bending too far.

Then good things happen all at once.

Chapter 14

Escape from Paradise

I want to move in to this hotel room. I could live in just the vast bathroom with its warm tiles and walk-in shower; a heated bathroom feels like pure luxury. Within an hour of arrival – after a ferry journey of over 16 hours – we are lounging around in fluffy bathrobes, and Stelios is forced to drink both glasses of the strong, clear spirit *tsipouro* they bring to the room to welcome us. I am happy enough seeing the Acropolis whenever I go outside.

After that long wintry month of February when we felt trapped on a storm-lashed rock with no reprieve, a change in the weather brought a wonderful gift from my mum: a cosy new duvet. Stelios also found me a hot water bottle at the pharmacy, so I went to bed warm at last. But then out of the blue I was commissioned to write an article about Athens that required a research trip. I was so excited. Stelios suggested we stay with friends or family out in the suburbs, but after last time, I insisted on staying in the centre in a hotel, to his bemusement. I needed a dose of city life.

We've been offered two nights for free in O&B boutique hotel thanks to the article I have to write. Most people in

Tilos don't seem very interested in what I do for a living; since I work from home and it's not obvious, perhaps they assume I don't do very much. The same happened when I worked from home as a freelancer once before for a couple of years in France. It's hard to explain the different aspects of my work. I don't mind any of this – I've chosen to live in a place where people are judged for who they are, not what they do – but it's nice for a change to be reminded that my work has value and is appreciated. Sometimes, working at home in Tilos, I feel my identity and self-esteem slipping away. Life with Stelios is full immersion: good for learning, but difficult and exhausting. It's a bit like learning Greek dances; gradually, I hope I won't have to concentrate so hard. No wonder I enjoy just walking alone around the island at times.

After a few meetings in Athens and a morning of writing, I arrange to spend a few hours on my own, and wallow in the pleasure of wandering the city. I realise that it is wonderful to be anonymous for a change. Nobody knows I'm pregnant, nobody tells me to be careful. I chat light-heartedly with friendly people in shops. It's important to remember that even freelancers in paradise need holidays, and although I love the island, it is a tiny place and it's natural to need breathing space from time to time.

In the evening, we walk to cafes and instead of boxed juice there are wonders like virgin ginger mojitos and fresh lemon juice and flavoured teas. The weather feels spring-like and we sit outside on the crowded steep steps in the Plaka in warm sunshine. In Psirri, around where we are staying, I marvel at more street art, walls playfully and skilfully painted with colour and imagination, and I'm happy to see a plot of wasteland reclaimed as a community vegetable garden. We eat so many different foods I hadn't dared to dream of while living on our tiny island in the winter – tabouleh and fresh coriander; strong salami; chocolate cake; marinated anchovies; fresh houmous and chewy, crusty bread – and all for reasonable prices.

Athens feels like a city people love living in. Though there have been riots against the austerity measures, they happened in a small area, mostly outside the parliament buildings; sensationalist reportage in the media affects people's livelihoods here unnecessarily – it's irresponsible. Of course there are seedy areas of the city; the area around Omonia Square feels unpleasant on a dark evening; but I've seen worse drug use on the streets in Germany, and there's none of the drink-fuelled violence of small towns in England. Greece is still such a safe place; on many islands, people don't lock their doors, and Athens remains for me a completely unthreatening city.

We dedicate an afternoon to exploring the Museum of Cycladic Art. I haven't visited for years, and we linger over the ancient artefacts from the central Aegean, especially the distinctive and mysterious female figures carved from marble in the third millennium BC. Then, as we're about to leave, we notice there's a temporary exhibition called 'Off the Beaten Track' – which includes Tilos.

Although we live within easy walking distance of important ancient sites in Tilos, excavated artefacts have been taken away for research and safekeeping, and little information is available except in the small village museum run by Stelios' mother. Harkadio Cave, where the skeletons of thirty-eight pygmy elephants were found – buried in the volcanic ash that probably contaminated all the food or water – is closed off until resources can be found to continue the work. The new museum there has stood empty for several years.

So it's fascinating to learn here that tools and pots made of trachyte, a durable volcanic rock from the neighbouring island of Nisyros, were also found in the cave, as well as pottery for storing, preparing and consuming food, believed to be from the fourth or early third millennium BC. This may suggest that humans co-existed with the elephants on the island. There are a few cups and jugs from around 1500 BC that show Minoan influence but were made in Tilos, found in an area called Garipa, near Megalo Horio.

The displays confirm that from the eleventh to eighth centuries BC, leading up to the time of Homer, a settlement existed on the steep slopes above today's village of Megalo Horio. It was a safe place to live, invisible from the sea and sheltered from winds, with two natural harbours nearby. Ancient graves have been found in the surroundings at Enousses, Pigi, Marmara, Ayios Apostoloi, Kena – names rarely used today. The graves were underground chambers carved into soft rock, one after the other in a tunnel formation. I've visited one in the Eristos valley with Charlie, an Englishman who has spent years exploring the antiquities of the island.

Fragments of pottery and carved stone suggest that Tilos was a flourishing settlement during the classical period, around the time when Irinna, the famous ancient poet of Tilos, lived her brief life; that the Tilos assembly approved an alliance with Rhodes in the third century BC; and in the second century BC, someone was honoured with a gold wreath by the *dimos*, the council or municipality of Tilos.

While pottery fragments and stone carvings are remarkable for the historical context they provide, the delicate gold jewellery takes my breath away. There's a gold diadem with intricate knots and winged cupid figures, dating from the classical period and found at Kena.

After the Roman poet Pliny referred to Tilos as Agathousa, 'the good', there were scant written references to the island for over a thousand years. In 1309, it's known that the island was conquered by the Knights Hospitaller of St John of Jerusalem, who called it Piscopie (the island is still known as Piscopi in Italian). In 1366, it was granted as a fief to Barello Assanti d'Ischia with the condition that he fortify and defend the island, and send hunting falcons and spoils from shipwrecks to the Grand Magister in Rhodes. That's when the castles were built, as were many churches. In the fifteenth century, after a deadly plague and Turkish raids, the islanders took shelter in Rhodes under the protection of the Knights, who gave them grain and forgave debts. In 1522, however, Tilos succumbed to the Ottoman Empire along with all of the Dodecanese, and would remain under Turkish rule until 1912. It was then occupied by the Italians for more than thirty years until World War Two, when German soldiers took over. It was finally incorporated into the Greek state on 7 March 1948.

Tough, resilient little Tilos, I think.

Then I hear a familiar voice behind me. There's a video playing as part of the exhibit, and Vicky is being interviewed. We feel very proud. Leaving, inspired by all I've seen and learned, I feel I've come alive again. It's good to get outside our little world from time to time – and to go back home.

On the last morning, we decide to buy an office chair for me and take it with us on the boat. Stelios thinks he can carry everything – since I'm not allowed to lift much these days – but I'm not convinced, and the kind man in the shop says he'll drive us to the port. Along the way, he says that business is so slow with the economic crisis, he's thinking of shutting up shop and moving with his Canadian wife to Montreal, where their son lives. But he sighs, thinking of it, arriving at Piraeus: nowhere has sea like Greece.

The sun is setting as our ferry pulls away from Piraeus for the overnight journey home. The last few days of sunshine have shown that summer is not far away.

I want to keep the positive energy I acquired while in Athens. In late March, I have my first quick swim of the year. The sea feels cold but energising.

I had no idea that exercise would be one of the things I'd miss during the winter on a little Greek island. I thought walking would be enough. But having regularly done boxercise and circuit training and body conditioning for the past few years, I'm missing something. So when one of the teachers starts to offer aerobics classes, I check resources online, which say careful exercise is not only fine but helpful in pregnancy, as long as you are used to it. Thanks to the international language that is aerobics, I actually know what I am doing – it's the first time I've been in a group of women in Tilos and not felt like an idiot. It feels good to move and stretch to music.

Rumour quickly gets around, and various island women tell me that I shouldn't be doing *yimnastiki*, or whisper behind my back as if I've done something terrible. Eleftheria in the shop tells me not to worry, however: she walked to Livadia and worked in the bakery when she was pregnant. There have been no signs of any problems, I tell her, and I cancelled the trip I was supposed to take to England for work. 'Good idea,' she says.

I buy some fresh eggs laid by Rena's hens, and feta cheese, and go home to cook what will turn out to be the tastiest omelette ever, with feta sprinkled all over it and a little sea salt and pepper. Sometimes the simplest things...

'*Teenafto?*' What's this? asks Stelios. But he's not talking about my omelette – he's pointing to the jar of Marmite.

'*Afto* – that?! Ah, *that* you won't like at all! It's something that only people who grew up in England can like – and some of *them* don't like it either...' I usually hide it away out of sight, but there it is beside the new toaster – and Stelios looks intent on tasting it. I try to explain this weird foodstuff. 'It's kind of like yeast, that you make bread with, and it has lots of vitamins in it!'

He tries a little on a spoon and doesn't mind it. *Antecho* is the word he uses, which means 'I can tolerate it'.

I think my Marmite supply is safe.

Perhaps he's getting used to my cooking, my different ways. The next day, when he's fishing at Eristos, he calls me on the phone. 'I'm thinking about that omelette you made yesterday… Can you bring me one?'

It gives me an excuse to get out of the house and drive to the beach for a walk. I cook an omelette and put it in a container with a fork and some bread. The sun is glinting on the sea as he rows to shore to pick it up.

The warm weather has brought out lizards: little ones that skitter across the path, feet barely touching the ground. The larger type, sometimes a foot long, is known as a *savra* – the 'saur' in dinosaur. They lounge on stone walls in the sun and when I change down into first gear to drive up the steep dirt track to our house, I see a *savra*'s big tail disappearing through a crack between the stones.

When I meet the little kids for English practice, they want to be outside in the sunshine, too, so we sit cross-legged in a circle in the playground, and I read them a story from a picture book about a spider that wants to be a family pet. Every time the family find the spider in a room of the house, they shout, 'Out you go!' The children don't just have fun, but they learn something: next time we meet, when one of them misbehaves, a smart kid puts up his hand and says, pointing to the miscreant, 'Out you go?'

It feels as though we have left behind that difficult winter as I stroll through the fields up to the village and say hello to people; I was too cut off during those cold days alone in the house. Although I like my own company, I need to make the effort to have more time for relaxation and social interaction.

Amid these thoughts comes an opportunity.

Chapter 15

Emptiness and Experience

Since he was a boy, Stelios has spent his summers at Eristos beach and the *kantina*: a little caravan selling drinks and snacks to the campers and other visitors.

Most recently the *kantina* was run by Vangelis and then his daughter Martina. Since her father passed away, Martina has decided to sell, offering it first to her friend and fellow cards player Stelios. He considered buying the *kantina* last time it was up for sale. There are many expenses involved, and he'd need to apply for the licence from the council. But he thinks it would be a good business for us for the future, another thing he can do without leaving the island – and something I can help him with, as it will soon be time for me to end the English sessions for the summer.

It seems a good idea, a positive move, and I admire him for his ambition. I offer to lend him some money if he decides to go for it. I like the idea of helping with an island business, investing in something that will keep one of its young people on the island.

Meanwhile, we have to take the early morning ferry to Rhodes again. We've got into the habit of taking our recycling over when we go and leaving it at the little depots at the harbour; it feels ridiculous, but it's hard just chucking things in the bin when I see all the rubbish that washes up on beaches – much of it from elsewhere, but it all goes somewhere. Since I'm not supposed to carry much, it's Stelios who has to take the plastic bags.

We're going for my third ultrasound, to find out whether our three-month-old baby is healthy – something that will determine the future of our lives – and I am a bundle of hyperactive nerves. Stelios doesn't seem to feel the way I do the momentousness of all that hinges on this scan. Instead of taking me directly to the doctor's, he *has* to go and get himself a spinach pie from a particular shop, which according to him makes the best spinach pies in Rhodes.

All the other couples in the doctor's waiting room look so happy, holding hands, so sure of what is happening. I feel that we must look out of place. I have that awful feeling again of having locked myself into this situation with someone who doesn't really understand me. Is it simply that I'm overwhelmed by the situation, by feelings of inadequacy and fear? It seems unbelievable that we've made it through the dangerous first three months without incident.

Stelios is fizzing with excitement as the doctor spreads the cold gel on my belly and an image comes up on the screen.

But I notice the doctor's mood changing. It's not the same as last time, the 'perfect' time.

'No,' he says. 'We have a problem.' He rubs his face with his hand.

I can't remember exactly what the doctor says after, when we go back into his office. It's possible he's speaking quickly in Greek to Stelios, but it's equally possible he's speaking English to me – it's all a blur. All I know is that last week I was three months pregnant. Now I'm not. We've just been very, very unlucky. From what he can see, the doctor believes its heart stopped beating a few days ago.

I will have to go to the clinic the next morning for an operation called *katharisma*, cleaning. Our little unborn baby is going to be hoovered out of me. And then the doctor can send it away to Athens for tests. He thinks he's seen something to indicate that it had Down's syndrome, and maybe that's why it wasn't healthy enough to survive, but we'll know more in a few weeks. This whole sad situation is going to cost hundreds of euros. I didn't do anything wrong, he says – not the swimming or the aerobics; most likely the embryo wasn't genetically healthy, and the body thankfully knew this.

I'm still numb when we leave the doctor's consulting room and go for a coffee. But my first caffeine in three months gives me the kick I need to ring my mum and let the tears start flowing properly. And they just won't stop.

We quickly leave the coffee shop and drive to a beach to be alone, but dark clouds appropriately enough cover the sky and it feels utterly bleak and cold. As I cry, Stelios tells me not to worry, we can try again, which makes me despair and think he has absolutely no idea what just happened. My feelings are incredibly confused and I can't talk to him, can't muster up the wherewithal to talk in

Greek about things I don't even understand myself. The tears go on and on.

I must fast that night from dinnertime, so eventually we drive to a quiet village and find an empty restaurant. The sun comes out and we eat and drink some wine and the pain stops briefly.

Late in the evening, the doctor calls Stelios and tells him we have to go and pick up a pill from the hospital. No one tells me what it is until we get there. I have a feeling the doctor has been explaining things to Stelios in Greek, assuming he'll pass them on to me, but I've been told nothing. Messages and calls from my family leave me feeling calmer, though, and as I lie in bed for the next 10 hours, hungry and cold but with Stelios' warm presence beside me, I let the thoughts flow through me.

The next morning, for an hour and a half, I lie chilled and terrified in a hospital bed, with a needle stuck in my arm. Then I'm in the operating theatre and a kind nurse is complimenting me on my Greek and leaning against my leg – how wonderful that warm contact feels. The doctor, whose face makes me cry now, tells me he will see me here again next year to deliver my healthy baby. A deep-voiced anaesthetist tells me I am having a light general anaesthetic and asks just as he's about to slide the needle into my arm if I'm allergic (has no one thought to ask this earlier?), then jokes, 'Enjoy your dreams...'

That moment of feeling nothing is sheer bliss.

For the next two days we must stay in a cheap hotel room in Rhodes as there's no ferry back to Tilos. I buy some clean clothes. At night, I feel that tiny bump that's now empty, think of that tiny thing that we already loved so much. Stelios meets up with his cousin and friends in the evening but I can't bear to be around people. I am terrified by how much I bleed, until Stelios calls the doctor on his mobile – he's said to call anytime – and finds out it's normal.

On the Monday, we go to catch the ferry and are completely baffled that no one's there. We've both forgotten what time the Monday ferry leaves, and have missed it. It's the first indication that Stelios has been going through hell, too, even though he hasn't shown it. When we return to town, we pass the recycling depot where we dropped off bottles before going to the doctor's appointment, and it seems like a year ago.

A few days after the operation, already my body and mind are, unbelievably, beginning to return to pre-pregnancy. My hair even feels like it's losing the haywire look it's been horrifying me with, and is going back to normal. How can something so big, so significant, with the potential to change the rest of your life, be over so quickly?

I am already losing all sense of why I was so unhappy from time to time during the past month. I suppose I did feel trapped, my life no longer my own, in the hardest days of winter. On our first day at home, after Stelios has been out working, he comes back and I hug him tight. I watch him barefoot in our garden, working on his onion patch, shouting for help every now and then. I feel better in myself, and wonder if it was just the hormones that were playing havoc with my mind. I am already feeling positive about the future; if I want to try again, I have to wait a few months for my body to heal. Friends write to say that miscarriage is not unusual but a normal part of the process of making a child, the body getting ready for a healthy pregnancy. In the meantime, I have a whole Greek summer ahead to get happy again – retsina, swimming, dancing. Three months when I don't have to think about it.

I love eating fresh eggs again sunny side up, the yolks still runny – something that was banned during pregnancy – with vegetables in olive oil. For ten days I'm on antibiotics and am not allowed to swim. As soon as I'm free, I walk to Plaka in the sunshine. I leave behind the shoreline and scattering of houses at Ayios Antonis as the road rises towards the little monastery of Kamariani, with the mountain on my left and the sea to my right down below, clear and peacock blue. The sound of the waves carries up clearly. It feels far from people, far from anything except goats. The road winds in and out with the contours of the hill covered in sage and thyme bush and eucalyptus trees. There are olive trees on the cliff-edge blown sideways by winter winds. Where the path slopes down towards the curve of beach at last, the hills are green and lush, and the water sharp and clean.

There's a short poem I saw once on the subway when I lived in Toronto. It caught my attention because it was called 'Sunlight at Sherbourne and Bloor', which is where

I was living, and the poet, Gwendolyn MacEwen, writes about cycling across the city and the bridge over the deep ravine, something I used to do. For some reason, it comes into my head today. She's thinking about the messiness of life, when it suddenly strikes her that each thing we do is built from the experiences we have and every choice we make; and because of that, every little moment is important. Or at least, that's how I interpret it. And I think that yes, taking this walk right now, seeing every beautiful thing around me, is the most essential thing I can do for myself.

Why does her poem come into my head that day? It's only later that I look MacEwen up to find out more about her. Lo and behold, she had a connection with Greece. She taught herself Greek, translated plays by Euripides and Aristophanes as well as writing fiction and poetry. After marrying first at the age of twenty-one to poet Milton Acorn, who was nineteen years older than her, and getting divorced two years later (spookily similar to my own first marriage), she later married again – to a Greek musician, Nikos Tsingos, and opened a coffee house with him. She lived on the Danforth, in the Greek neighbourhood of Toronto, where I moved to after Sherbourne and Bloor. She died in her mid-forties, around my age – on my birthday, 29 November.

She would often have cycled across the bridge over the Don Valley as I did. By the time I lived there, the Don Valley had a bike trail and wetland where I would go to escape on weekends from my sometimes frenetic city life. A few weeks after Gwendolyn was born, her mother had considered jumping off that viaduct, and admitted herself to a psychiatric hospital. Gwendolyn died in poverty not far away, drinking heavily, far too young. But I discover that she left behind some of the most beautiful writing I've ever read about Greece. It's in a book called *Mermaids and Ikons: A Greek Summer* about the happy summer months she spent on the little island in the Aegean Sea where Nikos came from, Antiparos.

She describes it as an island of fig trees, thyme and oregano; they stayed in a simple house in a half-abandoned village. Nikos went fishing for octopus and she became accustomed to the sight of dead octopus being smashed against rocks to force the 'grey-white soapy substance' out, which makes the meat tender enough for eating. They ate octopus and drank ouzo with the priest, Papa Stephanos, who told them hilarious stories of the islanders, crying at the same time in his 'boundless love' for his people, and they walked home watching silver moonlight on the water of the harbour. They caught and cooked snails after the rain.

Her marriage to Nikos didn't survive: her illness drove him away. But for a few months she had been happy in a place just like this.

I start going on long walks again. Green fields spread below the rugged mountaintops where clouds hang. I watch eagles in the blue sky above, and swim at Skafi where the sea is so clear I can see the pink sand underneath. At Eristos I find a huge dead turtle washed up, nature in the raw. The garden is suddenly thriving with potatoes and onions, peas and rocket and *radikia*, a type of *horta* like dandelion leaves, semi-bitter and delicious. The fields are blooming. And I am about to experience my first Easter in Tilos.

Chapter 16

Big Week

The holy week before Greek Orthodox Easter is called *Megali Evthomatha*, Big Week. In many parts of the world, Easter is heralded long in advance by the arrival of a plethora of chocolate eggs of all shapes and sizes in the shops. In Tilos, none of the shops has chocolate eggs, but I do spot a local farmer pulling the intestines out of a dead goat hanging from a tree – people prepare for the feast somewhat differently. When I hold my last English session with the little kids before the holiday, I ask them to draw pictures of what Easter means to them so we can write English captions. All of them draw churches, some with candles and biscuits. Little Yorgos draws a big crucifixion with a crowd watching underneath. This is my first indication that Easter might be a bit more serious here.

The last time I went to a church service in Megalo Horio four years ago, an old woman glared stonily into my face for wearing a dress that showed some leg above the knee, prodding a bony finger into the offending flesh and making a sign of the cross. I'd been to Greek monasteries where the wearing of jeans was forbidden for women, so

I'd assumed the dress was the only option in my holiday luggage. It's something of a surprise to find that super-sexy tight trousers and five-inch black spike heels are pretty much the order of the day at Easter services in Megalo Horio. It's an unexpectedly come-hither look.

The church service for *Megali Pempti*, Big Thursday, starts in the evening. After we hear the bell ringing, we leave our lonely house in the dark and take the motorbike down the dirt track. It's a cool and windy night. The church is smoky with incense; chandeliers and censers and crosses woven from grass hang from the ceiling; the dark old painted wood of the altar screen leans inwards; the haunting chant of the priest rises and falls. We light candles, and people kiss the icon. A cross with an image of Jesus is decorated with garlands of flowers. It feels very strange, and very mournful.

I go outside for a while, where Stelios is standing with a group of mostly men, but it's cold and dark and I feel alone. The service lasts several hours, and candles are lit from time to time. I find a place inside again, watch people coming and going, and gradually the trance-like effect of listening to an entirely sung service starts to feel less strange, more comforting. Unable to follow the words, and not being an Orthodox Christian or religious at all myself, I try a kind of meditation. In the two weeks since the surgery that left me feeling so empty, I've come to feel OK again. But a little space for mourning is in fact just what I need.

Church starts a little later on the Friday. For an hour or so, a service takes place around a representation of a funeral bier, which stands in the middle of the church covered in flowers. Children at either end hold candles, and I notice some of the older women stocking up on long, spindly red candles from the table at the back of the church. Then the priest leads a procession. Men carry the bier by its poles. We follow it up the steps behind the church, squeezing through the arched doorway, and along a dark alley through the village. There are few lights and now I know why the steps are whitewashed at the edges: so you can see where you're going in the dark. We pass the ancient wall of massive stones, then continue down towards the cemetery, disturbing the donkeys in the field.

At the graveyard, families disperse; people hold lighted candles in the dark. The priest circulates, stopping at each family and saying a prayer for their departed loved ones; his helper discreetly palms some money each time. Knowing little about Greek Easter, I am taken by surprise by this communal remembrance of the dead, and when I hear others crying it makes my own tears flow briefly. Stelios and I hug. It was a tough winter for everyone, with much loss. During the sad but beautiful ceremony, rain starts to fall and people repeat after the priest a phrase, *aeonia i mnimi*, eternal the memory, as we begin to follow the bier slowly back to the church.

When I ask Stelios what time we'll be going to church on Saturday, he says *to vrathi*, evening. In fact, the church bell starts ringing at 11 p.m. Everything in Greece starts so much later than I expect.

During the many hours in church listening to chanting I don't understand, I've been rather obsessed with watching the priest's helper deal with the candles. One night he's chopping candles into small pieces, which ladies stuff into their handbags; another he's keeping an eye on the candles we all light on our way into church, snuffing them out as they reach their last couple of inches and throwing them in a box. *Out, brief candle...* Tonight's candles, for the celebration of Christ rising again, are white but stained red at each end.

Something else is different tonight: the profusion of *vomves*, bombs or firecrackers. Stelios has been complaining about the lack of *vomves* this year, and indeed to him part of the appeal of standing outside the church is setting off *vomves* to the annoyance of people inside. That older folks come outside to complain from time to time just adds to their fun. I'm afraid Stelios and I don't see eye to eye on this one. To me, the charmlessness of something that simply makes a loud bang cannot be overstated. Being sensitive to the sound, I finally flee the church when a loud crack echoes in the doorway.

People greet one another as they leave the church with *Christos anesti*, Christ is risen, and *Alithinos anesti*, He is truly risen; then they go home to break the fast with a soup called *mayiritsa*, made from the entrails of the sheep or lamb that will be spit-roasted for the feast. Gradually, well after midnight, everyone makes their way to Bozi, the club at the edge of Livadia. Stelios drives our car and parks so close to the entrance that it would be impossible for anyone but a Greek to retrieve it several hours later when hemmed in from all directions. Suddenly, the solemn religious week erupts in celebration, and we drink ourselves silly enough to dance for several hours.

The next morning, Easter Sunday, is breezy but sunny, and I work in the garden for a couple of hours, clearing away weeds to find hidden tomato plants and forgotten shoots. When we arrive for lunch with Stelios' cousins in the Eristos valley, a whole lamb is turning on the spit over a bed of coals.

Nikos Taxijis is the cousin of Stelios' father Nikos – they had the same grandfather, and since children are named after their grandparents, they are both Nikos. Men tend to be known by nicknames to distinguish one from the other. This Nikos is simply known as 'Nikos Taxijis' because he drives the island taxi, though most nicknames have nothing to do with someone's job, and can even be handed down from father to son – but they're sometimes a bit cheeky and not used to the person's face.

'*Ela Jenni!* Here, try this,' says Nikos. '*Entera.*' Intestines look surprisingly appetising plaited and barbecued.

'Is that liver?' I ask, pointing to the darker pieces on the plate; I like liver.

'Yes!' says Nikos. My hand has already reached for a piece when he adds, 'And lung, heart...'

I take a bite and the taste is salty but not unpleasant. The round table in the garden at the edge of the orchard is spread with *horta*, salad, cheese, tzatziki and bread and fried potatoes. And a huge oven dish is packed with Flintstones-style portions of lamb – bones with hunks of meat, ribcages, an accusing eye and what I realise is a row of teeth. Nikos jokingly plonks a joint of meat suitable for a medieval warriors' banquet on to my plate.

'*Pameh!*' he says. Let's go! Thankfully a flagon of golden home-made wine appears from under the table with increasing frequency. '*Roufa!*' shouts Nikos – drain the glass!

The girls finally get up from the table with some effort and we drive to the beach with a pan full of Greek doughnuts in honey.

The church bell rings in the early evening of Easter Sunday. The service is in the other church at the top of the village, and Stelios says maybe I shouldn't come as there will be lots of *vomves*, but I have a trick up my sleeve – or rather, in my pocket. As we follow the alleyways and reach the courtyard, the views over the still-sunny valleys and hills and sea are beautiful. Everything is so much greener than the last time I came up here, during summer. For an hour or so, I listen to the peaceful singing of the service and breathe in the incense, our house just visible through the open doorway in the lee of the bare mountainside. I look around at the group of people who've lived through these days of Easter together.

Then, as the cracks and bangs of *vomves* outside grow more insistent, as if we're being besieged by an invading army, I put in my earplugs.

There's a little confusion over some readings and a mistimed ringing of the bell outside, but the priest smiles. We all follow him outside, and it's time to burn Judas. An effigy has been hanging from the belfry since the afternoon. Now as our small group of old and young

– some over eighty, some younger than ten, some in skin-tight white jeans and some in dark suits – all gather in the bright early evening, someone takes a candle and after a few efforts sets it alight. The clothes and the shoes eventually catch fire, and the straw inside, and we watch the body disintegrate and fall into the field below. One of the ladies I met for the first time this week gives me a reassuring pat on the leg and a smile.

Everyone says, *'Keh tou khronou,'* – And next year – a wish that we will be healthy and together again the same time next year. I've been on the island for a year now; last year just after I arrived, I went to Eristos Beach Hotel to buy olive oil and was given Easter biscuits. A year is something to celebrate, and I hope I will be here in another twelve months, too.

There have been challenges. Greek people are known for their resilience, which is perhaps why it's normal for them to shout at one another regularly. I might be resilient in the long term, but in the short term I am sensitive, hurt easily. I need to be more resilient, and learn survival techniques like the earplugs. I will be better prepared for next winter: wellies rather than umbrellas (not second-hand fisherman's wellies with holes in them). I've learned about modems and storms. I don't have to believe people when they accuse me of doing something bad.

It's time to let go of sadness and start to enjoy life again.

Soon after Easter one night, the house is surrounded by silence and darkness and I am settling cosily into the sofa. Since early morning I've worked, swum, baked bread, spent a few hours with the schoolkids, had a couple of glasses of wine to relax my nerves while Stelios cooks little red crabs in exploding hot oil, and now I'm feeling very sleepy. Then Stelios calls his friend Yorgos, whose family have the taverna En Plo, to wish him *khronia polla* for his name day, and we are invited over. There is an enduring belief that life on a Greek island is very quiet and slow. It makes me laugh.

I sigh, feeling that usual dread of summoning up the energy to speak Greek to people I don't know so well. 'I'll go and get dressed,' I say.

'*Mia hara eiseh*, you're fine as you are!'

I roll my eyes and explain that I am not going out, even if it is just down the road, in tracksuit bottoms and his old jumper, which I have now appropriated. I put on leather boots and jeans and jacket. And he likes the way I look, though he grumbles about the lipstick, which he hates.

'I'm not wearing it for you,' I say, smiling. 'It's for me.'

Despite my nerves, we pass a lovely hour or so at a convivial gathering, where Yorgia celebrates her name day – Yorgos and and his girlfriend Yorgia have different forms of the same name and therefore celebrate on the same day – by working non-stop to keep everyone supplied with plates of roasted goat, cheese pie, salads and then cheesecake. The youngest family member is already asleep covered in coats on the couch, while the eldest is well into a bottle of Cutty Sark. It reminds me of the regular Christmas 'do' at my grandmother's house in Manchester when I was little, with a buffet set out in the kitchen and glasses of whisky doing the rounds among aunts and uncles, the late-night cigarette smoke eventually driving me outside into the cold night with my cousin, or to the marginally less cold upstairs of the house to bed.

People help me to food and ask a few questions. I feel honoured to be part of this, and chastise myself for my reluctance to come. Those gathered at Yorgia's are no longer strangers, I realise. I know her sister from Ayios Andonis now, through the children. I'm beginning to know Yorgos' family from En Plo at Eristos, too. When I first arrived to live on the island, I knew nothing of the relationships between the people I saw around, didn't know who anyone was. My confusion over who is who is slowly clearing.

We leave early, as the next morning we have to be up at the crack of dawn. No, we have to be up *before* the crack of dawn, 4.30 a.m., as once more I'm joining Stelios on the fishing boat.

Chapter 17

Turning to Summer

As the boat chugs away from the harbour, the dark sky is full of stars. To the east, a glimmer of reddish light on the horizon shows day is on its way. It's a calm morning, the sea rippling lightly as we close in on the southern headland. Then suddenly I spot a pod of dolphins and they leap in front of the boat, silhouetted against the silver-grey sea.

The sky brightens to dark blue as we follow the curve of the island, pink and yellow dawn glowing on the horizon, with a low dark shape, the uninhabited islet of Antitilos, on our left. The land is still dark. This end of the island is all dramatic grey cliffs, so sheer that not much grows here. We continue over still, serene water towards the bay of Ayios Sergios, enter a cove and the fishermen start pulling up nets.

Honey-coloured tones begin to appear in twisted, layered formations of rock, the occasional patch of red scree or green scrub, low cloud on the horizon showing mauve. The colours of the fish – tuna, sea bass, an eel – are also beautiful against the painted wooden deck or the wooden boxes where they're stored before being packed in ice. The first splashes of direct sunlight hit a pale high ridge, showing a profusion of hollows and caves.

In bright-orange overalls, Nikos leans towards the water, gripping the side of the boat with strong, dark arms, and shouts out instructions as a yellow net is winched up from the water. It makes a triangle that glistens with diamond-like water droplets. A long and pointed *loutsos*, or barracuda, is thrown into the wooden crate along with a fish that's been half-eaten. The sunlight becomes golden, burnishes the water, and the pale rocky shore is reflected in the oil-smooth swells of the sea. The men are pensive, quiet. A couple of hopeful gulls start to follow the boat, but there's not much in the net. The men look disappointed. A large seal surfaces nearby. The fishermen busy themselves extracting what fish they can from the tangle of nets. The promise of the morning is sullied.

Each adult seal eats 20 to 40 kilos of fish a day, I've been told, and there are families of up to seven seals in some of the little bays. It's only from boats that they can be seen, in parts of the island inaccessible by land.

Nikos asks something I don't understand, and Stelios explains.

'If you can steer the boat, it will help us finish the last nets and get back to harbour more quickly. It's OK, Nikos will tell you what to do.'

I readily accept the chance to do something useful and learn something, too.

I sit at the back and push or pull the wooden rudder, stop or start the power according to shouted instructions from Nikos. *Krati* – hold it. *Apo tho* – this way. *Apo ki* – that way. *Isia* – straight. We seem very close to the rocky shore and it's scary but exhilarating.

Green scrub now almost glows in sunlight on top of a smooth headland, and the sea is so clear I can see the yellow net spiralling down into the deep. Up comes an angry-looking purple lobster. A moray eel is flung back into the blue. The fish come in ones and twos. Seagulls line up on the rocky shore, and a cormorant glides by. The boat gradually fills up with wound-in nets and floats. The day is not a disaster as among the fish are two *sinagrithes* – king of fish – one of them weighing 4 kilos and worth a lot of money. My reward for steering the boat safely is a *fouska* or *spinialo*, something like an oyster, perhaps a kind of sea squirt, with soft yellow flesh that tastes like the sea.

Back ashore, we drink Greek coffee under a cloudy sky at the *kafeneion* in Livadia. Nikos parks his flatbed truck across the road by the square, the fish on ice in the back to entice customers. Men and women lean in to look – an older woman called Anna who lives alone near Eristos beach, wrapped up in layers of clothes because she rode down on her scooter; Dimitris the headmaster in jeans and blue shirt, his ubiquitous belt-bag hanging under his belly, casting a curious eye over the catch on his way to the post office. A clever ginger cat sits patiently under the truck.

There are days when they catch very little. On other days, they might catch hundreds of fish, and have to work for hours against the clock, packing it all in ice to ship it off quickly to the markets – if they can get a good price. They only earn whatever they can sell the fish for. And sometimes they don't even go out to catch more if they have nowhere to sell or keep them. There's no welfare to make up for the bad days. It's an unpredictable, demanding life. An hour later, at home, I hear Nikos' voice shouting '*Psaria!*' as he tries to sell what he has left to the people of Megalo Horio.

An old lady is in conversation with Rena when I arrive at the shop, and I overhear her saying she doesn't go in the sea until it's summer.

'What's this?' demands Rena in her no-nonsense way, pointing out the door.

Though still early May, it's 28°C. *Protomayia*, First of May, has passed. *Protomayia* is officially the start of summer. We've just had the Ayia Irini festival, the first festival of the summer, which takes place in the afternoon of 5 May at a pretty little chapel surrounded by fields in the Eristos valley. Triangular religious flags in many colours fluttered in the wind and the sun was bright on the circular dance floor. This daytime festival – held while the island is quiet – feels relaxed, like a birthday party, and I enjoyed dropping in for an hour or so to watch the dancing.

The start of summer is also signalled by the power going off for an hour a couple of times a day, with restaurants opening again and people returning to the island from wherever they've wintered, turning on their lights and appliances; not just this island, but Kos and

Nisyros, as we get our power from there by undersea cable. The beaches are being cleared of the detritus that washes up over the winter. The young kids aren't allowed to play football in the schoolyard from lunch until five, because the same man who shouted at me for teaching on Ochi Day tells me *'kalokeriazei'*, it's turning to summer, and people will now be taking a siesta. I now know he's the father of Yorgos the nurse, and husband of the primary school caretaker who throws the keys to the school over the fence to me.

In fact, the older kids have exams coming up and the rest want to be outside. I don't blame them. It's no time to be cooped up in school. One day, driving to Livadia and wondering when we should finish English sessions for the year, I offer a lift to a couple of walkers with backpacks and it reminds me how much I'd like to be out doing the same, now that I can. I love feeling free now; I mustn't lose that feeling if I get pregnant again. I start to feel sure I want to try. It's easier to feel more relaxed when it's warm and bright, the sun shining.

The fishing has been going well, and Stelios has a few kilos of sea bass to grill – ones they can't sell, with little bites taken out. Of course, there is nowhere on Tilos to buy a barbecue, but no matter because apparently everyone makes barbecues out of old hot water tanks.

There is an island habit of discarding objects large and small when they are no longer needed, and leaving them wherever they fall. This happens with fishing nets, wooden pallets, washing machines and fridges, an old car Stelios once crashed, and of course the disused cement mixer which demarcates the turn-off to Skafi, helping me explain to people where I live. This habit comes in handy when you need a barbecue. Stelios finds a rusty old water tank lying around somewhere, borrows an extension cord from Pavlos for his circular saw, and starts attacking the rusty metal, with scant regard for the possibility of rusty bits of metal flying off and hitting him in the eye, or his fingers getting in the way. Sparks are soon flying. I can't bear to watch. But an hour or so later, ta-da! By sawing off a section of the boiler, he has managed to fashion something that looks more or less like a barbecue, albeit a rusty one that has to be propped up with a rock. As a piece of recycling, it's impressive. He is quite ingenious. He finds an old grill somewhere and scrubs it clean, then we drive down to Eristos beach to see someone who makes charcoal. He grills the fish, leaving the patio spattered with oil.

I keep getting confused between *tha psisoume* (we'll grill – what you do with a barbecue) and *tha psifisoume* (we'll vote). Elections are taking place, and Tilos is busy with people coming home to vote. There's a lively, celebratory atmosphere, as people meet friends and family they haven't seen for a while.

As for the elections themselves, though, people are unhappy with austerity measures and being bossed around by Europe. They are angry with what their government has allowed to happen over the previous decades while assuring everyone that things were fine, which has left the country in such a mess. Welfare payments only last for a limited time after you lose your job in Greece; after that, you must rely on family to keep you alive. So when the results of the vote come in, the current ruling party, PASOK, is firmly defenestrated from the political scene. It's a strong message.

The elections leave Greece in limbo. Neither the old, right-wing Nea Dimokratia party nor the new, left-wing Syriza win enough of the vote to form a government, nor are the parties able to form a coalition, so the people must vote again in June. The outcome could determine whether they stay in the eurozone; there's the potential for monumental change and it's tempting to hope for that path – the one that would allow Greece to forge its own future.

It's time for me to fly to England to see colleagues, friends and family again. The plane descends through white-grey cloud as I arrive, but I don't go to England for the weather. Seeing people face to face after several months apart is wonderful. I feel so lucky to have the best of different worlds in my new life.

Many people have fixed ideas about Greece and the Greeks, which they pick up from the media – people like to think issues are simple and a single article in a newspaper is sufficient to understand a situation. Rushing from one meeting to the next in London, I take a cab and have to pretend to check messages on my phone when the driver makes it clear he thinks the Greeks are lazy, layabouts – a familiar opinion. I think about the fishermen, about the people I know and the several jobs they do; and laugh, remembering when I caught a glimpse of Eleftheria, after working in the shop all morning, standing behind a mound of vine leaves and rice mixture and preparing dolmades for her extended family. No lazy nation would actually make stuffed vine leaves from scratch for lunch.

I meet up with a friend who works in the same business and lives in London, and we go for a drink. He's surprised when I tell him I'm still just settling in to my new life. Apparently he expected me to say I've had a year of living on a Greek island and have got it out of my system, and am looking for a job in the city. I try to explain the joys of my life: walking to beaches, watching eagles above my house. There's a pause, and he asks politely, 'And you like that?' Clearly, it wouldn't be paradise for everyone. Thank goodness.

At the end of the week, I find a great little camping shop and buy a cheap sleeping bag and tent that fit in my rucksack. Then I take a quick, budget flight to the south of France and make my way to a town by the sea to meet a friend to hike for a couple of days. Long-distance footpaths are one of life's good things. To think, someone has created this and we can use it for free. The path takes us away from the town and up to a picturesque village, then higher still to a ridge that looks out over hills covered with forest. Along the way we catch up, talk freely about our lives, not having to think very much. The sky is blue and the sun shines, glinting on the silver and gold-flecked stones of the path. Tired at the end of the day, we descend a steep, scree-covered track and plod, exhausted, until at last we find the perfect campsite, looking down towards the sea. We have the place to ourselves since it's out of season, and sit drinking red wine outside until sleep calls, waking up in our respective tents in the fresh air. After the troubles of the past few months, this is a gift to myself.

When I arrive back in Rhodes, I'm waiting for the bus when a tall, skinny cab driver approaches the bus stop and offers to take me and a couple of Swedish backpackers into town for two-thirds of the normal fare. He's fed up with waiting for business at the back of the queue, he says. 'Better for me to keep working.' He chats to us on the way into town and when the Swedes ask where to eat, he advises them at length.

The subject of the crisis comes up and the Swedish guy makes a gauche comment about how 'the Greeks will now have to work'. There's a pause while the driver wonders if he's joking, then he shrugs and says, quietly, that he personally works 12 hours a day, though takings are down 50 per cent.

As for the vote ahead, he says: 'It's crazy we have elections in the summer, the tourist season. And who can we vote for? This one steals, the other steals more. Anyway, I think is better to go back to the drachma. Sure it will be hard for years, but not as bad. People will go back to the villages – life is easier in the villages – and make things again.' Maybe in some ways it would be good for people to move back – to keep village businesses going during the winter.

When I return to Tilos, the restaurants already have customers from northern Europe. But will Greeks be able to afford the trip to Eristos beach this summer? The island waits to see what the summer will bring. No one is more curious to know than the new owners of the *kantina*.

Chapter 18

Red Tape and Red Mullet

Stelios signed the contract for the *kantina* and is preparing to open. It sounds like it should be easy: a temporary snack bar on a free-camping beach on a remote Greek island. Not so.

What he bought was the physical trailer along with fixtures and fittings – fridge, water tank, sandwich toaster, etc. I lent him half the money, but buying the *kantina* was the easy part – maybe even the cheap part. I cannot believe how much needs to be done, how much paperwork there is in order to be *nomimos*, legal.

He had to apply to the municipality for the grant to use the piece of land on the beach, get a licence to sell food, and insurance. He needed a tax number and cash register and accountant – all very expensive in Greece. Who knew that the cash register alone would cost hundreds of euros and that he would need to keep calling the accountant to get him to complete the papers in time? He's spent months procuring elusive pieces of paper, having tests for a health certificate, and doing other stressful and time-consuming things. There are also rules about what he can sell. There are three nearby tavernas, and he can't offer food similar to theirs. Nothing can be served on a plate with cutlery or in a real glass.

But none of that would put Stelios off. He's wanted to run the *kantina* for years. Now all the efforts are close to completion.

He asks me to pick up some things he needs for the *kantina* while I'm in Rhodes yet again for a follow-up appointment at the hospital with my doctor. I understand what he wants, but as I'm in a rush I don't write the actual Greek words down and can't remember them. This leaves me with only one option in the hardware shop. Grinning, I prepare to perform a party game where you have to make a person say a word without saying the word yourself, a cross between Articulate and charades, using my limited Greek and exaggerated mime.

'It's something you use to paint with...' No, not paint, but *pinello*, paintbrush.

'Something that you use to close something with a key...' *Klitharia*, lock.

'It's two plugs in one plug.' It's called a '*taf*' – the Greek word for the letter T.

Someone sorts me out with all I need and even makes me a frappé coffee. How civilised. I take it outside with me when my phone rings. When I come back inside, a few men standing around the front desk are chatting about something.

'What do you think?' they ask.

'Sorry, I didn't hear...'

'We were just saying that in other countries, if you do something wrong, the police actually come after you.'

They seem to be saying it's an unusual concept but a fine principle, if the police are fair.

I smile and shrug. 'I suppose so.'

It must be strange to grow up in a culture where you don't trust the system, but that is how it's been in Greece for a while; there's a sense that it's always better to look out for yourself than to follow the rules. It's what feeds tax evasion, when people don't trust the government to do the right thing with their hard-earned money. The Greek respect for cunning and outwitting one another is written into the oldest literature, in the heroic character of Homer's Odysseus – and the tendency to dodge authority is often attributed to the four centuries under Ottoman rule, when Greeks used their wits to dodge the tax-collecting overlords of the country. But corruption is still part of the system today. I've been reliably informed about doctors asking for a *fakellaki* or small envelope (of cash) to give treatment.

And while Stelios is going to great lengths to set up the *kantina* legally, the system of red tape seems somewhat onerous for what should be a simple enterprise. It's enough to make young people less enterprising. I've begun to learn that sometimes in order to get by, people have to break the rules, be a little bit 'unlegal' or *paranomos*. The free camping itself that provides the *kantina* with business is technically unlegal, after all; Tasos, the old mayor, encouraged it even though it's against Greek law and few islands allow it.

When I was first asked to help the island's children with their English, I discovered that actual lessons would not be legal without a licence and certification, so we had to find a way to do informal sessions – otherwise the children couldn't progress. In a similar way, legally people are not allowed to slaughter their animals without the presence of a vet, even though they've been slaughtering their animals for generations and farmers can't send their animals away on a boat every time they need to slaughter one. How sad it would be if the law killed the island's farming culture just because there's no vet on the island. Life has to work a bit differently on small islands – otherwise people couldn't live here and the islands would be abandoned more and more.

Sipping the last of my coffee, I walk back to town with my errands done, looking for the bus to the hospital. I find it awaiting its departure time beside the harbour. I've met crazy, funny bus drivers before in Rhodes, and this one is no exception: for him, the Number 3 seems to be merely a venue for his daily performance. I'm sure it's against the rules but he isn't sitting in the driver's seat when I get on – he's in the back with the passengers instead, and has a joke for everyone, explaining to one foreign woman in English, 'I am sorry, but I am original, I am Greek.' She offers him some chocolate. He is cheering up everyone's day, even on an otherwise mundane bus journey.

Eventually, the packed and sweltering bus sets off, reaches the outskirts of town and breaks down. As we wait, I ask the old man standing next to me if he knows what's happening. I explain to him I have an appointment at the hospital and may have to find a taxi. A replacement bus arrives and it's about to take us back to town, but the old man shouts to the driver that I'm in a hurry and they must take me where I need to get to. So – presumably breaking the rules – they do. Isn't life so much richer when things are not done completely by the book?

The doctor tells me my body has recovered well from the miscarriage but that I should wait another month to get back to full strength. The appointment brings back a lot of emotion: an excuse for shopping therapy. Anna is pleased to get a message from me and jokes I have another 'prescribed' month of excessive exercise and drinking before I have to start doing all the right things again, so I'd better make the most of it and she'll be on hand to assist. We'll go out for dinner at our favourite spot next week.

The *kantina*'s allocated place under the trees, where it's been for years, some 20 metres back from the shoreline, gets lashed by storms in the winter and waves wash pebbles high on to the sand. These pebbles must all now be cleared so that holidaying folks can relax in soft, sandy comfort as they sip their drinks. Stelios is anxious about how long it will take to move the stones, and fusses around saying he has to borrow a rake from somewhere; I estimate it will take an hour or two and we can do it with just our hands. But several hours later, our backs aching and hands chafed, I see what he means and we decide to come back and finish the job the next day. Thousands of pebbles, buried many layers deep, must be scooped up into crate after crate and carted away.

He also needs to find someone to help him bring the drinks fridge and the ice cream freezer and the wooden tables and chairs from the field where they overwinter, not to mention the *kantina* van itself. Then he's got to see if he can teach me to make a decent Greek coffee for customers who show up while he's out fishing in the morning. He can't afford to give up fishing until summer brings enough business.

He's so worried that he's thinking about taking up smoking again. 'I was much less stressed when I smoked,' he says. 'And the doctor says I've got to be careful about my stress.' The two sets of *komboloi* or worry beads he bought in Athens don't seem to be helping.

It seems it's not possible to make an arrangement in advance to get help to move fridges and furniture. Maybe Stelios knows that such an arrangement would be unreliable, so he grasps an opportunity and when he sees his friend Yorgos from En Plo with not much to do, enlists him immediately. So all of a sudden we are at the beach, amid a frenetic chaos reinforced by shouting and cursing as the two of them heft massive pieces of metal and wood off a flatbed truck and on to wooden pallets in the sand. Somehow, in an hour, it is all done and they curse one another again good-humouredly as Yorgos drives off in a cloud of dust.

After we've cleared the rest of the pebbles, or at least agreed that we've done the best we can, I am bedraggled but oddly happy, washing out the insides and shelves of two rather dusty fridges on the beach, when someone I know walks by.

'What *are* you doing?' he asks dramatically, swinging a lily-white towel over his lightly bronzed shoulder. He has a beautifully restored house at the top of the village, which he visits for a few weeks a year in breaks from his busy job in his sophisticated urban life. 'You're not some sort of Greek wife, you know.'

'Well, I sort of am, actually.' I laugh, thinking how much fun I'm having doing some physical work for a change – not for money but being part of a new venture, another way of getting to know the community. This is exactly what I want to be doing.

My contract with my old employer has gone down to three days a week, which was a bit of a blow and not what I expected; I'd been working so hard, trying to show I could contribute in ways that are different from my old job. I will have to grow my freelance business; a new business is always tough and it will be especially challenging from here, but I can only do my best and see what happens.

When I arrive for my *kantina* lesson the next day, Stelios and his cousin are sitting around smoking and drinking beer. Things don't look promising. But gradually they load up the big fridge with beer and soft drinks. The first customer comes by – a friendly English chap who wants a Greek coffee for himself and a lemonade for his wife. He shows me photos he's taken of an owl on the way down to Skafi, and even leaves a tip. Someone else stops by in a truck and asks if the beers are cold yet. Another friend of Stelios, who works at the nursery school, comes for a coffee and a sandwich and leaves €10 – a particularly magnanimous gesture given that her salary has been reduced by so much ('We don't talk about that!' she says). By mid-afternoon we leave with things sort of in place, and Stelios has a few euros in his pocket.

At dusk, Stelios out fishing, I water my vegetable patch and the roses. There's been no rain since April and we're unlikely to see any before October. I've noticed the dandelion-like *radikia*, which provides an abundant supply of leafy greens, has blue flowers that open in the morning and disappear in the evening. I put up more bamboo canes and fishing nets over the tomatoes, and sit on the terrace in the warm evening air. In the distance, in the deep-blue sea, a big cruise ship crosses the horizon. A bat flits by.

Maria shouts 'Jennifer!' and when I look up she is at the end of the path, arms laden with two types of cucumbers, green peppers and courgettes, straight from the earth. I make a huge salad with the cucumbers and peppers along with onions, rocket and boiled potatoes from our own garden, and the first of the tomatoes from the farm on the road to Eristos. Red mullet are in season; Stelios brings home a handful of them that can't be sold because they're not perfect: they've had small bites taken out of them by other sea creatures. It makes them tastier, he says, because they then absorb a little salt from the sea. Red mullet are the dolphins' favourite food, he says, and I think they might be mine, too; sweet, dusted with flour and fried in olive oil (most people don't fry with olive oil, but Stelios does). I'm so hungry I eat them standing by the stove as soon as they are cool enough.

The temperature's been well over 30°C for weeks now; the upstairs of the house is very hot and there's barely any breeze through the windows, even here where we usually get a breeze all summer, so I set up my little tent in the garden. We do now have an air conditioner, but the noise and flashing lights when you turn it on are a bit distracting. I prefer to sleep with a view of the stars through the netting of my tent.

At six in the morning, a cockerel crows and bees buzz around the flowers. I walk up the stone steps to the roof terrace, and sit on the raised ledge. Pink-orange light hits the craggy tops of the limestone hills and the castle, slowly revealing the remains of walls from earlier centuries and terraces of old farms. From the fields, there's a smell of damp herbs and grasses. Wisps of cloud cling to the hilltops, birds sing, crows flap overhead. Looking down the Eristos valley, I see the sea still pale and misty in the early morning.

I go back downstairs and sweep out the house – a mix of sand, garden-earth, dried seagrass and most likely a few ants. They've been exploring my computer and kettle, the muesli and bread now both must be kept in the fridge, and I've become accustomed to carrying the occasional very small pet on my arm or leg.

Then, taking a bag of ice cubes from the freezer, I drive down to Eristos, making a quick stop at the farm to buy tomatoes, peppers and onions. Stelios has to see the accountant, so I must open up the *kantina* for him.

Chapter 19

Endless Afternoons at the Beach

When I arrive at the *kantina*, the vast sandy beach is empty, pale-blue sea lapping calmly at the shore, the mountain to the south still pale grey and mist lingering in the tops of the trees, leaving a gentle haze over everything. The sun picks out silver drops of dew in the trees.

It's early in the season but we decided it would make sense to learn the routine before it gets busy. I unlock the fridges, clean things we might need, organise the food, put ice in the bucket... and finally make a practice frappé and sit at one of the wooden tables, looking out over beautiful Eristos beach. Birds are twittering in the trees, and cicadas start to rev up. I can't imagine a nicer place to sit. Who cares if no customers come?

Just after nine, while I'm at the wooden table with my feet in the warm sand, a big bear of a man with a gruff voice and elaborate tattoos arrives with his pretty young daughter. Stephanos has a house on a lonely part of the hill nearby. He buys a beer for himself and an ice cream for Irinna. Then he asks for a *skini*.

I'm confused. A *skini* is a tent. We're on a beach. There are tents around, but... I try to look as if I'd like to help but am not sure...

'For the hammock,' he adds, as if that clarifies things. A tent for the hammock...? 'There's usually one,' he says.

I'm baffled.

Stephanos walks around the back of the *kantina*. *'Na to!'* Found it. A coil of rope. Ah!

I am embarrassed and try to pretend I knew what he wanted all along. I should have noticed: *ena skini* is a rope, *mia skini* is a tent. But now Stephanos wants a knife to cut the rope. I'm not sure if I should let him, as Stelios probably needs that rope and surely the hammock is fine without it... Although with his tattoos and early-morning Amstel, Stephanos doesn't look like the sort of man you'd cross, I say it's perhaps not a good idea. He leaves and I hope I've not done something wrong.

Fifteen minutes later, he's back – with a rope from home. He ties it to the tree next to the hammock so that Irinna can swing herself back and forth. He sits down to watch the sea with another beer, and then Irinna joins him and they play chess together. I ask if everything's OK.

'A fou pino bira, eimeh kala,' he says. I drink beer, therefore I'm fine.

It's quiet, so I read. There's a brief power cut, but thankfully no one needs a toasted sandwich or frappé coffee.

Over the next week, Stephanos will become a familiar and welcome face around the *kantina*, always friendly and good-humoured; he likes this spot. And slowly, tourists begin to arrive. Some, in addition to wanting a sandwich or a cold drink, are interested in information about places to see, and I love talking to them. So many are keen walkers and make the most of the trails. I'm chatting to a retired couple who live in Boston and are island-hopping for six weeks, when the bus pulls up and a gang of the high school kids troop off towards the volleyball net. I hear shouts of 'It's burning!' as they run barefoot on the hot sand. I know them all now, care about them. Soon a few come up to the *kantina*.

'*Yeia sas kyria*!' Hello, miss! Just as I'll always care about them, they'll always address me with respect, even if instead of marching them through grammar points, I am now making them sausage sandwiches. I feel funny asking if they want ketchup or *mayonesa*, but for them it is perfectly normal, having grown up in a place where people do a bit of everything, where someone working for the council may also work as a waiter – perhaps it's because the council workers aren't being paid, but people are who they are, not what they do.

It's good to see the kids relaxing together as always. It must be hard for them to lose that close group of friends when they leave the island. They are polite and open and resourceful – a credit to Tilos, and a mark of the success of small island life. They reinforce the idea that this is a good place to bring up children. Now that I'm no longer helping them with their English, I have a little free time and feel lucky to do something else that takes me away from my desk and gives me a point of connection with people.

Nectarios, a local honey-maker – you couldn't make up a better name – stops off in his truck to grab a frozen bottle of water. He's helped Stelios a lot recently and gave us a big jar of honey for nothing, so I say I don't want any money from him but he insists.

A woman from Ioannina in northern Greece who's staying on the beach for a few weeks comes by at mid-morning for her *kafedaki* – she uses the affectionate diminutive form, which shows you how much she likes her Greek coffee. She tells me carefully how she drinks it, with very specific instructions about the water/coffee/sugar ratio. I've learned to mix the deeply aromatic powdery coffee and sugar into the water in the little long-handled pot, the *briki*, stir slowly as it heats over the flame, then leave it until it is just about to foam at the edges. Though later Stelios' friend Stratos tells me the only way to make a Greek coffee is 'with love'.

One of our regular customers, a woman in a long dress and floppy hat, is in fact secretary to Alexis Tsipras, leader of the left-wing opposition party, Syriza. In the second elections in June, a coalition was formed. Enough people voted for the right-wing Nea Dimokratia that the new government could try to meet Europe's bailout terms; but Syriza got a massive show of support, increased even from May. It feels as if they are waiting in the wings.

'How can you be here now?' I ask her.

'I told Alexis I must go to Tilos for the month of June, as I do every year.' I've seen her sitting on the beach just looking at the sea, perfectly peaceful. 'He understands.'

On the summer solstice, as I reach the village in the evening, sheep come hurtling and clattering down the road, making me laugh. Invited for a birthday celebration with an international group of neighbours, I think that I am now enjoying more of life than I have before, that I have a fuller life, through a mixture of luck and determination.

While Stelios continues fishing in the mornings, I open the *kantina* for him. If there's no one around, I jump in the sea to wake up and then work at a table in the shade. The woman who comes for her *kafedaki* is still asking for infinitesimal improvements on the way I make her coffee. Is it possible Greeks take their coffees a wee bit too seriously? There again, I grew up in an England in which you were grateful for a drinkable coffee; an England into which Starbucks arrived as a sort of emergency Beverages Sans Frontières; we don't have a tradition of 'English coffee' and perhaps it's just as well I'm learning to make *elliniko*, Greek coffee.

A Swedish couple arrive by bus from Livadia every morning, swim and sun themselves at their favourite spot right at the edge of the sea for a couple of hours then come to take a couple of Mythos beers back to the beach and fall asleep. They are blissfully content having a swathe of beach to themselves and cold beer a few steps away. This is the joy of the *kantina*. There's also a young couple from Athens camping on the beach for a week of 'recharge', living cheaply and simply on coffees and sandwiches. Yes, there's 'the crisis' in the economy, but we've still got to have fun.

A regular visitor from Athens called Stephanos is in his seventies, thin as a rake and deeply tanned. He sets up camp at the end of the beach for a few months every year, building a pebble floor for his dining room, improvising a kitchen in the tree branches, cycling up to the farm for vegetables. Stelios takes me to meet him and he feeds us *revithosoupa*, chickpea soup with onions and garlic.

The *kantina* doesn't serve traditional Greek food – but the prices are good and it's quick and laid back. If it were my *kantina*, I'd want paper cups only (no polystyrene), fresh juices, fresh fruit cocktails... But Stelios says that's not what people want. Paper cups wouldn't keep your frappé coffee cold in the heat of summer, so everyone would complain. When I ask if he's costed things to determine how much he needs to charge to make a profit, he thinks I'm being absurd. I ask why he can't order food and drinks more cheaply from Rhodes rather than through the local suppliers. But with only one boat a day, he explains, you need someone reliable who will deliver things quickly when you need them. His cousin brings bits and pieces over from Rhodes – backgammon boards and *pagokipseles*, plastic bags for making ice in the freezer at home in the absence of an ice machine.

When Stelios roars up on the motorbike to take over, I have a long swim, and then if it's a weekday I drive back home for my working day proper; with the time difference, I'm back at home just around the hour people in the UK are checking their emails. Most people at Eristos have no idea that I have a serious job, though some do ask how I'm lucky enough to live here. When I don't have to rush back, I spend the afternoon reading, going for long swims and lying on the sand.

One Saturday Stelios calls to say he'll be held up on the fishing boat for a while, as they've caught lots of fish and lobsters, and because they were fishing deep they've got lots of cleaning to do. So I handle the lunchtime rush. I look out from the hatch of the *kantina* and see all the seats full, people enjoying themselves. It's a satisfying sight.

Locals also use the *kantina*. Eleftheria's husband brings their son and lets him play on the beach while he sits with friends. One morning I arrive to open and see a very recognisable car belonging to another local man parked nearby. The car's owner emerges from a tent that I know isn't his, and buys two coffees with a smile on his face.

Some afternoons, the chairs are filled with guys playing backgammon. A shy young Greek couple sit romantically entwined in the hammock. A young boy asks if he can get his mum's ice packs from our freezer; campers charge their phones. A guy with dreadlocks asks if his girlfriend can set up a stall selling hand-made jewellery; fine if they are customers, says Stelios. Another camper fashions us some ashtrays out of empty beer cans. Erikos and Angeliki walk by with their little dog on its lead, carrying bamboo for the walls of the shelter they always build; they are dedicated naturists, sleep out under the stars, and even the dog is vegetarian.

Beyond the *kantina*, the beach is clothing-optional. An older couple sit on little deck chairs under yellow umbrellas with their picnic cool bag and their drinks holders, and you could almost imagine a tartan blanket and thermos, except that it's nearly 40°C and they are both completely naked. Beautifully toned young people with all-over tans step glistening out of the water and make their way up the scorching sand. I start to feel overdressed if I walk down to the end of the beach in a bikini.

Gradually as July progresses, the long stretch of beach – which in spring was empty, the tamarisk trees broken by winter storms (we won't tell the tourists about the dead turtle) – is transformed. The bus drops people off in ones and twos with their backpacks. Twice a week the big ferry from Athens brings families and groups of friends in 4X4s. Campers hang their Indian-print sheets in the trees for shade, string up their hammocks, build shelters out of palm fronds and plant solar-powered lights in the sand, looking out for scorpions. Antonis, who has long silvery hair and runs the communal bar on the beach with its pirate flag sticking out of the sand, has been coming for over twenty summers and can't imagine life without it.

I am camping, too, but in comfort at home, as usual. When it gets too hot indoors, I go out to the cool of the garden under the moon and the stars, and sleep in my tent on soft quilts until I wake with the bees at six. After a couple of hours at home, I drive to Eristos with ice cubes, stopping quickly to buy three kilos of tomatoes and one of peppers.

'Oreia kopella simera!' says Michalis at the farm, surprised to see me in a dress with my hair up and lipstick on. The *kantina* is becoming a bit of a show, and it's more fun when I'm dressed up.

Continuing down the road, I pass a few campers out for a walk, and they wave and shout '*Yeia sou*, Jennifer!' Much as I usually love my quiet life, it's fun to be doing this, to be part of it. The free watermelon that Michalis gave me graces the counter, and I think it might be nice to cut up watermelon and offer it to customers. There's nothing quite like the sweet tang of watermelon straight from the fridge to cool you down on a hot day.

Sundays are different, I learn: Greeks wake up with a coffee and cheese and ham toastie mid-morning, then chill for a while. A young man pads down the sand to get a frappé and *tost* for his girlfriend, who's still in the tent. 'We drank a lot last night,' he admits. I'm worried I'm not making the frappés very well, but he says they look fine. The preferred amount of sugar and Nescafé – for Greeks, instant granulated coffee (as opposed to real Greek coffee) is always this brand and is referred to as 'Nes' – has to be added from the start, along with a small amount of water; then you must froth it just the right amount before topping up with ice, cold water and milk if desired. I must concentrate hard to understand people's specific instructions in Greek.

I'm rather impressed that Stelios is actually remembering all the things he needs to buy for the *kantina*, even if he still constantly forgets where he's left his mobile phone. He dashes about to pick up food, rings the supplier to restock the drinks fridge. He seems to have evolved quite naturally into a businessman. He tackles everything in a rather stressful way, with the same air of urgency and chaos that I've become accustomed to by now, but he's flourishing in his new role as *kantina* owner, the capitalist on the hippie beach. It's great fun to watch him charm customers, speaking in English with a heavy accent.

'The hamburgers are home-made!' he says, as they peruse the menu. I cast him a quick glance as he turns to light the gas burner for the grill. He says quietly in Greek to me, grinning, 'Well, they are, they're home-made by the butcher's wife...'

The free camping is a hit this year, not surprisingly; people keep coming to ask us if there's anywhere else to camp, as most spots are taken. There's no longer a quiet end of the beach. And the quiet times at the *kantina* get shorter. One Sunday, we actually run out of hamburgers after a dozen Belgian performance artist types descend upon us. I watch one of them, a pale-skinned girl with red hair, doing handstands and cartwheels by the edge of the sea.

The standard of conversation is raised when a large group of language and literature students arrives; young Greek people love spending time in a big group, a *parea*. Another group of less serious students arrives and half-naked girls drape themselves across their boyfriends. Stelios cuts away part of a watermelon and fills it with *souma* for them to drink through straws. The students tell me I'm the most smiley person they've seen on the island, which makes me happy. I'm not so smiley the next morning when I arrive to open up and find their stuff everywhere: empty cigarette packets, the odd shoe, and one of the young girls sprawled out in the hammock. She remains fast asleep until mid-morning, blissfully unaware of tattooed Stephanos sitting next to her playing chess with his daughter.

Stelios puts a halt to fishing for the summer and stays late at the *kantina*; I open up for him in the mornings, stomping around and cursing the mess of beer cans and cigarette butts. We cross paths briefly and swap notes. We have no time to cook for ourselves, so we eat *kantina* sandwiches. Sometimes I return to the *kantina* in the late afternoon when we have a beer with customers.

'I have gossip!' says Stelios.

Someone's wife is involved with another man. I'm shocked and amused when I hear the details, as all the parties involved are well over sixty and fairly earthy farmer types.

'Sorry, I shouldn't laugh,' I say, 'it's serious...'

'And funny,' grins Stelios.

So much for the quiet life on a little island.

Chapter 20

Rat on a Hot Tin Can

I've joined the ranks of islanders who spend all summer running around for work; I watch tanned, relaxed holiday-makers strolling down the road to Eristos, when I am whizzing past in my dust-coloured car.

Occasionally I think of offering someone a ride, out of habit, then wonder whether they'd really want to get in. The car stinks from ferrying home bin bags full of empty drinks cans for recycling, a concession Stelios made to me after I complained about the amount of rubbish we were creating. He set up recycling bins and he figures we can find a way to get it all transported to Rhodes at the end of the summer, so for now we're piling the bags in the empty building next door to our house. In the heat, it doesn't take long for a beer can to stink. Thank goodness we can leave the car windows permanently down.

There are usually one or two people waiting when I arrive in the morning to clear up the *kantina* and open at nine. So in late July, the busiest week when people come for the festival of Ayios Panteleimon, I leave home early, hoping for a bit of peace and quiet before the customers arrive. As I drive up at eight, I see to my dismay that already half a dozen people are sitting around waiting for their coffees. Turns out they had a big night and they're ready for a few special sandwiches as well – omelette and sausage with all the trimmings, and fresh juices. The only thing to do is laugh and get on with it.

Stelios agreed finally that it was a good idea to offer fresh juice and we commandeered our cheap juice machine from home, although it has to be cleaned after each use so as not to attract flies and ants. It also means I have to buy crates of oranges, in addition to dashing about with ice cubes (hurrying so they don't melt), bottles of water and 5-kilo bags of tomatoes.

People congregate each morning for their coffee with its little variations; I've learned that for Greek people there's not just 'medium' and 'sweet' coffee but also 'medium towards sweet' and 'medium towards bitter'. Occasionally, when I can't quite catch what someone is saying and they roll their eyes, exasperated at my incomprehension, I've felt 'medium towards bitter'. But there are plenty of other people who tell me that I am always smiling, which never fails to make my day.

When Stelios arrives, we rarely have time for a quiet catch-up of news: it's a question of pointing out the outstanding orders in the book and working together while I pass on any messages. By the middle of the day, when we've got the toaster and gas burners going inside the small metal box that is the *kantina*, it's like a sauna. Then I escape, walk straight across the sand and plunge into beautiful blue sea. It makes me more relaxed when

I go back to my computer – gives my life balance. And something different happens every day as people come and go. One day the bay is dominated by three huge boats, apparently belonging to a Russian aluminium tycoon – I wonder if he wants our recycling?

One evening, I come home in the dark and at the corner of the house see an animal's eyes caught in the headlights – a little animal sitting on top of the fence, it seems. After I park the car, close the gate and walk up the steps to the front door, I shine the light from my mobile towards the fence and there it is: a rat with a long tail, perched precariously on the wire and not budging. Bizarre, but I don't even have time to dwell on it. I feel a bit dazed and caught in the headlights myself.

August is hectic, and Stelios usually works until the early hours. He takes me for dinner at Eristos Beach Hotel, the lovely family-run hotel set among lush gardens. The taverna has some of my favourite food, moussaka and stuffed vegetables, *gemista*. Hippocrates, the grandfather who busies himself with growing fruit and vegetables and olives although he's in his eighties, gives me a handful of ripe figs, and it's only then I remember that it's fig season. Because I've barely had time for walks, I haven't been brought to a halt by the heavenly aroma from the trees and reached up for the warm fruit. Driving down the dusty track to home, I realise I'm not going to get any if I don't do it now, so it's a question of hit and run – stop the car and leave the engine running while I grab a few figs off the tree, and eat them straight away.

One night, it takes a power cut for me to stop and notice the sky, incredibly bright with countless stars, and the Milky Way like a splash of white paint across it.

In mid-August I'm at Harkadio Cave in the early evening for a festival being held in the open-air theatre – an evening of dance performances. It's the first time I've been here at this time of day, and I realise what a spectacular view there is towards Megalo Horio, with sunset colours over the sea at Plaka, and the broken peak of Nisyros island in the distance. But we're not here to enjoy ourselves: Team *Kantina* will provide the souvlaki stand. Stelios and two friends set up a long charcoal barbecue, filling huge buckets with ice blocks supplied by Nikos the fisherman, and hundreds of cans and bottles. The pork souvlaki are juicy and tasty, but we only have time to taste one before customers start arriving – schoolchildren who'll be performing dances and are already hungry and thirsty. My job is to help people to drinks, and take the cash. There's a brief lull when I go to watch part of the show, and I'm thrilled to see the teenagers I know perform impressive dances. Two hours later, I am laughing as I struggle to add up in my head the cost of seven souvlakis, two beers and a Coke, trying to make change in the dark with fingers numb from rummaging around in the buckets for well-chilled Amstel. But we sell out of souvlaki and the evening is declared a success. My learning curve this year has been rather steep, but it's rewarding being involved.

Soon it is the festival of Panayia Kamariani, which goes by in a blur of dancing and greeting new friends. The *Koupa*, a couple of nights later in Megalo Horio, feels relaxed and intimate, now that I know more of the community. There's a familiar sense of anticipation as the evening starts in the *kafeneion* overlooking the church, the young musicians warming up. As always the older men walk down the stone steps, arm in arm, singing their way into the square with its smooth grey sea-pebbles. They stop, arms clasping one another's shoulders, their deep voices finding the last words of the song. There's nothing ceremonial, nothing forced or for show; things simply happen this way, the same way every year, and everyone knows what to do. Just as Fotis will be the first to lead the dance, and his wife Maritsa will be watching from her seat where she's been waiting patiently for hours. It makes me feel goose-bumps and a lump of emotion in my throat.

Continuity: it's something I consider a lot here. It's hard not to, when I look out from my house to the cave and the stone walls on the hillside where people have lived since prehistory to the present day. The children of the island who I've come to know will help shape its future. It's hard not to think of continuity when we have spent our summer running the *kantina* on Eristos beach that Vangelis ran, welcoming old friends and new. Although things change, the island's traditions are strong and keep the community together – just as in the circular dance of the *sousta*, arms bind the line together, old and young.

I grew up in a community with history and traditions specific to the north of England. There was a procession from one village to another every Whit Friday, a feast day after Easter – I remember as a little girl carrying a posy of flowers and holding the ribbon of a banner – and there was a big brass-band contest in Dobcross at night, while we kids ran around firing at one another with peashooters. In August there was the Rushcart, which brought morris dancers from around the country to compete, and push and pull the cart of rushes up and down hills from one village to another, stopping to drink beer and dance. My family left Saddleworth when my father's job moved to London, but I've returned for Rushcart and it makes me happy to see festivals that still celebrate a community's heritage.

Perhaps it's something we all think of more as we get older: the continuity of life. Continuity is part of my reason for wanting a child, because I love my family and want to keep it going; I'd want my own child to have the kind of old-fashioned freedom and days playing outdoors that I had in the Saddleworth villages.

Here in Megalo Horio, the jolly priest Papa Manolis, in his black cassock, his long grey hair tied in a ponytail, is an energetic dancer and gives the young men in their casual shorts and jeans a run for their money. Stelios' father Nikos dances rarely but with great feeling to his favourite song, and I feel I've come a long way when I'm able to dance alongside him and Vicky, and Telis and the priest. For me, it's the best *Koupa* yet. And in true, traditional style, two old guys drink too much, there's a fight and they have to be pulled apart. A *Koupa* wouldn't be the same if someone didn't get punched in the nose.

I hear a chanting one morning soon after, from the direction of the village. I check my diary and see it's 27 August, the anniversary of Saint Fanourios, finder of lost things.

Among the panoply of saints in the Greek Orthodox Church, Ayios Fanourios stands out head and shoulders above the rest for his precise and irresistible brief: I will find what you are looking for. I've certainly found happiness and a home. Somehow, miraculously given that I've barely seen Stelios, my period's late – in fact it's something of an immaculate conception given that mostly we sleep at different times and in different parts of the house. Over the summer, without any expectations, I've been hoping that without any fuss, without all the stress of last time and the worries, I am quietly pregnant with a healthy baby. Last time, the laboratory in Athens confirmed that the foetus had not been healthy enough to survive. I've tried to balance a positive attitude this time with not getting overly excited, and kept the news from Stelios for as long as possible.

The good thing about sleeping outside in my tent in the cool night air is that Stelios needn't worry about turning on the light in our little house and waking me up when he comes home very late. I also needn't worry about mosquitoes. It's usually a very soothing way to sleep. But I am going to bed as usual in my tent one evening, with my comfy pillow and a torch and a book to read, when I notice an odd noise and can't work out what it is.

I unzip the tent and go outside with the torch. It seems to be coming from the empty building where we keep the recycling. As I approach, it gets louder – a sort of, well, crunching sound. I shine a light and get the distinct impression that something is happening inside those black bin bags of beer and soft drink cans. I pick up the wooden handle of a garden spade, and gingerly poke the bags.

Out flies a rat.

It dashes past me, and I notice the noise has stopped. On investigation, I find it has eaten through the bin bag and been gnawing its way through the drinks cans. Aluminium has been turned into metallic confetti. Presumably it's been having a party with all that sugar and beer. Thinking about it, I realise that the building must get very hot during the day, and even the sugar has probably fermented into something potent. The rat has been getting sloshed on the dregs. Rat-arsed. The booze explains, I suppose, the way it was dazed on the fence. The next morning there had been no sign of it; it was probably nursing a hangover.

Living surrounded by fields in a rural environment, you get used to strange, unexplained, screeching noises in the night, and creatures coming in and out of the house. I've had goats in the garden and birds in the bedroom, ants on my arm and bees crawling across my computer screen. But something will have to be done about this. For a start, unfortunately it means an end to the recycling plan. Meanwhile, the rat is emboldened and is soon breaking into the house whenever it feels like it, eating its way through the metal screens on the windows, even eating through the wooden window frame. It has become a bionic rat.

I mention something to Pavlos, as we have to explain why there are now large holes in the window screens.

'*Poddygoss prepei na'neh,*' he says. Must be a mouse. A large mouse with a long tail.

Early one morning, I hear it moving around in the kitchen. As I go downstairs, it hops through the rat-sized gap in the window screen and on to the windowsill. I grab a broomstick and manage to corner it in a little space behind the wooden shutter. Got you, I think. I prepare to give it a knock with the end of the broomstick that it won't forget in a hurry. But I hesitate, wondering how much force to use. It takes one look at the broomstick, jumps aboard and comes running down the handle towards me, at the last minute making a comedy dive, limbs akimbo, and dashing off to safety.

Chapter 21

The Cheese Thief and the Rabbit

At Eristos, suddenly the Greek campers are packing up to take the ferry home. But there's a steady stream of visitors from northern Europe again, those who dislike the midsummer heat and prefer the quiet. They linger over sandwiches and beers and bottles of retsina, looking out at the sea. All summer, we've been meeting interesting people. I can see why Stelios has made some of his best friends on this beach over the summers.

He will keep the *kantina* open for the first half of September, without placing any more big orders. Meanwhile, I'm writing an article on romantic, historic boutique hotels, and am enjoying a little indulgence at a place in Rhodes Old Town that housed the Sultan's harem in the nineteenth century, when the island was still ruled by Ottoman Turks. The current proprietors of Nikos Takis Hotel have decorated it in an extravagantly eastern style, all cushioned divans and sequinned wall hangings, and tasselled four-posters trailing with gauze, pinks and greens and yellows. From one window of my suite I can look out at the Palace of the Grand Masters from the days of the Crusade, a mosque and various ruins. From the bathroom, with its blue tiles and flower patterns, I can see ships come and go in the harbour. It's a shame I can't drink the complimentary champagne – but my second cousin and great aunt can, sitting out on the terrace with its view over rooftops.

I wish I could just enjoy all this – my family and this luxury – but although I'm seeing the doctor for a scan tomorrow, I'm not feeling as pregnant as I did before. The symptoms don't seem to be there. It could be that my body's better prepared this time, but when I called the doctor about my concerns he said to come in right away.

And the next day, I find out that it is true: I'm no longer pregnant. The foetus is not developed enough for them to determine what might have been the problem. They will do a long list of other tests over the coming months: the doctor apologises but they don't do them until you miscarry twice. I realise I'd been kidding myself about not getting my hopes up. It feels very, very bleak, and once again I collapse with grief. Stelios asks if he should close the *kantina* and come over to be with me but I tell him I'm fine with family here.

It's better, really. My second cousin Catherine, who's the same age as me, has had health scares; my great aunt Cath tried to conceive for years before having Catherine in her early forties. Talking about these things helps me feel less of a freak, less of a failure – not the only one who got it wrong, surrounded by happy pregnant women and their friends and children... They are staying at a resort hotel in Kallithea, and over glasses of wine on their balcony that evening, we talk and laugh – which is very good medicine. I'll have to have surgery, then once again let my body recover. For the rest of the week I move into a pension in another part of the Old Town, the Stathis Hotel, which is just off Saint Fanourios Street and I visit the church somewhat tearfully. There's a friendly bar nearby where they let me plug my computer into the wall, so I can distract myself with work, and in a dark corner, nobody can notice that I'm crying over a heaped bowl of comforting pasta.

I've stayed at the old-fashioned and simple Stathis Hotel several times over the years and know Yorgos, the man who runs it. He has to go to the hospital the same morning I do for a problem with his leg, so he'll take me in the car. I explain I need the private hospital – my doctor only works at the private one – but he takes me anyway as he has plenty of time, which is very nice of him. I ask him what it's like at the public hospital and he grins. 'It's a good hospital. There just aren't any doctors.'

This time, I know the procedure: fasting from nine o'clock the night before. Hungry, cold, dehydrated, I make my way across the polished lobby and through the empty corridors of the clinic, numb as I undress and lie in that cold, bare room, waiting; I feel so pathetic in the surgery room, waiting again while people come and go, chatting. I feel sheer release when the anaesthetist puts me out of my misery; I'm starting to love anaesthetics.

My cousin and great aunt meet me afterwards at the hospital, and we laugh at the 'Greek Night' at their hotel that evening. I enjoy the week with them, joking about how kind Yorgos talks to me through the window of my bedroom when I'm getting dressed and has pinched half the cheddar cheese Catherine brought for me.

Anna emails, asking if I'm at home having a nervous breakdown, and whether after a week of being brave I might be able to handle the distraction of the last festival of the year in Tilos. I'm still away, I explain, though I would have loved to go to it with her. The last *paniyiri* means summer is drawing to a close, but it also means we can go on walks again, so we make plans to walk to Gera when I'm back.

Another thing puts a big grin on my face unexpectedly one day: the Saturday outdoor market, or *laiki*, at the end of town by the cemetery between some ancient Hellenistic walls and Zephyros beach. September is a wonderful time of year for produce: fruit and vegetables, bowls of eggs and jars of home-pickled capers, vine leaves and fruit preserves.

'*Rodakina, glyka san emena!*' – peaches, sweet like me – shouts a man. Peaches are in season and piled high, filling the air with a heady aroma, and only €1 a kilo. There are colourful peppers, some long and twisted like witches' fingers, tied with string, for 50 cents a bunch; and gigantic squash pumpkins. I stop to admire fat green olives and thick green olive oil in plastic water bottles. I'm invited to taste the olives and they're delicious, meaty and tangy. *Fetines*, explains the man – this year's.

Men and women, young and old, wander the rows of stalls and stop to chat to one another. A young woman rides her moped up to say hello to a friend and is handed a bag of nectarines. There's a beautiful display of woven strings of garlic, their dry skins not bright white like the imported stuff but pinkish-grey and earthy. Fresh fish stalls glisten with sardines.

One stall has only grapes, pale green and ebony black, strung in bunches all around. A fellow passer-by comments, 'Now *that's* a shop!' I ask if it's OK to take a photo, and get a free bunch of grapes.

In a market in Provence the previous year, I was chastised by a cheese seller for photographing his stall, so I'm careful now to ask permission. But here no one minds at all. The garlic seller even tidies his stand especially for the photo and asks to see the picture so he can show it off to his friend. Greece, I love you.

The melons, with their orange-coloured flesh, smell delicious and I apologise to the stallholder that I can't carry one back with me – my bags are already heavy. He cuts me a slice anyway, and the juice drips down my fingers. It's sweet but not too sweet, and I notice from the sign that it was grown in the fertile area near Kameiros. I am powerless to resist, and ask the melon-seller to choose me the smallest he can find; somewhat missing the point of my original protests, he throws in a second melon for free.

The previous autumn, Stelios rummaged around in my dictionary one evening to explain to me that he was a 'failed rabbit killer'. Killing rabbits is illegal in Tilos because all the wildlife is protected, but he had almost hit one accidentally while driving home. If he had hit it by mistake, he could have made stifado with it – one of his favourite foods, a stew made with onions, tomato, spices and red wine. Remembering what skinned rabbits looked like in butchers' shops in France, I shuddered at the thought.

This autumn, the rabbits seem to have a death wish. Like the partridges that fly out of hiding when you walk down a path, the rabbits seem to wait at the side of the dirt track until the car is near, then dash out in front. Stelios accidentally hits one, and asks me if it's OK to skin it. I make him do it outside and take it to his parents rather than put it in our fridge. A couple of nights later, I can't avoid hitting one, too. It seems a shame for it to die in vain, so I tell Stelios and he goes to collect it.

At last, the drinks fridge is pretty much empty, and it's time to close the *kantina* for the season. There remain a few delightfully oddball naked characters staring at the sea on Eristos beach, but not enough business to make it worth staying open and we both need a holiday. I'd like to see more of Rhodes, and he wants to taste *souma* to order for the *kantina* for next year. So we take the ferry, borrow his cousin's car and drive to Embona.

We pass Kameiros as we make our way down the coast, then turn inland, winding up into hills covered with pine trees and vineyards as the views become more spectacular. Remote Embona is high under the peak of Attaviros, the highest mountain in the Dodecanese islands. The village's sunny climate is perfect for traditional winemaking as well as olives, fruit and honey. The light is clear at 800 metres and in late September there are few tourists. We find rooms, have a lunch of grilled pork, salad and tzatziki with local wine, and lounge in the late-afternoon sunshine by the swimming pool, looking up at green trees tapering out into a bare mountain ridge, and the sun setting over the fields that slope towards the distant sea.

Everyone in Embona drives a pickup truck for hauling around grapes at this time of year. As we're wandering the quiet streets the next day, considering which winery to visit, a truck stops beside us. The driver is from Tilos, and married into one of Embona's wine-producing families, Merkouris. He and Stelios know one another. He tells us to continue up the road to the winery and find him.

Behind the shop, we find a few outbuildings and inside one dark room is the *souma* still. A hale and hearty old man, with an extravagant grey moustache that reaches his sideburns, invites us in, and shows us how the intense heat from the furnace creates the fiery liquor that trickles from a pipe below into a bucket. The clear liquid coming out now is the strongest, at 70 per cent proof. We take a tentative sip – it's not really for drinking at that strength, but is usually mixed with water or with weaker *souma* to create something around 40 per cent. At full strength, old ladies rub it on their aches and pains in the winter. But Stelios insists on buying a bottle.

While he talks and tastes, I head back into the bright sunshine and find the man who invited us standing in the shade of a pergola thickly covered in overhanging vines, taking crates of black grapes and emptying them into a stainless steel press, where juice spurts out. His face is tanned and his white T-shirt stained with purple. He shows me the wooden wine barrels inside, and the wide plastic barrels out in the sun, surrounded by olive trees, where the *souma* ferments. I want to drink the wine from here. Before leaving, we buy a few 10-litre containers, which the lady in the shop fills from huge barrels.

I'm keen to walk on the mountain; the old man told Stelios about an ancient sanctuary so we park the car and walk up through the forest, but after an hour or so he's not sure we're on the right path, so we turn back and drive on. At the village of Ayios Isidoros, we slow down as we see a little stone-and-wood taverna called To Aletro on the bend as we enter the village, and a man leaps out and beckons us inside.

'Bah! They don't know how to make wine in Embona,' he says, as we tell him about our day. Intrigued by his challenging statement, we sit down for a light lunch and are brought excellent glasses of light, dry white and rich, deep red. We eat stuffed peppers and tomatoes and vine leaves, lavishly flavoured with oil and fresh herbs, chickpeas cooked with onions, soft roasted potatoes – all for an excellent price, with a view over fields. I want to come back and stay longer in this peaceful place with its clear mountain air and superb produce.

But in the meantime, we have a wedding to attend.

Chapter 22

An Island Wedding

Yorgos, the youngest of two tall, handsome sons from the taverna at Eristos, is marrying Yorgia, the youngest of three beautiful, dark-haired daughters from the taverna at Ayios Andonis. Forty goats are killed for the feast. The whole island is invited. It's the stuff of myths and fairy tales: there are rumours of 5,000 vine leaves being stuffed.

Yorgos the groom, the *gambros*, is Stelios' good friend – this is the Yorgos who invited us to celebrate Kathari Deftera and his and Yorgia's name day, and who helped him with the *kantina*. So on the first evening, we join the crowd gathered outside his family's house on the road through Megalo Horio. Guests have arrived from far afield. While musicians play and an older lady sings, we walk with the groom under the bougainvillaea-covered pergola and down to the house of the bride, the *nifi*, at the bottom of the village. Everyone's olive skin has the colour of summer, set off against pastel dresses and grey suits. According to custom, the groom must fight his way to his bride past her sisters, who try to grab him for themselves. Guests leave money on their wedding bed: the ceremony is called *krevatia*. There are drinks and dancing until late; old Hippocrates is leading the dance while young kids play mischievous games in the dark.

The bride is quite heavily pregnant. Often a modern Greek couple don't marry until they're having a child, but it also occurs to me that both families have been working flat out at their seaside tavernas for the past six months, and couldn't have taken the time for a wedding before now. Perhaps I'm more attuned to this now that I've seen how normal life is suspended when you have a summer business.

The next afternoon, we drive on Stelios' motorbike to the windmill at Ayios Andonis where we meet friends to wait just as the late afternoon light is turning the bare tops of the mountains golden. Eventually we see a tiny red car, covered in a huge ribbon of white netting and trailing a tin can on an old fishing rope, and a train of vehicles. We tag on to the back and we all make our way up the cliff-edge road to the monastery of Ayios Panteleimon. The little red car slowly leads the way, with the mountainside to the left and blue-and-silver sea far below to the right. We stop and park near the gates, where the groom gets into the back of an open buggy dolled up in more white gauze and flowers, powered by a couple of bicycles. His best men sit all dressed up in grey suits and cycle up the last section of hill, given a final push by friends through the stone archway of the monastery.

White ribbons and flowers hang from the leafy branches of tall trees. People crowd into every available space in the courtyard and the terrace above as we wait for the bride.

When Yorgia arrives, the priest stands before the couple at a table covered in white cloth to lead the ceremony. Two simple white crowns, *stephana*, joined by a ribbon symbolising the linking of their souls, are held over their heads, then exchanged to seal their marriage. They both sip from a common cup containing a little red wine, and eat honey and nuts from the same spoon. Bride and groom circle the table and everyone slaps the groom on his back.

When we go to congratulate the newlyweds and their family, I ask Stelios what you're supposed to say. He jokes it's *'Keh tou chronou'* – and the same next year. Cheeky. *'Na ziseteh'* it is – may you live. And people say to unmarried people, *'Seira sou'* – your turn next.

Then the party moves back down the hill – thankfully while it's still light – for the celebration at the little monastery of Kamariani. Guests pin money on the front of the couple's clothes – in the old days, it would have been coins attached to the bride's dress, but now it's large-denomination notes. The rest of the night is all about eating and drinking and, of course, dancing. Everyone comes together, holding hands, the talented at the front of the line showing off the fanciest footwork.

The celebrations continue the next day by the harbour at Ayios Andonis, for the tradition of the 'false groom' trying to steal the bride away. There is more music and dancing, and once again it strikes me how important a part of community life the traditional Greek dancing is. Knowing the dances means you can join in.

There is hot sunshine one morning when I walk down to Livadia – a social occasion with everyone waving or stopping to say hello or offer a lift. When I arrive, the bay is mirror-like, cats sit in the middle of the road, birds are chirping, there are oranges on the trees and someone singing outside the *kafeneion*. A woman is cleaning fish under the little bridge on the seafront with an audience of cats, while a man cycles over it with his son on the crossbar.

Days are still hot but when I walk to a beach, I won't find anyone there. And there is time for walking again, and for slowing down to talk to people. One day, I stop to see if Michalis, the farmer, has any vegetables. He doesn't, but he's happy to go and pick me some tomatoes and peppers. I wait, sitting in the sun and watching a little cat playing, happy there's nothing to rush away for. The peppers smell zingy, and I make a salad with olive oil from Hippocrates, thyme that we gathered and dried ourselves, and olives and capers from Rhodes, and we eat it with fried sardines caught that morning.

Finally I have time to walk to Gera with Anna, just days before she must return to England for work. I didn't see her much this summer – I was hardly ever in Livadia, busy with the *kantina*; she spent her days quietly, sometimes out on a friend's fishing boat, although she did come to Eristos to confirm that the reputation of Stelios' legendary hamburgers was deserved. For the festival of Ayios Panteleimon, she stayed down in Livadia for a smaller *paniyiri* and danced until the early hours; she came to Megalo Horio for the *Koupa* and since it was so crowded, we danced on the roof of the *dimos* offices.

Stelios decides to come with us to Gera, and we take the path from Livadia that winds up around the headland from the tiny harbour by Faros taverna, and skirts the edge of a mountain. Gera is another abandoned settlement, one that was used by the people of Mikro Horio in the summers. I think about all the abandoned places in the Aegean Sea – the sheer number of the islands leading to many being only partially inhabited – and how that sense of dereliction appeals to some of us, some of us who choose this over a mainland life.

Stelios says his grandmother had a house at Gera – she was from Mikro Horio, while his grandfather was from Megalo Horio, rival villages. He picks some 'wild pears' for us to taste, so sour they stick your mouth together. The houses, deserted half a century ago, still have strong stone walls with kitchen shelves and chimneys, wooden roof beams overlaid with tree branches and twigs: people built well with the simplest materials in those days. Golden sunlight spills over the trees and grain-threshing circles and the terraces where previous generations grew their summer crops. The sea below is a deep, almost navy blue today, and clouds dash across the sky.

We have a taste of winter: cracks of thunder and a deluge of rain for half an hour. The next day there's a soft, grey light, and the temperature is a little cooler. There are birds of prey above again, and the grey smoke of bonfires. Stelios calls to ask if I'll bring him some of the rich red octopus *pilafi* or risotto he made last night for his lunch.

They're fishing at Eristos beach, where the road is flooded and all is grey except the bright paintwork of the boat and the fishermen's orange overalls.

The new season brings the pale-green-skinned guava, the first lettuces and still-green lemons. We have mounds of *horta*, leafy wild greens, boiled and served with grated garlic, half a lemon and a generous amount of green olive oil.

The seasons are distinct here, the cycle of life more pronounced. It's a circular dance with set moves. And each year, you learn them better. This year, I hope I'll know what to expect of winter, know its twists and turns and how it goes.

Of course, there will always be surprises. After a few days of rain, I see to my horror that my beloved tent, left out in the garden though I've been sleeping indoors for a while now, has been torn to shreds. What could have happened? I consider the evidence at the scene of the crime. Snails always come out when it rains, and they seem to have been crawling up the walls of the tent. Cats must have gone after the snails, and slashed the thin material with their claws. This is my guess – otherwise maybe it was simply the wind, as the tent material is very fragile after a summer of being burnt by the sun. I salvage what I can, a groundsheet and string and pegs, for reuse at some point and the rest goes in the bin.

After the rain, people start ploughing their fields and planting. Stelios has been hesitant to do much with the land his father has given him until all the legalities have gone through, as it's all confusingly tied up with the complicated paperwork for his father's pension, which at least one accountant and lawyer are trying to untangle. But having decided it's now safe to plant more at the *horafi*, he's bought fruit trees: two lemon, four orange (two sweet, two bitter), half a dozen olive, a dozen vines, a walnut tree and, at my request, a fig tree. I volunteered to dig the holes – and then had to dig circles around each to hold in water, and water them, of course. Well, I did ask to help.

This winter, someone else will help the children with their English, so I have more time in my week for walking. Although the days are getting shorter, it's an in-between temperature that's perfect – maybe a few clouds scudding across the blue sky, but no need to carry much water or look for shade. One greyish lunchtime, on a whim, I take the road to Ayios Andonis where the sea is muted and calm and beautiful. Men are fishing on the beach, and I scramble over rocks to a hidden area – since I don't have a swimsuit with me – and dive in from there. I return up the hillside path, where eagles circle in slow motion above. Reaching the village I see Nikos, Stelios' father, cheerfully on his way to the *kafeneion*. I get home at dusk, full of happiness. Another day, on the way to Eristos, I veer up the dirt track over the empty headland and follow the path marked by piles of rocks down to the pebbly, secluded bay of Ayios Petros, and take a fast dip in the sea, which is silver where it meets grey cliffs. Goats graze in fields that are brilliant green with new grass.

On an afternoon when it's blowing seven or eight Beaufort and I'm not sure how much energy I have after a late night the night before, it's good weather for making *gigantes*. I used to love eating the tinned butter beans in tomato sauce, but one of the benefits of working at home is that you can cook things for hours – warming the house at the same time as infusing it with aromas of garlic and herbs.

Afterwards, I go out in jeans and a jumper and sweatshirt and head up the road. Maria and Pavlos pass me in the car and stop to ask what I'm doing out in such weather. Gradually this year, green signs have been appearing all over the island, pointing out footpaths – there's even one at the end of our road, pointing the way to Skafi, which makes for a better class of landmark than the broken-down cement mixer. I notice one near the helipad and it gives me the idea to walk up to the 'Italian house' – the hilltop observatory from the Italian occupation. In spite of the dark associations, it's known as one of the most spectacular peaks on the island but I've not yet made it to the top.

Stones mark the edges of the path, and cairns or red spots on the rocks show the way. I keep heading uphill and get into my stride as the views of hill and sea get better and better. The path gains height fast and the effort-to-view ratio is a persuasive argument to keep going. As always, the only blot on the landscape is the unused reservoir; in an unplanned twist, it's turning into a wetland for birds.

Halfway, an old information board in Greek and English left over from when a 'nature interpretation trail' was set up here points out wildlife – *phrygana* bushes such as Jerusalem sage and thorny burnet, and creatures that hide among them such as *perdika* (insular chukars, like partridge) and *krokodilakia*, 'small crocodiles', the local name for the large lizards. The ground is colourful with wild crocuses. Soon I can see the island's harbours to the north, west and south, and other islands beyond. Tilos is a complex, twisted shape with promontories stretching out here and there, creating fresh views when you walk a new path.

I still have an hour of daylight, I estimate, as I approach the top, tiring a little but hoping the eastern views to Turkey will be just over the next rise – and then I'm hit by a gale-force wind. I crouch low to the ground but there's no way it's safe to continue to the top. I'm close, but I'm not going to risk being blown over. Maybe next time. I head back down happily, almost fell-running on the best bits of the path, exhilarated to be watching the clouds turning pink and mauve as the sun sinks.

Chapter 23

Winter Sunshine

I dash down to the port with a giant suitcase. The ferry dock is busy and friends ask, 'Are you leaving?' I grin and lift up the suitcase with a finger – empty. I'm going to spend a couple of days of filling it up.

I'm now free to travel whenever I need to, and I have to go to Rhodes often for blood tests. I make the most of the opportunity to wander around shops buying things you can't get on the smaller island, go out and listen to music and the buzz of chatter, read a newspaper and people-watch; pick up a sandwich or salad with different ingredients whenever I want. Rhodes feels good in the winter. It makes me happy to see Greeks swimming and reading at the beach in November. The empty walls of the Old Town glow in the crisp winter sunshine. Now that it's cool and quiet, locals dress up and sit outside, talking together over coffees and cigarettes.

First, I need a massage and a yoga class to fix my aching muscles: my back and shoulders are paying the price of all that digging for our trees. The yoga instructor is an English woman I met who was camping at Eristos during the summer, and through her I connect to a Romanian massage therapist and a Swedish photographer, members of a small network of fabulous expat women in Rhodes, mostly married to Greeks.

I now have an opportunity to visit the modern art museum, located near the casino, not far from Elli beach and the old Turkish cemetery. Among the collection the pieces I warm to most are paintings by Theofilos, playful portraits of soldiers with curly moustaches; and a painting of supper on the first day of Lent in 1950 by Spyros Vassiliou, a simple table laid out with plates of food on a balcony, with a view across the city of Athens to the mountain. As I leave I get talking to the man on the ticket desk, and he reads me some of his poetry.

Later, I go out to a cafe-bar housed in an Italian villa with ancient mosaic floors displayed under designer-cracked glass. I sit at the bar, once again enjoying the different way of life and anonymity here, and chat with the barman, who's from Athens but came to live in Rhodes for the lifestyle. The owner of the bar tells him to offer me a drink on the house.

It feels easy to get to know people in Rhodes town, and when people ask me where I'm from, saying I'm English but live in Tilos generally leads to some interesting conversations. I glance in the window of a shop next to the hotel, and the owner ends up telling me his father was from Kalymnos and was sent to teach in Tilos at the school in Mikro Horio during the Italian occupation; he says the Italians sent clever people to the little islands where they couldn't cause as much trouble. Another man I meet in a health food shop tells me his cousin has a house in Tilos but, even after living there for two years, has never been invited to anyone's house. It reminds me a little of last year's birthday party. I think perhaps people have to preserve their privacy more on a small island. It's certainly not a lack of warmth or friendliness.

On my break in Rhodes, I find even chores can be charming. I need ink for my printer and like to buy from Cartridge World because they're cheaper and recycle the cartridges. But when I call to check what time the shop closes, I find it's moved out of town – too far to walk. I ask the man on the phone if there are buses.

'Where are you?' he asks.

'Mandraki.'

'No, where *exactly*?'

'Er, the Hermes Hotel.'

'OK, I'll be there in ten minutes.' He comes to collect the cartridges, and brings me what I need later in the day. Now that's service. 'Lazy Greeks', eh?

I've been shopping for two days, filling up my suitcase with purchases: a reading lamp, a casserole dish, a tasty Cretan cheese covered in black peppercorns. On my last day, I discover another, slightly smaller street market just outside the Old Town, near the Gate of St John. I admire all the colourful fresh produce, buy some plants for a few euros each, and perhaps because of the big smile on my face I receive a marriage proposal and a cheeky elopement proposal – which make my smile bigger.

But when I get back to the hotel, I realise I've hit the retail wall. There is no shopping left in me. I have lost the will to shop. I've enjoyed my time here so much. But home is calling.

However much fun I've had, I am happy to be back on the island where olives are being harvested and startled goats make me laugh out loud. I go to my Greek dance class and drive back through hills bathed in silver moonlight that picks out every detail, making them seem unreal. I never knew before coming to Tilos how moonlight transformed the landscape.

I drive through the gate of the honey factory and Pavlos looks at me oddly as he notices me getting out of the passenger door – the driver door doesn't open any more. But I reckon the car has done well this last year, considering it's subjected on a daily basis to the equivalent of rally driving, bumping over rocks and ruts through dust clouds. Pavlos is tending his passion fruit trees, and we get on to the subject of pomegranates.

'The mice ate all the pomegranates this year,' he says. 'They run up the trees. I pulled down a branch to pick some fruit and a mouse ran out!'

I wonder if it was a marauding relative of our drunken rodent. I change the subject, asking where the beehives have disappeared to.

'*Rhodos*,' he says. 'On holiday! This time of year, there's not much for them to eat here in Tilos so they go to Rhodes.'

Sounds like an extended gourmet break. Do bees have any predators, I wonder, apart from the colourful bee-eater birds?

'The *krokodilakia* get them,' he says – the big lizards. 'They sit outside the hive with their mouth open and close their eyes – they have a thick skin and the bees can't sting them, it's only their eyes that are sensitive – and they eat the bees as they come out of the hive.'

I love the image of the little crocodile sitting outside the hive with its tongue out and eyes closed. Sometimes I'm so pleased that I understand all this in Greek that I later wonder if Pavlos was winding me up. It's hard to tell sometimes.

It's still dark and I'm in bed when I hear Stelios on the phone to Nikos as they arrange where they're meeting for fishing.

'No, I can't take the car, Jennifer needs it…'

I'm puzzled and mumble, 'I don't need the car…'

A few minutes later he's upstairs. '*Moraki mou*, babe, could you do me a little favour…?' And I learn why I need the car.

So I'm driving to the post office in Livadia just after eight, and am so glad I had to do him a favour as the centre of the island is breathtakingly beautiful. The early *igrasia*, the moisture in the air, has turned the grass all silvery white in the sunshine, and the trees are darker than usual so their reddish-brown autumn leaves glisten.

When I arrive, young children are gathered in the square for some event and a few shout '*Yeia sas, Kyria Jennifer!*' Savvas from the post office is watching them, but breaks off to help me do Stelios' money transfer. Then I take advantage of being in Livadia to go for a swim off the rocks. The water is glassy calm, clear enough to see fish down below without a mask, and I swim as far as a rock stack, where I get close to a cormorant. The only sound is a fishing boat chugging across the bay. Some men are fishing off the quay in the hazy morning light. My heart fills up with emotion for this place.

In late November, it's Stelios' name day; Saint Stylianos, from which Stelios derives, was a helper of children, and patron saint of children yet to be born. Last year I had no idea it was his name day until he told me, so I put it in my diary this year.

'Don't you have a name day?' asks Stelios.

'No, we don't do that. I don't think there is a Saint Jennifer anyway.'

Once again, living on a tiny island neatly eliminates the commercialisation of celebrations since there's nothing much to buy. I bought him a book last week on the ferry, so I make him chocolate brownies – they were supposed to be chocolate lava cakes but the measurements are tricky when you don't have scales.

For my birthday a few days later, he buys fresh fish called *balades* from another fisherman. Their eyes are huge, for seeing at over 200 metres deep – but they're tasty.

'Oh, I forgot, I got this for you when I went to the shop, *moraki mou*!' A Kit-Kat emerges from the pocket of the holey fisherman's pants. It looks like it's been there a while. But it's always the thought that counts. We have fish, wine, salad, chocolate and laughter... a perfectly relaxing evening.

I'm looking forward to our coming month-long trip, to England for Christmas and then to France for the first half of January, to break up the winter and miss some of the days that felt tough last year on Tilos. We need to spend more time together, after this busy summer.

I'll see my colleagues, too, to try to iron out some issues in our working relationship. My experiment in working from home in Tilos seems to me a success and I still love the work; I've brought some successful projects to the company and have been lucky that there's never been a power cut when I have a Skype meeting. But I realise that I did have more influence when I was in office meetings; it is easier to discuss a project and convince your colleagues in person. It's only natural to get a little frustrated if you believe in your own abilities. They want me at my desk at particular hours in case they need to reach me urgently, but they never seem to need to. I wonder if it would be better for everyone if I moved on. But I worry about losing an interesting job, one that gives me a steady income.

One thing I know, however, is that right now, it's all worth the risk. I'd rather deal with difficulties, and live on a remote, empty island without many cars or houses, in a house with a view of mountains and sea. A day spent walking never feels wasted. Having a beach to myself is something most people can't buy with all they earn in their work. I know life here wouldn't suit everyone. But if it was easy to live here, everyone would do it and it would be just like everywhere else. I'm glad it's not.

There's no doubt that I'm more and more at home here. One day, old Hippocrates from Eristos, who seemed gruff at first, stops his ancient moped to offer me a lift to the village. It feels like a breakthrough, though I decline, not sure the moped would survive. In Livadia to buy my ferry ticket, I chat with our friendly policeman Christoforos, who is fishing, and Stelios Stefanakis in the ticket office beckons me behind the counter to see a video on the computer.

Thinking about our upcoming trip to England, Stelios and I laugh as we have 'fish and chips' for dinner. Much as I love English fish and chips, I am very happy for my fish and chips here to be fresh fish caught that morning, potatoes newly dug from the garden, both fried in local olive oil with local lemon squeezed on top, and oregano from the fields around the house. Next summer he's going to gather salt – so even the salt will be local. I make mulled wine with honey and orange, cinnamon and cloves. Stelios likes it as much as I do.

'Maybe we should wait until after the holidays to try again,' he says, 'so you can drink.'

I want to try again for a baby as much as he does, but I also feel a need for adventure this coming year. I plan to buy a new tent.

On the last day before we leave in mid-December, the bay at Eristos is bright silver in warm sunshine and, as I have my last swim of the year on an empty beach, I think how hard it is to leave. When Stelios gets home from fishing that evening, music is on, a glass of wine poured. A romantic evening? When I head upstairs, he's fast asleep. Oh, and of course he's going out fishing tomorrow morning before we catch the 11 a.m. ferry. Why wouldn't he?

Chapter 24

Nectar for Christmas

The car – which looks delightfully dilapidated, with a missing wing mirror, dirty seats and only partially functioning locks, but has never failed to start – is often full of wood, oddments left over from the *kantina* or mysterious tools. I make Stelios take most of his tools out so we have some space for our bags.

'But where will I put the tools?'

I suggest the house, since we won't be there for a few weeks, but he's nervous – his tools are his pride and joy and I'm surprised he isn't taking them to England.

Of course we can't drive straight to the port, because we have to pick up more bags from a friend in the village to put on the boat as a favour, plus his parents want a lift down to Livadia. As I stop for them, Pantelis comes over to the window to ask where we're going.

'If I'd have known, I'd have given you a gift to take with you,' he says, sending his greetings to Mum and her friend Hermi, saying they must come again next year.

I drive across the island, the car packed to the gills. Everyone's talking at once – Nikos explaining about a TV quiz game he won money on, Vicky telling me a joke

Stelios no longer talks about moving to England to make money, as he did when we first met. Having been to England, he finds the weather grey and the society restrictive – for example, he can't smoke anywhere he wants. He's happy now being a businessman in Tilos.

A summer of speaking English with customers has given him confidence and he generally charms all my friends and family – I do love this man. And it is quite funny that he brought a plastic water bottle of *souma* to contribute to our family Christmas lunch in London. But when everyone politely declines, preferring to drink good champagne as they banter merrily, he continues to thrust the slightly grubby looking bottle at people, saying they must try it because it's nectar. You're not at the *kantina* now, I think. It's probably quite funny but I feel caught between him and my family. I wish he could appreciate my culture, too; enjoy my family's way of doing things, as they enjoy his when in Tilos; do something to make his girlfriend happy. I love his world, the life we have in Greece, but it's not the whole of my life; I also have a life outside it, and he doesn't seem as able to share that.

Every relationship has its ups and downs. In our daily routine, we're a good team but when we spend time alone together as a couple – going out at night or on holiday – we don't get along so well. I don't know why – perhaps we've grown apart with spending too much time doing our own thing, or maybe it's just the pressure I have put on our relationship because of the urgency to get pregnant, making the stakes so much higher. Certainly the miscarriages have cast a shadow over how things were. Boxing Day morning sees us sitting at my dad's kitchen table, each of us angry and unhappy, talking about splitting up. Eventually we decide to try again and go to France together as planned.

We fly to Marseille, a city I've always liked, and Stelios likes it, too. It was founded by the Greeks 2,600 years ago. Coming from England, it seems as though we've arrived back in a Greek city, a Mediterranean place where people with black hair wear leather jackets and take their coffee drinking seriously. They even smoke illegally in the bars like Greeks; we see empty juice bottles set out on tables as surreptitious ashtrays. We have fun gorging on delicious North African food: lamb tagine with couscous, chicken and almond filo pies, Tunisian sweets made from thin pastry and almonds, everything cheap and fresh.

When we take the train north into the Luberon, though, with a few exceptions, there's nothing he can't get better in Tilos. The Provencal wine generally disappoints him. He enjoys the fillet of trout, duck breast and a risotto made with foie gras and truffle shavings. But the French yoghurt to him is completely tasteless; finicky fat-free faiselles and fromage blancs, nothing thick except the ones labelled Greek yoghurt. He complains about the oranges, which are actually from Spain, tasteless to him compared with Tilos oranges straight from the trees – though I'm sure French oranges are good straight from the tree, in the right season. One day I take him to a shop with regional products, thinking perhaps he'd enjoy tasting the different olive oils of this region of Provence, but he's unimpressed and tells me why Greek olive oil is the best in the world.

We have sunshine almost every day, often seeing the white top of Mont Ventoux against a deep-blue sky; while back in Tilos, according to daily phone calls from Megalo Horio, it rains. Every morning we wake to the 'wack-wack' sound of hundreds of ducks gathered on the frosty grass around the pond we can see between the pine trees. At Fontaine de Vaucluse, where a crystal-clear river rises from a spring of unknown depth below tall cliffs, we walk up the hill to the remains of a medieval castle and then eat lunch at a *kantina*, Snack the Big Fred, and Fred has his photo taken with the Tilos *kantina* man.

The original plan was to spend a couple of weeks in France. We are very lucky to have free use of an apartment in the complex where my mum has her place, surrounded by open countryside. I will work during the days and Stelios can amuse himself. But as he sits playing online *biriba* on his computer, he complains when I won't let him smoke indoors because it's against the rules; I complain when he leaves bits of tobacco from his roll-ups and grubby handprints all over the table, or spills red wine on the couch. It makes me so angry that we almost split up again. My head is also spinning with trying to translate French into Greek and vice versa, resulting in a melange of the two that leaves me hitting my forehead in despair. It's a slight relief when he decides to change his flight and return to Athens early to see friends and eat a big plate of Greek-style lamb chops. I'm looking forward to some time alone.

On a bright, sunny day, after queuing ages for train tickets, we head back to Marseille and eat wonderful food again from the North African market – paella, fluffy pancakes stuffed with spicy vegetables, veal stew with peppers and olives and potatoes, all for a few euros each. The friendly vendors like it when Stelios banters with them about prices, saying he's from Greece and has no money. We walk to work off the food, then ask a man in a wine shop to uncork a bottle of Côtes du Rhône and take it back to the hotel, where Stelios wants me to read aloud to him – translating into Greek – a book I'm reading about a journey to Constantinople, and I'm amazed that finally he doesn't want to watch TV or play on the computer. We kiss and hug goodbye at the airport, and make silly duck noises.

It's Sunday morning on the big ship *Diagoras* and the church service is on the television in the corner of the dining room where I'm eating yoghurt and honey for breakfast.

It feels strange to have been away from Tilos for over a month – the longest I've been away since I came to live in Greece, coming up for two years ago. My break in France was lovely, peaceful writing days on my own and a few days with my mum who flew out to see me, and I'm enjoying my journey home from Athens, with a good book to read for work. A little time away always makes me see things clearly again, appreciate the details. When we docked at Kalymnos at seven this morning, I went up on deck and the sky was a wintry dark blue with a shaft of sunlight breaking through heavy rain-clouds, church bells beginning to ring from the many churches around the port, fishing boats setting out to sea.

I drink tea, look out at the islands we wend our way through in light rain. Men from rural islands are eating eggs and bacon together on their way back home, a raucous phone blaring out from time to time, a relative ringing to find out where they are, if they're past Kos yet. The dining room staff – all men in blue jackets or stripy waistcoats – are joking around at the service counter. I've got to know them pretty well over the past couple of years. It must be a strange life going up and down the Aegean Sea twice a week, continually plying the route between the capital and the Dodecanese, living on the ship: the one who stands behind the food counter, telling people about what he's cooked that day, the cashier, the ones who collect your tray. I wonder who folds the napkins on top of the counter into swans. I read recently that the crew haven't been paid in months.

Stelios' mother and father have been having a holiday in Athens, and are also on the boat. When Stelios told me 'You'll be travelling together!' I experienced an attack of nerves, but I'm learning that when Greeks say that, they don't expect you to sit with them for the whole 18 hours; it's just handy to know someone else on the boat, in case you want somewhere to leave your bags or company for dinner. I see Nikos smoking a cigarette on deck; he's being naughty and not following the doctor's instructions, but at least it gets him out on deck in the fresh air...

The sun breaks through the clouds when we arrive at Tilos towards the end of the morning. Stelios is still busy with the fishing boat, so I say I'll wait for him and we can drive back together. I leave my bags at the car. The cliffs around the island had looked stark and barren from the ship, but within the bay the hillsides are green, the grassy verges bright and sprinkled with yellow flowers. Everything is peaceful.

As I walk around the seafront I make friends with a playful dog who follows me. He's got floppy ears, big dark eyes, a white streak down the front of his head to his cute nose, a sleek black body and ruffled white fur around his neck. He goes for a dip in the clear blue sea, torments all the cats along the way, grabs a long piece of grass and dares me to take it from his paws. I spend an hour or so running up and down with him. He's adorable. He reminds me of the friendly dog we stroked daily when walking from the apartment to the town in France. We've talked in the past about getting a dog but I said it was too much of a commitment, too difficult when I had to travel. This floppy-eared dog makes me think about it again. Who knows, in the future perhaps...?

The sky is blue as we arrive back at the house next to the honey factory, surrounded by the usual clutter of old beehives, bits of wood and the red scrap car. On the lush green slope across the Potamia valley, the white houses of Megalo Horio almost gleam, everything washed clean by the January rains. The sea sparkles between dark grey hills. I think I have become an island woman, a *nisiotissa*.

Chapter 25

Life Will Never Be the Same Again

It's time to fall in love all over again with the island. In the village, sheep wander around the rough car park. On the hillsides, euphorbia bushes are bright yellow and green, contrasting with the bare branches of oak trees. The meadows are thick with parsley-like grasses and Bermuda buttercups with their clover-like leaves, and anemones, nodding flowers in white and pink and mauve with black centres like poppies. The sea is pale blue and so clear that from up on the rocks you can easily see the pebbles on the sea floor.

Stelios comes home one night with pieces of *galeos*, dogfish or small shark – good with *skordalia* or garlic sauce, he says. You can make *skordalia* with breadcrumbs, but also with potatoes – and we have plenty of freshly dug potatoes from the garden. I quarter and boil them until soft, then mash them with a few garlic cloves that I've smashed in the pestle and mortar, and vinegar, pepper, and olive oil.

'Does it need anything?' I ask Stelios. Stupid question.

'More olive oil. But it's good. Though I prefer it with bread.'

I love mashed potatoes, so for me it's perfect. The fried *galeos* is a little fatty for my tastes, though I eat it, but I could eat garlic mashed potatoes forever.

We finally have to admit we have a problem with the car that needs fixing: it regularly stops. The mechanics who live on Tilos have looked at it and say it needs to go to Rhodes. I'm not ready to leave Tilos again so soon, but we must. In Rhodes, the mechanic changes the oils and filters and the battery, and we hand over what feels like a substantial amount of money. I don't even use the car very often any more except when helping Stelios with the *kantina*, and I'm still feeling uncertain about money since my work contract was reduced six months ago and other income is up and down. I'd feel more comfortable spending less for a while.

Afterwards, he wants to go shopping at a big supermarket out of town; although they stock some things you can't get in Tilos, I've eaten plenty of different foods lately and don't feel the need. Sometimes I prefer to reduce the choices to what we have at home in Tilos. As we pass through the entrance, a security man says I can't go in with my daypack as it's against the rules: you can only carry a handbag. Stelios sides with the jobsworth but I fight for my rights – it's no bigger than any of the handbags people are walking through with – and leave. Stelios does his shopping and I wait outside in the sunshine, smug that Carrefour aren't getting my euros.

We are barely speaking after the Carrefour Incident when we continue down the coast road towards the turn-off for Embona. Stelios wants to order *souma* and buy wine. The day doesn't feel any better when we have to swerve around a dead cat and dog, hit by a car and left in the road. I feel sick. And as we arrive in Embona, the battery light is flashing again, so apparently the mechanic hasn't fixed the car after all.

After an OK meal that seems expensive after paying so much for the car that's still not working, we are settling in to the hotel room when I realise there are no towels, so I go back to reception and pick some up along with the code for the internet. When I return at 8.30 p.m., Stelios has fallen asleep. The internet doesn't work anyway, so I lie in the dark.

The next day dawns bright and sunny, though, and the mountain air is beautiful. We stop at the bakery for cheese pies, and drive back towards Rhodes town with a tantalising view of snow on the mountaintops of Turkey. The car will have to go to the *ilectrologos* at Koskinou junction. We find the electrician working on another vehicle, and he says he'll look at ours as soon as he's finished. I leave him and Stelios talking in Greek about things mechanical, and saunter back out into the sunshine. There's not much to do at Koskinou junction but at the end of the row of businesses there's a pet shop, so I wander inside to kill some time.

It's years since I've been in a pet shop, but instantly there's that unmistakeable pet shop smell of sawdust and feed, the squawking of exotic birds in cages and the scurry and scratch of tiny hamster feet. Cages house parrots and budgies, lizards and snakes. And alone in a cage at eye level is the cutest puppy, a chubby ball of pale fur. The poor little thing seems terrified and all the torn-up newspaper in the cage is wet, but when I poke my finger through the wire to be friendly, the pup responds immediately by licking it.

The man behind the counter comes to open the cage door, lets the puppy out so I can hold her – she's a girl. What a beautiful, affectionate creature. I am certainly feeling drawn towards dogs at the moment, though I wouldn't buy one from a pet shop when there are so many strays that need homes. After playing with the pup for a while, I thank the man and he puts it back, and I go back to see how Stelios is getting on.

I've almost made a clean getaway when the man from the shop catches up with me.

'The dog you were looking at – I just wanted to let you know we're not selling her, we're just trying to find a home because her owner couldn't keep her.'

Could we give her a good home on Tilos? I take Stelios to meet her and he, too, falls for her. We say we'll think about it for a while, and we do; but we only have a few hours because we're leaving on the ferry early the next morning, before the pet shop opens, and in the afternoon we have an appointment. The man in the pet shop can give her inoculations. Could we keep her in the hotel overnight? We could wait, think about it some more; but something is telling me to take *this* dog home now.

Life at the honey factory may never be the same again.

We buy her a large collar that she'll grow into as there's nowhere to buy collars in Tilos. The big blue collar hangs off her like a hand-me-down from a much larger sibling.

She fits easily in my hands, on my lap, as we drive back to town. She's scared, but seems to rest happily.

When we reach the hotel, we have 10 minutes to go before meeting Malena, the photographer. Stelios looks after the pup outside while I dash to the room to shower and change. The photos I need are for a magazine article and I've been asked to wear a summery dress. Malena suggests we take them on the old stone fortification walls by the sea, and the dress feels a little inadequate in a freezing cold January wind, but there's a deep-blue sky and our gorgeous puppy puts a big smile on my face as I hold her in my hands.

From there, we drive to see a friend who can lend us a cat box for travelling; it turns out to be just the right size. I've resolved to stay overnight in the car with our pup if the hotel won't take her. We walk into reception with her in the box, and explain that she's shy and scared and probably won't even leave the box all night. They say that's fine.

As soon as we get into the room, it's as if she now knows she's safe and free and not going back to the pet shop, and she runs a merry dance, wanting to jump on the beds. I follow her around, cleaning up after her. In the end we have to lock her in the bathroom so we can get some sleep.

On the ferry next day, though, she happily submits to being in the box on the seat next to mine, and in spite of the waves she doesn't get sick. She's an island dog.

We decide to call her Lisa, which Stelios says is a good name for a dog. I wonder if it's because a young female dog is a *skilitsa*. Lisa the *skilitsa*.

How come puppies don't know where to go to the toilet, but instinctively know how to do all those puppyish things like playing with broomsticks and wrapping themselves adorably in jumpers? The only way to calm her down is by rubbing her tummy, which acts like hypnosis.

Everything, *everything*, gets bitten. The broom, the fringe of my scarf and my wellies are fair game, as are feet and anything reachable. When I take out the mop to wipe the floor after her, she thinks it's a fantastic toy to grab with her teeth and hang on to. The track pants we tend to wear around the house in winter soon have holes all over them from her sharp little teeth. I now understand how maternal instinct kicks in. I will happily sit in a wet jumper with cold bare feet as she snoozes in my lap, just to stop the little blighter doing any damage for a while.

For such a soft, furry creature, she has very sharp teeth and scratchy nails. I take a picture of Stelios beaming as he holds her to his chest, and it looks like she's kissing his neck, but in the next picture she's wriggling away and the one after that he's grimacing as he tries to extract his finger from her mouth.

House training happens quickly. Since I'm working at home, I can swivel my chair around every few minutes to see what she's up to, and when I see her peeing on the floor I leap over and carry her outside. She gets the hint within a week.

I have some big old cardboard boxes left over from moving here, so I make one cosy with woolly layers and it becomes her bed. She howls and howls at first when left alone in it, so loud I think she'll wake the village across the valley. Old jumpers that I don't wear very often get recycled into bedding. She's sleeping on cashmere.

She's most likely a golden retriever or Labrador crossed with something else; something that bites a lot – a shark? At eight weeks old she's quite plump with a tiny head. Her fur is the colour of thick, pale, creamed honey, offset beautifully by big dark-brown eyes that look outlined in kohl, and a healthy black nose, white fur around her whiskers and chin, and her ears are perfectly floppy. There are splashes of white at her feet. She is dwarfed by my tall wellington boots when she sits beside them at the door. She's so tiny that I realise I can't leave her outside in the garden alone in case an eagle swoops down and takes her. I also realise the old well is a disaster in the making and have to find some wooden boards and rocks to cover it with. I see the house differently with an inquisitive puppy around; it suddenly seems fraught with hazards for small creatures. When I hang up washing on the line, I can't leave anything hanging tantalisingly close to the ground or she'll pull it down.

She prances and dives around the kitchen as I make bread and put some dinner in the oven – pieces of pork roasting with potatoes in olive oil, fresh lemon, oregano and garlic, easy, tasty, and good for warming up the house on a February day. Having a puppy is a totally absorbing activity and there is little time for complicated cooking, even if I wanted to. Although I helped with our family dog when I was growing up and have looked after my mum's dog, I anticipated a mere fraction of the challenges involved in learning to care for and train a puppy.

The area of the Greek vocabulary that deals with dogs is soon mastered. I very quickly learn the words *gavgeezee* (she barks) and *gleefee* (she licks). People are forever asking *'Dagonee?'*, does she bite? Well, she bites everything except people. I decide that it's best for us to teach her commands in Greek, as not only is that our common language around the house, but then she'll understand when one of the locals speaks to her. So we gradually introduce *ochi* for 'no', *kahto* for 'down', *ela* for 'come' and *pereemeneh* for 'wait'.

She can't walk very far at the beginning, so I develop a new appreciation for the meadows around the house, Lisa bounding like an Andrex puppy through a green field full of daisies (though on the Andrex ads, they never showed the ticks you have to pull out afterwards).

She needs things to play with constantly. She gets hours of entertainment out of a plastic jar or an old spiral-bound notebook. We have a good supply of cardboard boxes from modems that burned out in winter storms, and these are perfect puppy playthings because of their many interesting compartments. Sweeping up torn scraps of cardboard is the price I pay, but at least she's amused for a while. A stuffed toy lemur I find at the back of the cupboard under the stairs becomes a favourite item to wrestle with. When I see rubbish washed up on beaches, I now see it as a toyshop. Old shoes? A fishing buoy or tangled fishing nets? The terrace begins to look like a junkyard. Other things I find useful are patience; the ability to move faster than a puppy; thick skin; and an ability to function on little sleep.

In return, however, the entertainment is non-stop. She's such a wriggly thing that when she stops for a moment and looks pensive – no doubt planning her next evil move – it's hugely comic. When I've told her off for biting the vacuum cleaner cable, I turn around 10 minutes later and she pretends with an innocent face that she's not really biting the vacuum cleaner wires at all but her toy, which just happens to be right next to the vacuum cleaner cable. When I find her with the pieces of something she wasn't supposed to destroy, and tell her *'ochi'*, she tilts her head at me quizzically as if to ask 'Why not?'

On a calm, sunny day, I carry Lisa halfway to Eristos and she stretches out flat in the soft, cool sand, making the doggy equivalent of snow angels. We have the beach to ourselves, and the only sound is the waves sweeping lethargically into shore. She burrows with her front paws and sticks her nose in the wet sand, digging further and sticking her nose in again, ears flopping down over her eyes, until the hole is big enough to fall into. She sniffs around the waves, letting the water wet her feet. Exhausted, she curls up on the sand in the warm sunshine, her little front paws curled under her chin, a smile on her face. I love introducing her to her new island home, her playground, and watching what she makes of it all. It's good for me, too, getting outside on these glorious days when the sky is blue, walking slowly enough to see the orchids at the side of the path.

Locals ask, *'Ti ratza eineh?'* – what breed is it? And *'Afto megalonee?'* – will it get bigger? Many say she has big feet and that shows she'll get very big. Having big feet myself,

I hope she doesn't get upset from people continually commenting on it. *'Eineh bez?'* they ask – is she beige? I get rather defensive about this, too. Buttermilk, pale caramel, straw – she isn't plain old beige. *Thilika*, I soon learn, means female, as opposed to *arsenika*, which means male (well, that one's easy to remember...).

As soon as her femininity is determined, the usual comment to follow is that she'll be making babies. I figure we'll cross the neutering bridge later – she's only two months old. Then again, when I take her to Livadia and introduce her to the floppy-eared dog that I now know belongs to the policeman, there is clearly some mutual admiration. He looks big enough to eat Lisa in two mouthfuls, but they paw one another delicately and whisper sweet nothings into one another's ears (and behinds). When I finally sweep Lisa up into my arms and take her into the safety of Petrino Cafe, the big dog makes sad eyes from the doorway.

Chapter 26

A Happy Household

The island is green, the almond trees covered in white blossoms. Shoots are appearing on our orange and pomegranate trees. As soon as she's big and strong enough, I walk Lisa to Skafi. We stop halfway down to sit on a rock where the sea appears deep blue in the distance, and drink some water – I now have to carry water for two, and a bowl for her. She rests her tiny, rounded, smiling face on my backpack and looks like a happy dog.

Under a cluster of tall pine trees on the track towards Skafi are the remains of a bar that existed about ten years ago. I've walked past it many times but Lisa suggests we explore. The benches and tables are all still there, the fridges and the entrance sign, all abandoned and left to the elements. There's a little patch of grass where I lie when the sun's warm. How beautiful it would be to live here, or run a cafe-bar until sunset. Stelios says once it was one of three bars in Megalo Horio; there were more young people in the village a decade ago.

Like most outsiders, I love the abandoned places, the ruined stone houses, the empty valleys. When Delos told me they were planning to concrete over the road to Skafi,

I was horrified. It's another seahorse conundrum: what works for the locals doesn't always appeal to outsiders. For Delos, a concrete road is progress. I hate to see electric signs where once there were hand-painted ones at restaurants in Livadia, but for them it's just business. In a book about Greece called *An Affair of the Heart* published in 1957, Dilys Powell wrote of idealistic travellers, who romanticised it as a 'simple, pastoral country', selfishly resenting Athenians for daring to put hotels, buses and other amenities at the foot of the Acropolis.

Concessions to the twenty-first century in this wild place make it possible for people to live and work here year-round, so that it's a living community, not a dying one. In my own way, I contribute what I can to the island through working from here. And you have to take the whole package or not at all, for richer, for poorer, for better, for worse. Thankfully development on Tilos is a slow work in progress, a dance that takes one step forward and two steps back. Even if they build the concrete road, the old broken-down cement mixer will probably remain at the end of it as a landmark.

The island has no taxi now – taxi drivers Nikos and Toula have retired because the costs made it financially unviable – but if you set off walking down the road, someone will often stop and offer you a lift. I love living in a place where there's an old sofa outside the petrol station where Nikos the owner sits when he's not busy, and the disused petrol station at Ayios Antonis is frequented by goats. Where sometimes you have to wait for someone to cut you fresh tomatoes; where if you turn up late at Omonia, the old-fashioned restaurant with its stencilled 'We have a card-phone' sign, Michalis tells you you'll have to wait a long time.

When the power goes off for an hour or two and there's no internet for working, I just go for a walk, and remind myself that I love living in a place that isn't like everywhere else.

On Valentine's Day, Stelios beckons me over. 'Can you help, *moro mou*?' He asks me to hold the body of an eel while he chops its head off. Sharing a house with a fisherman is full of interesting surprises, though thankfully this isn't a Valentine's Day gift – he's taking it for his parents. Having Lisa has brought us together again and we're back in our routine. He brings home some fresh tuna they've caught – about a foot long, a type of tuna called *palamitha,* which I think we'd call bonito. His plan is to boil the hell out of them for an hour, then whip the flesh up with mayonnaise from a jar, parsley and onion, to experiment with it as a new sandwich filling for the *kantina*. I manage to grab a few pieces of fish before he boils the lot, fry them lightly for a few minutes until just cooked through, then eat them with lemon.

This winter, with no aerobics class but unfortunately plenty of time at home to do things like bake bread and cakes, I started doing exercises to music at home, in the tiny space behind the door, between the kitchen and my desk (the ceiling's too low upstairs). The first time I try exercising with Lisa around, she barks like mad, then stands on my chest when I lie down and try to do sit-ups. I can't tell if my muscles are aching from the exercise or from laughing so much. As she gets bigger, she learns how to climb the stairs, if not to descend again, and she pokes her head through the wooden railings of the mezzanine to look down.

On a warm, sunny day, extraordinary for February, Stelios has a day off so we take her on a walk up the hill towards the Italian house, to see how far we'll get; it's hot for her and she's not yet capable of going far at all. We turn back quickly and have a late lunch together instead, sitting outside in the sunshine, sipping wine. It's the kind of thing we never do. The only sounds in our empty part of the valley are birds calling, goats in fields, and waves rolling into shore far down on Eristos beach. It feels like a much milder winter than last year's, and a happier one. Dusk brings a brilliant crescent moon in a pale-blue sky.

Daily walks with my dog are just what I wanted. One clear morning, the sky is deep blue and I take Lisa up the track towards the castle. Down in the valley the fields are bright green, contrasting with the barren grey rock of the mountaintops.

Walking back down into the village beside an ancient wall built of massive rectangular stones, I see something that makes me laugh out loud. A little car has been tied up with ropes in intricate knots, Houdini-style – is this Tilos security? Ropes are easy to come by in Tilos, as they're used by farmers and fishermen, and often wash up on shore. When Lisa chews her way through her collar one day, I simply improvise with an old length of rope to make a collar and lead. People tell me it's wrong, but why not – and what else to do?

My companion loves clambering over rocks and lying on the beach, and she makes me laugh. We walk to Eristos to take lunch for Stelios, and the sun gleams silver on the blue bay between smoky grey hills. We sit in the sun, Lisa perching with her paws up on my leg, then lounging with her head resting on my knee. We return along the dirt track so she can wander freely without my worrying about a car coming around the corner. The fields on either side are lush with the winter rains. Back at home, she stands almost upright with her front paws on the low wall of the terrace, surveying her territory and scouting for intruders with her head in the air like a meerkat.

I look at our happy pup in her country house, with the village across the valley, and feel content with life. Within a couple of weeks she has already lost some of her rounded puppy look, and is turning into a beautiful young dog. She's decided she likes sleeping on the beanbag with my best wool blanket, instead of in a box, and she can make her way up the steps to the roof terrace. She also loves to sit in the corner of the sofa with her chin on the arm, looking at what we're doing. By late February, her legs are longer and she can jump up on walls when I take her up the mountain path from Kamariani, and she rolls in the green grass amid white daisies and the mauve anemones.

The ferry service is affected by storms further north, and it's hard for the fishermen to get the fish to the markets of Athens in time. In this season, the fish are full of eggs and will go off more quickly, and if they're not perfectly fresh, the price will go down, making it less worthwhile. So the fishermen take a few days out to mend damaged nets. On an overcast day, the long purple fishing nets are spread out on the quay in Livadia and men stand holding the nets up like cat's cradles, then sit on the ground and weave strong threads through them. I watch for a while, then walk with Lisa around the bay. A cormorant skims the surface of the still, blue-grey water. At the tiny harbour of Ayios Stephanos, another group of men are cleaning octopus on a jetty. Each man holds a rope that's heavy with the weight of several dead octopus, and they lift and drag them on the ground over and over to tenderise the meat, leaving a trail of white foam that flows back into the water. It's a strange sight. Lisa and I scramble up a hillside filled with cyclamen, their flowers like white flames rising from bright pink fire, or bright-white feathers in the pink band of an Indian headdress.

I get up when it's still dark on a cold winter's morning for the Friday ferry. My bag already feels quite full with Lisa's things – a shawl for her to sit on, a bone to chew, a cuddly toy... No room for a book for me to read on the journey. It feels like a taste of motherhood.

As a woman who never had the urge for children until late, I assumed I just wasn't mother material, so it was strange to hear people say, when I first got pregnant, 'You'll be a great mother!' Could I really do cartoons, games, the school run? Yet I'm learning, from having Lisa, that it all comes naturally. I am perfectly capable of baby-talk with my dog. I wonder if having her will help some mothering hormones to kick in.

When we arrive in Livadia, dawn is beginning to fill the sky with blue, yellow, orange and mauve, a few tiny clouds lit up red and gold. Lisa is fascinated by all the activity outside Remezzo, the cafe on the quay, and hoping for some attention. She now looks a fine young dog, with smooth, pale fur, a white flash down her chest, and a beatific smile on her face. She's beginning to grow into her Greek-blue collar. As we pull away from the harbour, the island is bathed in sunlight, the south-facing cliffs deep red.

Normally I'd try to get another hour or two of sleep on one of the comfortable couches in the lounge, but Lisa's still so small that I don't want to leave her alone in one of the cages they have for animals on the deck, and will have to sit in the outdoor cafe with her instead. Gradually she curls up on my shawl and goes to sleep. When she wakes, we go for a stroll, and she seems to understand that the lack of grass means she'll just have to wait to relieve herself. Over the course of the journey, lots of people come up to see her and to pet her, including one of the crew, who shows me pictures of his own dog.

Rhodes town is at its best: a warm and sunny winter's day. Our main task is to walk to the vet's for her check-up, and while we're there we stock up on dog treats, collars and leads. Around town, people smile at Lisa, comment on how lovely she is, ask what breed she is; I've never had so many conversations with strangers. After an hour or two, though, I have a problem. Lisa can't walk any further. I carry her for a while, looking for a cafe where we can sit, but of course it's difficult to go inside with a dog. Eventually I sit down in a doorway, and realise that with Lisa's plastic water bowl in front of me, I look homeless. I laugh to myself, too tired to care. I find a bench at one of the entrances to the Old Town, and we sit beside the medieval walls, soaking up the sunshine. On the ferry home, it's cold up on deck but I sit with my furry friend as she curls up again to sleep.

Back home in Tilos, I spend much of my day outdoors in wellies. There are still a few vegetables and herbs in the garden. I cook up aubergine, tomato, onion and green pepper into a tasty stew with *revithia*, chickpeas. I am hoping that Stelios' *horafi*, field, will have better earth for growing things, though at the moment it's overgrown with grasses and wildflowers except for a corner we cleared to plant potatoes, onions and carrots. When strong winds came during the winter, Stelios had to strap the young trees to canes, and they all survived; the lemon trees have little buds on them, and the vines and fig tree are sprouting leaves.

This time last year, during that cold winter, I spent too much time indoors working. It has been a milder winter, but now we also have better heaters and a duvet for the nights, and I've been outside enjoying the days a whole lot more. The March colours are astonishing. Some days the beach, sea and mountains will transform from grey to silver when the sun breaks through. One early morning, there's a thick bank of cloud in the sky, but the dawn turns it pink and mauve. The path to our field is bright with poppies and daisies and sage flowers. I watch Lisa grow and change from day to day. Every day is different.

At the beach, Lisa tries to eat everything – seaweed, dried-out starfish and cuttlefish bones. She loves walks, grabs the rope with her teeth to pull me along. Delos and Pavlos like having her around the honey factory. Having our very own honey monster has been a job and a half, but I've loved it.

Another thing that has cheered this winter is the opening of Kali Kardia (the 'Good Heart') in Megalo Horio, a tiny taverna that serves souvlaki, skewers of grilled meat wrapped in warm pitta with tzatziki, tomatoes and onions. It's good to have a place to eat out and see people in an impromptu way at night.

We've been a happier household these past months, as a family. When we wake up, it's to an upside-down dog: lying on her back with her hind legs stretched out and her front paws pulled in high on her chest kangaroo-style, so there's plenty of belly to rub.

What a difference a dog makes.

Chapter 27

People Who Care

When Stelios goes away for a week, I enjoy having the car if I want to drive to Livadia in the morning to buy fruit and vegetables from the farm trucks. Like most dogs, Lisa adores driving along in the car with her nose out of the window, ears flapping in the wind. In fact, she tries to stick her whole body out of the window, so I have to keep the window up halfway. I'm in the square one day when Vassilis, who runs one of the seafront restaurants, asks her name, and then says in English.

'What, you call your dog "rabies"?'

Oh! It turns out *leeza* is how her name should be pronounced; *lissa* means rabies. It reminds me of the time when Stelios seemed to be telling me he'd been mending a leaky boat with pizza he found washed up on a beach, which seemed very odd; not pizza, he explained, but *pissa*, tar.

Stelios has been in Athens, trying to make progress with the interminable problem of his parents' pension paperwork. He jokes that the government hope you'll die before you collect your pension.

It's been pleasant having the house to myself, going to bed early and reading. I like to be a hermit from time to time, to switch off from the news of the outside world. When Stelios is away I find myself quite oblivious sometimes, too, to the news on the island; often I hear news of Livadia in emails from Anna in England.

I'm taking things easy, pretty sure I'm pregnant. Each time the three months of recovery time is up, it seems to happen like clockwork. My doctor in Rhodes confirms with his magic scanner that there's something with a heartbeat in a sac in a good position; but he says, '*Fovameh*' – I'm worried. All the months of tests have confirmed everything seems normal, except that my hormone levels reflect my age and something called thrombophilia may be causing my body to reject the foetus. No one is certain of anything, but we should try whatever we can. He gives me progesterone tablets, and anti-thrombophilia syringes to inject into my stomach daily. I used to have a fear of needles, but with so many blood tests I've become more resilient. It makes me feel sick, though, pinching the skin under my belly-button and pushing in the big needle that doesn't always go in easily, making me cry in frustration. But maybe this third time will be it.

Back when I was first pregnant, people seemed so keen to be involved; since miscarrying, few people here have talked to me about it. So when I meet Menelaos, the goat farmer who keeps his animals on the way to Skafi, while out walking, he surprises me with his sensitive words about our losses. He asks if I'm all right, tells me it's natural and that many families have these difficulties – it's up to God to decide.

Back from Athens, Stelios drives me mental looking after me, though he means well, forcing me to eat pungent wild asparagus. All I want to do now is eat and sleep, which I take as a good sign. There are thunderstorms and rain and a power cut, which gives me a good excuse to go to bed in the middle of the day. When the rain stops, I take Lisa to the bottom of our dirt track and the Skafi road has turned into a stream which she has great fun jumping around in, chasing the current. The hillsides and fields almost glow green. By early evening, the clouds have passed and we have pale-blue skies and sunshine.

In the mornings I often walk Lisa just 10 minutes or so past the abandoned bar to an old spring below a chapel. The stones have two bowl shapes worn into them where rainwater gathers, providing a drink for her. One day I sit on a boulder while she finds a grassy spot in the shade of a pine tree. Around about are broken stone walls and tall dark cypress trees and I wonder how long this spring has been used and who drank from here in the past. The only sound is of bees buzzing around the water source and a breeze through the trees, and the air is fragrant with wild herbs. I let Lisa lead me further up a gully, pushing through sage bushes. We emerge at a flat area with a view of nothing but hillsides, and the deep blue of Eristos bay in the distance, no sign of man anywhere. It's one of the most beautiful places I've seen.

Following the path back down, I notice white, yellow and orange butterflies, little lizards, lots of dragonflies – the first I've seen this year – and an overwhelming variety of flowers, blue, white, mauve and yellow.

This empty valley, home to Menelaos' sheep with their tinkling bells, was what attracted me to the house, when Dimitris came to check it out for me and described it as 'located in the earthen road... three minutes until the alone cypress tree'.

Stelios, home from fishing, shows me the contents of a plastic bag: a long silvery fish with sharp teeth, which he says is called a *riki*, related to the tuna but 'the best of the species'. They caught some off Lethra this morning. Within minutes, there's blood as he fillets it; later he tells me he found a big whitebait in its belly. Everything has to be done *now*, fast, as in a couple of hours they'll be going to put out the nets again. I hope he's not going to boil it for hours into a broth, or cover it with mayonnaise. But no, he cooks it in the oven in foil with onions, garlic and parsley. Meanwhile we agree to make *spanakopita* together.

'I'll clean the spinach...' I say.

'... and I'll make the pastry! *Teriazoume* – we're a good match.'

I spend half an hour cleaning mounds of spinach leaves freshly picked yesterday, and put it into a pot to steam for a few minutes. (My other job will be to locate all the things Stelios can't find in the kitchen, even though they are always in the same place... Oh, and – feminists, please look away – cleaning up.) He makes shortcrust pastry with wholewheat flour produced in Rhodes, then fries up some onions. When the pastry has rested in the fridge and the ingredients have cooled, he makes up the pie with a thick layer of spinach, the fried onion and an egg or two, and it's ready for the oven. And the fish emerges from its foil package in the oven, juicy and delicious.

Happily exhausted, full of the joys of spring, I sleep the deep sleep of the two months pregnant on the ferry to Rhodes for my appointment with the doctor. It feels right this time. I've been cautious, taking gentle walks, sleeping a lot; taking my tablets three times a day, injecting myself, and any time left in the day has been devoted to eating folic acid-rich foods. Without allowing myself to think ahead too much after the heartbreak of last year, I'm hopeful that this is the one.

So I'm not prepared for the doctor telling me an hour later that this one has stopped developing, too, and there is no embryo left, no heartbeat. The doctor, who was always so positive in the beginning, has nothing reassuring left to say. He has no idea what the problem is, and when we sit in his office afterwards to make an appointment for the next morning to do the *katharisma*, he suggests I try specialists in Athens. I get out money to pay him as usual and he pushes my money away. He can see how hard this is for me.

I wish more than anything that I was still pregnant and this wasn't happening. For many years I used to feel acute pain at the ending of a relationship. Now, that holds no fear for me. But this... It's the hardest thing I've ever gone through. Worse things happen every day to people, I remind myself; I am still lucky in so many ways. I call Stelios with the bad news, and he says he can come over on the boat in the morning but I tell him I'll be OK – I know the routine now. Wishing I could just go home – at a time like this, it's hard living on a remote island – instead I walk and walk through the town, cry unstoppably, eventually finding the strength to sit in a cafe-bar and drink some wine to calm myself down. It knocks me out for a couple of hours in the hotel room before the rest of the sleepless, fasting night.

At the bus stop in the morning, I ask a driver which bus I need for the private clinic. He thinks, perhaps notices that I look like I need cheering up, and tells me to hop on. It's a school bus but he can drop me off at the right place. We set off to pick up the children from sunny neighbourhoods and he turns up some rock music loud, and I enjoy watching his banter with the children as they board the bus. When he stops at the clinic, I try to buy a ticket but he flicks his head and shoos me off. Amazingly, I arrive smiling.

But my smile soon fades. From my last visits, I already dislike this clinic that looks like a corporate headquarters outside; inside the vast, shiny marble lobby, the dolled-up girl at the desk directs me down to the cold basement and instructs me to go to the *tameio*, the cashier, to sort out my paperwork. Previously I paid after the surgery, but they seem to have changed their system. Now before you see the doctor, they want to know how you're paying. The accounts room is full of people queuing, all clutching their differently coloured insurance books; I can't help thinking that a smart bomb wiping out the entire Greek paperwork system would do everyone a lot of favours.

The queue doesn't move in half an hour. I'm tired and sad and dehydrated from fasting and weeping, and I'm finding it hard to stand in line for so long; my body still thinks I'm pregnant, and is used to good rest and frequent meals. I probably should have asked Stelios to come after all. As the time for my surgery nears – the doctor had said he would try to do it before nine as he has a packed schedule after that, which is why I arrived early – I push to the front to ask one of the girls at the desk what I should do.

'You have to sort out your paperwork first. Just wait.'

Another half an hour passes. I go and ask another girl; they all look as if they should be working in the cosmetics section of a department store, as if they'd really care if they broke a nail or missed a hair appointment. She snaps at me harshly. I wander, unable to think what I should do. This is not a place that cares about me as a patient. It gives me the chills. I wonder if I should get on a plane to the UK; maybe a doctor there would be better able to analyse my problem in my own language. But it's the weekend tomorrow, and the doctor told me before that it's dangerous to wait too long. I go outside and sit on a wall, not knowing what I should do; unable to speak to Stelios as he's out fishing with no signal, and my phone is running out of charge. When I need food and am tired, my mind doesn't function properly, and I'm in such an emotional state my thoughts won't settle. I wish someone could help, tell me what to do. I think of calling my mum, but it would only upset her that she's not here with me and can't do anything. I suddenly see a taxi and grab it, and ask him to take me to the General Hospital.

I usually like hospitals, as my grandmother, my mum's mum, worked in one as a physio nurse when I was a child and I spent time there with her. This tired old building feels like a real hospital. A kind nurse at a desk with hand-drawn posters and religious icons tells me I can see the doctor; I easily buy an appointment ticket, which costs very little. At least I have a chair to sit on during the next two miserable hours, as the waiting room fills with happy pregnant women walking in and out of the doctor's office to ask questions and have ultrasounds; just yesterday I was one of them, but now I am the failure, the one who can't have a baby. My body aches.

At long last, I see the doctor, a very busy man who's quite matter of fact about things. He can't help me if I've had three miscarriages, he says, but he can do the D&C surgery (dilation and curettage – *katharisma* in Greek) and after that I can try going to Athens to see a specialist. He directs me to the paperwork desk – where I wait for only 5 minutes before a friendly woman sorts out what I need – then up to the ward. More kind nurses do thorough pre-surgery paperwork, asking about allergies and illnesses and giving me a cardiograph. They also need to take blood. I am weak and the older nurse takes her time with the needle in my arm as she is teaching two trainee nurses how to do it. The blood doesn't flow; this happens to me sometimes – I was actually forbidden to donate blood the last time I tried in England. I try laughing about it but instead I go dizzy, lose my vision and faint. I'd forgotten how horrible it feels to faint. Then they give me a bed to rest in and I sleep a while – pure bliss.

When I wake up, I realise there's a newborn baby with the young woman in the other occupied bed in the room.

Over the next few hours, I look out the window at the blue sky, and listen to the woman and her baby and her family who come to visit. One of the women comes over and strokes my arm, tells me not to cry. I feel selfish for casting a shadow over their happy moments, but I'm too sorry for myself to stop.

As the afternoon passes, I'm confused that there's no sign of my surgery, and worried about catching my ferry back home to Tilos tonight, as there isn't another for three days; I just want to be at home with Stelios and Lisa. I ask a senior nurse at the desk and she laughs.

'In your dreams you'll be in Tilos tonight! In your sleep!'

I ask for more information but she says she's really busy and I know she is; there's a woman fit to burst in a room nearby, hooked up to a machine broadcasting a loud heartbeat. I go downstairs to where I saw the doctor, but the whole corridor is deserted. I remember what Yorgos at the Stathis Hotel said about it being a good hospital except there aren't any doctors. Their salaries certainly would have been drastically reduced, some would have left, and their workload increased as resources are scarcer. There's no soap in the bathrooms and little toilet paper, though the place is spotlessly clean.

By the time it's dark outside, the senior nurse is not so busy and is more sympathetic. I say I haven't eaten or drunk water for 22 hours. She offers me something but I say I'll wait in case the doctor comes, and I go back to bed. Later, someone puts a glycerine drip in my arm, and my body is able to sleep. The doctor wakes me at one point and explains the hospital needed the operating theatre for more urgent things today, but he'll definitely do it by eight in the morning. I sleep on and off. And although it is heart-breaking, it's also a wonderful experience to be in the same room as a newborn baby all night, hearing its frightened cries as it realises it's not safely inside its mum any more, then calming down as it suckles her breast.

A jolly, older man wheels me down to surgery in the morning; I am so weak I can't figure out how to get my arm and glycerine drip through the sleeve of the gown. 'Don't worry,' he says. I don't have the energy to explain that I'm not worried about the surgery but about my future. As we squeeze into the lift with another orderly and patient, he compares bellies with the other man, who agrees that he's fatter but sexier. I laugh and he realises I understand Greek, but he tells me he also speaks English so he can joke with the international patients sometimes. 'It's true, isn't it? You see a good-looking man, he is cold inside. But an ugly man, he is warm...'

After the surgery, when I wake up from the light anaesthetic, I'm moaning in pain as I'm wheeled back upstairs. Abdominal pain makes me howl – how on earth would I handle labour? Another kind nurse offers me a painkiller injection, which I readily accept. When I wake up again, she gives me my prescription and signing-out paperwork, but the senior nurse says there's no need for me to go and stay in a hotel until the next boat, I can stay here in the ward. The people here have been unbelievably kind and I know I did the right thing by coming here. They probably haven't been paid properly for months, and yet they care. I thank her but explain it's hard to be around pregnant women and babies now I've had my third miscarriage. She says there are women who've had ten, twelve. How do you handle that, I wonder?

'You'll have a baby,' she says. 'You're healthy and it's all up to your own body; wait six months and try again.' She and the other nurse, whose parents are from Tilos, give me chocolates and home-made honey cake to eat.

When I smile, they say, 'You have such a nice smile.' So I start smiling again, in spite of everything. I'm alive and healthy, and I'll be going home to Tilos soon, to my furry little girl.

Stelios tells me that once he understood what I was going through yesterday, he asked the mayor to help, and she actually rang the hospital and spoke to the doctor on my behalf.

Swimming, sex and wine are all forbidden of course for a few weeks after the surgery while I'm on antibiotics again. Hang on, how can you have life on a Greek island without swimming, sex and wine – isn't that what it's supposed to be about?! I joke to Stelios that I might be ready to do all three at once as soon as the time is up. All my maternal instincts will be showered on Lisa the pup, who makes me smile and laugh every day.

Chapter 28

Wild Beauty

We've had a recurring conversation for a while now about chickens. I was thinking we should maybe start with two. Stelios was thinking a dozen. I thought we should learn a bit about keeping chickens. Stelios figured it's easy. Three days ago, he was helping someone dig up potatoes and was offered half a dozen chickens in return. That's his story anyway. Just as I had the final word in the dog conversation, he had the final word in the chicken conversation. I have an inkling as to who will end up walking to the *horafi* to feed them every day. The same person who waters the trees and vegetables most days... But it's a good walk for Lisa and an exercise break for me.

Stelios will need to build a *kotetsi*, a chicken house. Recently he spent a couple of days carefully constructing a wooden doghouse for Lisa. She hasn't been in there yet, but the idea is that when she's old enough and it's warm enough outdoors, we'll make it hers. There again, we weigh up the likelihood of this dog – who will sneak up on our bed at any opportunity – ever taking to a doghouse. There's more likelihood of us sleeping in it.

So another decision is quickly made to use it as the chicken house.

Tilos doesn't have any foxes, so there are no ground predators; but the crows and the eagles will go for a chicken, apparently, so the run has to be sealed well overhead. And because the chickens will be in the field with our vegetables and trees, they need a strong fence to keep them in their coop. Stelios carefully seals off an area around the chicken house underneath a big old tree that will provide shade in the summer. He's not just a pretty face, Mr Fisherman-*Kantina*-Man-Plumber-Chicken-Farmer.

Their first night in their new home is a cold, windy one; down in Livadia, the catamaran managed to stop in the afternoon but broke a rope doing so, and everyone on board was sick. Anxious to know if the chickens have survived the night in their new home, we drive to the field first thing in the morning, Lisa jumping up and down with excitement that we are going on an excursion. The chickens are right as rain. We bring Lisa inside the enclosure while we feed them, so she starts to get accustomed to the birds and learns not to harm them. She's only interested in eating their food.

On a bright day in late April with a deep-blue sky, we head out to gather capers on the cliffs at the edges of Eristos bay. Here, as in many Aegean islands, it's not just the round buds and berries but also the young stalks and leaves that are pickled and used in salad or with a meze. Caper leaves have been used since ancient times.

Caper bushes are obvious as splashes of bright green halfway down steep red cliffs. I try scrambling up, but the rock crumbles and, after a few scratches, I play it safe and look for more accessible bushes. I can't bear to watch Stelios reaching further and further into the most dangerous places, especially when Lisa's following him gleefully.

'I came here to gather *kapari*,' he says, grinning, 'so I'm going to gather *kapari*!'

We pick the newest shoots and buds, which snap off easily in our fingers; we manage to find just a few jars' worth, though I find a better cache later in the week and we go back to gather more. Picking does the bushes good, like pruning a tree, and as the shoots grow back quickly you can collect again from the same bush within a week or two throughout May. We leave the leaves in pans of salted water or seawater to remove bitterness, changing the water twice a day when a strong ammonia smell comes off. After five days, we put the caper leaves in old honey jars with a mix of brine and vinegar; a few days later they have turned a dull shade of green and are ready to eat. We now have a supply of delicious Tilos capers to add to the onions, lettuce, rocket, tomato and carrots in our own garden salad. All of it *viologiko* – no chemicals. We have locally gathered salt – a gift from someone, as it's illegal to gather it to sell... And I hope to have fresh eggs soon.

May is the time to gather *rigani*, or oregano, when the white flowers are just coming out and it's at its most pungent. So *gather ye rigani while ye may* – we take armfuls of the stuff from the fields at the back of the house, then hang it in bunches from the rafters of the empty house next door. When I want to use it, I snap off a head of dry buds and crumble it on to the food.

Lisa enjoys gathering wild food, too: she loves to eat the dead lizards she finds at the roadside. I never knew there were so many. I know we have an abundance of live ones, including a large *savra* who takes to sitting on the bathroom window, but there's no way she can catch those. She is part hunting dog, we now know from the vet, and gets excited when she sniffs the trail of a rabbit or a snake.

Along the way to feed the chickens at the *horafi*, we pass by the well-kept farm of Grigori, husband of Sofia, who has the *kafeneion*. Apart from growing all sorts of vegetables, he has an enclosure for goats. They have young kids in the pen with them now, and the babies bound around playfully on their spindly legs. Lisa's about the same size as a baby goat at the moment so they all eye one another with curiosity. One day a few big elder goats with beards and horns gather around and take a good look at her, before turning away, as if to say, 'Naah, not one of ours...' This time of year, when the goats have milk for their young, is when the islanders make the fresh *mizithra* cheese. With a set-yoghurt texture and an extremely goaty flavour, it's an acquired taste, and I haven't yet had time to acquire it, as Stelios scoffs the whole half-kilo on its own, with a spoon, in two days flat.

Easter feels happier and less strange and gloomy to me this year, perhaps because it occurs later, in early May when the evenings are already bright and warm. On Easter Sunday, we are again invited to lunch with Stelios' cousins Nikos Taxijis (although he's now an ex-Taxijis), Toula and family to eat baby goat; this time it's stuffed with rice and roasted in the oven, and the rice and liver stuffing flavoured with lots of fresh herbs is delicious. Also at the lunch is the priest, Papa Manolis. It's a very convivial meal, and I'm surprised when Stelios argues with the priest about religion on Easter Sunday – but the priest doesn't seem to mind a bit. He's very friendly, and as we're chatting, he asks me if I'd like to read in church that afternoon. Apparently there's a section of the service, the *evangelio*, that should be read in different languages. I say I'd love to and immediately curb my wine intake, even though the service is not for several hours.

When we get home, I ask Stelios if I understood correctly. He wasn't listening, though, to that part of the conversation, so he doesn't know. The time of the service comes around, so I dress smartly and make my way up to the church – alone, as Stelios says it's too early. I get the sense that he doesn't approve. I stand at the back of the church, thinking surely it was a mistake, but the priest comes over and brings me to the front of the church. It feels such an honour and I love those old words, about the disciples who saw Jesus come back from the cross, and Thomas who wouldn't believe unless he felt the wounds with his own hands. I am bursting with pride, even though there are so many firecrackers going off that no one can hear what I'm saying anyway and the plaster is practically falling from the ceiling.

Summer is beginning again. I take Lisa to the beach daily. When it's warm, she races into the sea and sits in the water. If it's really warm, she'll swim, and the half-drowned look of her, a seal-like thing with floppy ears hanging over the water, makes me giggle hysterically. She gets out and shakes herself all over me. I take the precaution of zipping my shoes and clothes into my bag so she doesn't steal them or eat them while I'm in the sea. If I lie on the beach, she has a habit of coming up to me and standing on my chest to say that I may rub the fur on her throat now. She also makes it clear when she doesn't want to leave the beach, standing and looking at me with her tongue hanging out, and glancing back over at the water. She never wants to leave – she's even more of a beach bum than me.

Before *kantina* season recommences, I make myself go away for a few days' holiday. It's always hard to leave, but breaks are good, especially after a difficult time, and I need to explore more islands for writing assignments that are coming up with greater regularity now.

Where do you go on holiday when you live on a tiny island? Perhaps an even tinier island, Pserimos: with a population of only twenty, a few kilometres long by a few kilometres wide, one of the smallest inhabited islands in Greece. It's halfway between Kalymnos and Kos, close to the shores of Turkey. Searching for information online, I find an obscure reference to someone called George who helps travellers to Pserimos, and an email address. He responds at once saying Tilos is nice, but Pserimos is a different experience – bold words! Because I'm thinking I'll have to bring Lisa, he says I'm welcome to set up my tent in the scout camp he runs. At the last minute, though, Stelios says he can look after Lisa.

I set off on the *Diagoras* at night, pass Nisyros and Kos, and reach Kalymnos in the early hours. Camping on the little town beach is forbidden, but I hope no one will notice if I lie on a sunbed in my sleeping bag and leave early. I sleep for a few hours, buy treats at a good bakery, and soon it's time to board the *Maniai*, the little ferry. The view on arrival is tantalisingly lovely: a horseshoe-shaped harbour with white sand and shallow, clear water, surrounded by smooth, low hills.

The bay is both a natural blessing and a sad curse, because it draws day-tripper boats and there are stalls of trinkets. An old lady beckons me over in a friendly way, then tries to sell me some herbs. When I set off walking to a quieter cove, it is sullied by debris brought in by the sea and dominated by views of a Turkish resort. But taking another path, I notice gardens of fig and prickly pear and grape vines, goats with long, twisted horns and farms with dry stone walls reinforced with old furniture to keep them out. A farmer lies snoozing with his dog under a tree, and waves to me as I pass.

Gradually, the little island grows on me. The few vehicles on the island include a truck with a ram's huge horns on its fender, and a scooter with a trailer that has a goat riding inside. I arrive back at the harbour when the day-trippers have left, and I have the soft pale sands to myself. I eat a good meal at Sevasti Pikou's taverna: vine leaves, which they call *fylla*, stuffed with rice, meat and tomato – the best I've ever eaten. Under the tall, aromatic pine trees of the scout camp, I fall asleep listening to the wind blowing through thousands of olive trees, kept company by wandering chickens.

The next morning, I have the bay to myself for a swim, watch the boats bringing in octopus and sponges and fish; when tour boats arrive, I take George's directions to an empty stretch of pale sand backed by low cliffs, with one half of a white chapel perched picturesquely on the edge – the other half having fallen into the blue sea. Locals stop to talk when they see I'm still there. I follow another path over the hills in the other direction – when I ask an old man the way, he warns me *'Tha berdepseis poli'*, You'll get very confused – to another stretch of beach I have to myself. I grow to love the sound of the wind in the olive trees during the night, and remember how good camping is – as well as the freedom of having nothing to do but walk and read and notice all these things. I am very happy I came to Pserimos for a few days, and resolve to return sometime.

On Sunday, I decide to work and get a head start on the week. After a couple of hours' emailing, I have to drive to Livadia to take some photos of the apartments Eleftheria runs. While I'm there, I run into various people I know, go for a quick walk down the seafront and a swim in the sea. Back home, before getting back to work I remember I have to gather sage. Just as I am going to get down to work, my Albanian friend Bubuque, our neighbour at the *horafi*, arrives and asks if she can use our internet connection to call her family. Afterwards, I drop her and her son back home, since I have to go and feed the chickens and water the trees. Lisa naughtily gets into the chickens' food box while I dig up some of the enormous evil thorn weeds that are taking over our field. Back home, I clear up the mess of bits of wood and rope that Lisa's been chewing on, then I water the garden, make a salad... Finally, I admit that work will have to wait until tomorrow after all. I open a bottle of cheap bubbly from Rhodes, my latest treat, and sit and watch the lights come on in Megalo Horio. There certainly hasn't been a dull moment since I arrived here.

Sometimes, nature red in tooth and claw gets a little too much when my office is part of my home, especially living with the two forces of nature that are Stelios and Lisa. In one day, Stelios explains to me how an octopus sucks the flesh out of a lobster, and I find Lisa with a rat's tail in her mouth, and a dead hedgehog in the nets over the vegetables; there's a massive meat cleaver in the sink, and a whole freshly slaughtered piglet in the fridge, thinly masked by the plastic bag it's in. I've always wanted an unconventional life, and now I've most certainly got one. The past couple of years have been an adventure in themselves, a very different experience full of wild beauty and immersion in rural Greek island life.

Although all the gardening and cooking and dog-walking can be distracting, getting away from my desk can give me a different kind of space for thinking. One day, an opportunity to write a story for a major newspaper comes up, as long as I can find a good idea. It's as I'm feeding the chickens that I come up with one. I email them on my return and get the commission.

It isn't a travel story, but about the pregnancy struggles. There's often a stigma about 'leaving it too late', but for me and other people I know, it wasn't a choice. I finished the long-term relationship of my thirties when I decided it wasn't stable enough to bring a child into; I was also still focused on building a long-term career because that's necessary for a good life, too. My next partner ended our two-year relationship unexpectedly around my fortieth birthday. Then there was Matt. Matt knew that the most important thing in my life then was to try for a child; that discussion led to our getting together. When I didn't conceive, he dragged his heels about getting test results – until I found out that he couldn't have children, at the same time as he dropped a few other bombshells. I finally realise that I am angry that he took those crucial years from me, and it's good to be able to write about it.

With Stelios, I don't seem to have any problems getting pregnant – but I have a problem keeping it alive. What has become apparent from my reading is that no one really knows what causes this kind of miscarriage. There is much disagreement among the specialists: some people claim success in one field of treatment, others in another. Now that I've experienced being pregnant, it is hard to let go.

Maybe I was never able to have children. Or maybe I still could. Not knowing is hard – and, I suppose, part of the great mystery of life. I just have to decide whether to continue trying, how much more I should put myself through.

I usually try to judge if I'm doing the right thing by asking myself: if you knew you only had a year to live, is this how you'd spend it? It works for jobs and relationships, but most people wouldn't spend their last year trying to bring a child into the world and I wouldn't spend it having treatments, seeing more doctors and perhaps going through the torture of miscarriage again. It only gets harder each time, because three unexplained miscarriages is more hopeless than two.

Each time I've been pregnant, it's drained me of energy for a couple of months and I've had to be careful and put things on hold rather than live life to the full, and all for a painful ending – though I try to make up for lost time afterwards. It's tempting to keep trying: who knows whether next time we'll be lucky? It's also tempting to give up and enjoy my life and my freedom. But what if I wish later that I'd kept trying?

We have, of course, discussed the adoption question several times. I've always liked the idea, but our lifestyle would be a major obstacle. Stelios says it's extremely difficult to adopt in Greece. We're not the model couple adoption agencies are looking for. We can't even have a complex conversation without a dictionary. So that's just not on the cards for now.

Although we love one another, I still have doubts about how good we are as a couple. Yet everyday life is good, and that's important. I remember one time he taught me the expression, '*Ouden monimotera apto prosorino*' – There's nothing more permanent than the temporary. It was only supposed to be a night on Eristos beach, and here we are with our chickens and lemon trees, and our dog.

Chapter 29

Investing in Freedom

One of the first customers at the *kantina* this summer is a man from Athens, who tells me over his morning coffee that in early June he wasn't just enjoying the sound of the sea and the stars above, but from his little tent was involved in trying to keep alive the signal of ERT, the Greek national television station.

A former computer programmer, he was always politically active but decided to do more about it when the work dried up during the economic crisis; he started taking photos of what he saw happening on the streets, recording the frustrations people were experiencing and their fatigue at being hit from every direction under austerity measures. When the government suddenly announced it was shutting down public television, 'the only unbiased medium' as he puts it, a group of journalists protested and tried to maintain the signal online, hoping eventually to set up a website with reliable information about what's happening in Greece.

'For young people it was very important,' he says.

The coming years in Greece will be hard, he continues, but most people in the cities think there is nothing left to lose. People with no work have to rely on the pensions of older relatives to survive. Properties are empty, shops closed. The *Dromografos* or street reporter tells me he finds his new way of life incredibly rewarding, though he's surviving on minimal income.

'I've learned many things I didn't expect,' he says; there is still stress but he feels great about his work – it's tiring but fulfilling.

His words resound in my head, because after taking the first two weeks of June off work, I realised I wasn't happy to be back at my job: after almost nine years with the company, it's time to ask for more responsibility, a bigger role, if I'm going to continue. It seems like insanity to keep doing the same thing, not growing and learning. I have inspired people with my story of moving to a Greek island; people have written to me saying they've been encouraged to change their lives. I've said that life is too short not to reach out for what makes you happy – and that's the ethos I should live by. It's time to speak up. The relationship isn't healthy if I don't say what's on my mind. A phone meeting is set up between me and the head of the company.

The conversation doesn't go quite as I'd hoped, and suddenly, I'm working out a month's notice. My income has been reduced by two-thirds.

It's both exhilarating and terrifying.

But as soon as the shock of becoming completely freelance is over, it's liberating. This is it. I am now completely free either to make a mess of things or make them better. It's in my hands. I can work when and where I want. I've always been scared of losing a regular income, but after all I've achieved since coming here, I should be able to fend for myself. I've cut the lifeline that I needed at first, making a firmer commitment to a new way of life.

Someone I worked with tells me that a shake-up of life is always good for opportunities. Almost immediately after going entirely freelance, I reach out to a potential client and am hired to complete a project later in the year that will stretch me more than I am used to. My judgement is being sought and valued and it feels like a good sign.

What I came here to do also, I suddenly wake up and remember, was not only to spend more time outdoors but to be more creative, to get away from the endless cycle of work and have more time for writing. It's not going to be easy – there are going to be dry periods between paid work, when I worry that I'll have to go back to England and get a job. But here I can get by spending little, in order to invest in creativity. With a lower cost of living, I can also live life more. When I want a break from work, I can step outside and be walking and swimming, being fitter and healthier for more of the year and with time and space and freedom for thinking. I can close the computer and walk away into the wild beauty I have found here. This, for me, is real life. It is time to grasp life by its goatish horns.

Here in the South Aegean in the height of summer, the habit of taking a sleep in the middle of the day is almost a necessity, and certainly a pleasure not to be taken for granted. As the heat intensifies, sleep begins to call. A midday meal and something to drink help you sink into slumber. And now, if I want to take a siesta during the hottest hours of summer and work later in the day, I can.

I can take my time to enjoy the rest of the summer, have a break while I adjust. I can rush around less, do things more thoroughly, spend more time with people. In the middle of July, we have a lively evening at the *kantina* with a good crowd: an English couple who are hoping to spend more of their time on the island when they retire; our Austrian friends from last year; a Greek couple, he a musician and she a model-like beauty who adores playing with Lisa; a muscular Greek interested in books of esoterica and philosophy. I have a late swim and a cold glass of wine, put on some good music. Lisa loves all the attention. When she's not meeting new people, she's doing important work digging holes. It's funny to think that when she first saw people at Eristos she barked at them – she'd spent the first few months of her life thinking the whole vast beach was ours alone and she must defend it against intruders.

As happens pretty much every year, there is controversy about the free camping. Some island residents see it as a waste of a good beach. Our mayor, Maria Kamma-Aliferis, writes in a Greek newspaper that the campers contribute to the island, bring business to local shops and restaurants, respect the place and clean up after themselves, and have become friends of the island.

Again this year, *kantina* customers include locals who use it like a *kafeneion*, a place to sit and drink coffee, talk and play backgammon. People staying at the hotels nearby, or arriving on a yacht or on the bus for the day also frequent the *kantina*; the atmosphere is different from the more mainstream beach at Livadia, which has its own appeal. We have a couple of French authors who are working on their latest books – Philippe writes about alternative communities and is fascinated by how things work on Tilos in general and Eristos in particular – brushing shoulders with young Greek men with tattoos and girls with dreadlocks. It's a fantastic mix of nationalities, families and couples and groups of friends. For many, making new friends or meeting up with old ones at the *kantina* really makes their summer complete. And although mostly when I go to the beach I prefer to be alone, to read and appreciate the natural beauty, it provides a welcome opportunity to meet new people.

For example, there are Kostas and Stavroula. Kostas used to have a wine shop in Exarchia, a hip, alternative neighbourhood of Athens, but recently had to close it down because the restaurants he supplied weren't able to pay their bills. Stavroula is a junior school teacher who hates having to explain to her kids why the school is now providing their lunches (because their homes can't). They've come here for the free camping with a budget of just €15 a day, and will stay until their money runs out. They gather thyme and walk to peaceful, secluded beaches. 'It's psychologically good just to feel ground under our feet here,' Stavroula says.

There's another Kostas and his partner Koula. He spends his days snorkelling, observing the sea life, while she creates clever jewellery out of recycled tin cans, and mouth-watering desserts, and has been hand-painting a sign for a women's co-operative shop to sell local products at the entrance to Megalo Horio.

And there's Nikos, a clean-cut and now out-of-work mechanical engineer, who is on his second visit to the island and who enjoys the nature and tranquillity (stop barking, Lisa!). He sits reading a book in the shade, apologises that the English he learned doing post-graduate study in Canada is rusty, then expounds eloquently on such diverse topics as the Antikythera Mechanism – a computer-like navigation device from a hundred years BC, found in a shipwreck – and Plato's dialogue on etymology. Then he introduces me to the modern Greek poet Odysseas Elytis, writing down a few lines for me from the famous work 'To Axion Esti', where in 'The Genesis', God creates the sea and in it the 'small worlds' of the islands, looking like the curved backs of dolphins.

My stereo sits on the counter of the *kantina* and people sift through the pile of my old CDs balanced on top to find something they want to put on. One day I'm looking for something when the teetering pile starts collapsing, and in my effort to save them falling into the sand, I clip the open CD holder and break the mechanism. It could be a disaster, but Mitsos spends the afternoon fixing it – no problem. It's a supportive community. Eighteen-year-old Eleonora has exams coming up in September but people have been helping her study: there are computer programmers and several physics teachers among the campers.

This year, I've enjoyed the company of the younger campers. Michalis, in his early teens, shows up sometime in the course of the morning and sits on a barstool to wait for his chocolate frappé or *tost* with Nutella – new additions to the menu that Eleonora and I came up with. Another young teenager, Ory, has been ill for most of the summer so sighs a lot, but tries to be cheerful. Tiny Orpheas usually has a very serious face as he lists the ingredients he wants on his sandwich; I see him with a cute smile on his elfin face, walking round and round the *kantina* first in one direction and then the other... Casting a spell, I wonder? Yes, they watched *Harry Potter* last night.

An angelic-looking little Italian boy called Rodolfo, about three years old, comes to the *kantina* daily with his parents for lunch. He speaks at me in Italian until his mother explains I don't understand. Apparently he's always telling his mother she's beautiful (which she is). 'Don't change!' I say. His father often ends the meal with a glass of *souma*, poured from a water bottle. One day Rodolfo perches on one of the stools in front of the *kantina*, dwarfed by a huge motorbike helmet, takes one look at a water bottle and asks if it's *souma*. Oh dear, we may have corrupted him...

Of course, there's still the occasional rude person to deal with. Precious Anastasia asks me to make tea for her for free using her own tea leaves, looks incredulous when

I say I don't have a tea strainer, and demands a plate and knife and fork so she can eat her own fruit among the other customers before she sets up her jewellery stand. She spends an entire euro at the *kantina* on a bottle of water in return – then the next day hassles me for hot water for her tea while I'm making coffees for people who ordered them first and will be paying. I ignore her. Stelios has this year given me carte blanche.

For the summer, Stelios and I don't really have a conversation that doesn't revolve around the *kantina* – about picking up some oranges, paying a supplier, washing the hammock, bringing some new music... He still worries about it, but I look around and see relaxed, happy, interesting people enjoying themselves, and I assure him he must be getting something right.

And my Greek is a little improved this year (though Stelios' friend Stratos says it's still not very good). I'm more confident, anyway. When things are busy, I smile and use a phrase I heard someone in Rhodes say once, '*Ena leptaki!*' One little moment.

At dusk, Lisa and I walk back home, where there are welcome warm breezes. I have a shower, some simple food, and sit peacefully, making up a poster for the *kantina* to advertise the ice cream, as Stelios asked. When he comes home, I hear his hiccups first. He barges in the door, almost trapping Lisa's head in it by mistake. I laugh and ask him what happened – he admits he's been drinking *souma* since early evening. Like many Greeks, he's not much of a drinker, so when he's spending long hours imbibing alcohol to keep customers company, he doesn't handle it well. I mention a message someone asked me to pass on, and he starts shouting, thinking I'm accusing him of something. Lisa cowers outside.

'The things I have to put up with,' he slurs. 'I reckon I'll be going to stay in the tent again...'

Tents seem to be a running theme in our relationship. He disappears back to his tent next to the *kantina*. Next morning, he arrives home again, sober, head aching, asking what happened exactly and asking for forgiveness. It's dangerous stuff, that *souma*.

When in early August we run the souvlaki stand at the festival at Harkadio Cave, it only takes three of us – one of Stelios' friends is a master of barbecuing souvlaki and works with him on that while I do the drinks and cash again. This year, I can keep up a bit more with the frenzy when everyone's demanding their dinner, even when we run out of water and bags and can't see a thing when it gets dark. I wrote myself a cheat-sheet multiplication table for totting up souvlaki prices, and there are hardly any exasperated customers. I'm learning. A simple achievement like this can be very rewarding. Working in an esoteric field that means little to most people, at home on your own, it's refreshing for a change to be judged on your ability to satisfy a crowd of hungry customers.

As I pull on my wellies to go to the field and feed the chickens one morning, I wonder yet again why they still haven't produced any eggs. I've researched online and bought a book to see if the coop needs any additions, and tried improvising perches for them using old bits of wood. I wondered if they might be sick, as they've been losing a lot of feathers, especially one of them – but as Stelios advised, it is August and pretty hot.

I reckon Grigori, whose farm I pass by every day, might be a good person to talk to. So I ask him if he wouldn't mind coming to have a look at the chickens when he has time. He stops off while driving by and strides across the field. He then scans the six of them quickly, and announces: 'Jennifer, you've got five cockerels.'

Apparently, when chickens are small it's hard to tell if they're male or female, and since ours are different breeds, they're different sizes anyway.

'But why's the one hen not laid any eggs?' asks Stelios when I tell him.

'Well,' I suggest, laughing, 'she's probably quite tired…'

A few days later, I'm recounting the story of the cockerels to a group of friends who've been camping next to the *kantina* and are taking the ferry back to Athens. We're sitting in Omonia, the restaurant off the square in Livadia.

'I don't think you could do it,' says Irini. She doesn't think I'm up to slaughtering a cockerel.

'Neither do I,' says Stelios, but with a glint in his eye, knowing that the one thing likely to make me kill a chicken is being told I look like someone who can't.

Chapter 30

Learning to Live Small and Think Big

I'm off at 7 p.m. to do the slaughtering, the *sfaximo*, or at least to help while my Albanian neighbour Bubuque shows me how.

I decide to start with the weakest two cockerels, which have twisted legs. Bubuque grabs the first by the wings. I am usually squeamish; I used to hate butchers' shops and faint sometimes at the sight of my own blood. But the skilled, quiet way Bubuque goes about this business is fascinating. She stretches the cockerel out; holds its legs down with her feet; with one hand on its upper body to stop it thrashing around, she cuts through the neck, blood gushes out on to the ground, and immediately it's not a living thing but meat. She snaps off the feet at the joints. I grab the second bird. Bubuque's daughter, back from university, has brought out a bowl of boiling water, and the slaughtered birds get submerged in the water to loosen up the feathers. We talk for a few minutes while we wait. Bubuque learned from watching her mother, she says, and has been able to slaughter chickens since she was a teenager. I ask her daughter if she could do this. She shyly shakes her head.

The feathers come out easily. To remove any last stragglers, she lights some pieces of paper and burns them off. Then comes the tricky part – removing the insides to make it good and safe to eat. There are little bits to cut off, parts to remove for eating, parts for the cat. The hard-looking round stomach is peeled away leaving a ball of undigested corn that the other chickens can eat – no point in wasting it. I'm full of admiration. I'm amazed not to feel queasy, though it does feel odd later cutting meat off the carcass, which is still slightly warm. The fresh meat is tough, but I boil up the rest of it the next day and it makes a heavenly soup, with our own potatoes, some black-eyed peas, onions and courgette. It's another step towards a wilder life, that's for sure. And another fear has been met head-on, so to speak, and overcome.

Unfortunately, I start to grow fond of our remaining useless cockerels, and poor Bubuque, who lives next door to our *horafi*, has to listen to their racket. They are now huge and stand waiting for me when I arrive to feed them, climbing all over the coop and the table that I left for them when I was trying to give them something to perch or roost on. But, as Stelios says, our chicken coop or *kotetsi* is now like *Big Brother* – who will get voted out next?

Lisa, our eight-month-old resident comedy canine, is in heat and rather popular with male dogs, especially with a young pup currently staying in a tent right next door to the *kantina*. So now I can no longer take her to the beach in the mornings. Her boy next door leaps up when he sees our dusty red car, and looks at me with sad, accusing

eyes when he sees Lisa's not in it. At h[...]
become almost nocturnal, sleeping all [...]
day and waking up ready to play as soon as [...]
going down – a challenge if I've had a long d[...]
to take her for her walks in the early evening t[...]ches
with few people to disturb and no dogs – easy to find on
Tilos at any time of the year except August.

'Why don't you take her to Lethra?' asks Stelios one day.
At first it seems a crazy idea to go for a long walk as I'm
utterly exhausted. Stelios is, too – he's had to work even
longer hours at the *kantina* this year to make it pay. In the
afternoons he lies in the hammock and when someone
wants something, he tells them to help themselves and
put the money in the box.

But I haven't been to Lethra for ages, and had forgotten
what a stunningly beautiful path it is. We pass sheer rock
faces where goats climb nonchalantly. Lisa runs ahead,
legs, ears, tail and tongue all flying in different directions.
As we trot down the path at 6.30 p.m., everyone is leaving.
One couple I know stop and comment on my T-shirt with
its heart motif, and kiss me on both cheeks. Lisa leaps
up at the sight of Maria, an Athenian teacher who's been
at the *kantina* every morning all summer (a coffee with
one spoon of coffee and two sugars, and a sandwich with
omelette, cheese, tomato, salt and oregano). Lethra is
in shadow when we reach the sea and it feels like dusk
is coming, but it's beautiful for a swim, and as we walk
back, there's sunlight on the tops of the hills, and the
moon in the sky. I'm getting very fit from these longer
walks. I drive back across the island and catch the sun

...gain before it goes down over Ayios Andonis. Back at home, the sky is soon dark blue, and the lights of the village and castle come on, silver and gold.

Inspired by that glimpse of the sun going down, another late afternoon I drive to Ayios Andonis and walk half an hour to swim at Plaka. On the way back, all I can think of is the food at Elpida restaurant. I like this place near the old windmill because it's right on the sea, which can be rough and tempestuous with a north wind blowing, and Sotiris, the owner, catches his own fish. I also like the hand-scrawled sign whose words don't quite fit on the lines ('Spaghetti with Lob/ster'). Sotiris allows me to sit at the edge of the terrace with Lisa tied to the tree next to my table, and I order food and a cold beer. With the waves rolling in, I can't think of a better way to end the day. Looking back towards Plaka, the promontory and little island offshore and, further away, the island of Nisyros, are different shades of soft grey. The sun starts to set in a glory of gold and orange and pink as I take my first bite of fried calamari with tzatziki. It's the most romantic spot for a dinner for two: Lisa and me. Love is... giving your partner the last piece of calamari.

As always in the last weeks of summer, music is continually going around in my head with all the festivals. On the full moon, we have live music at the *kantina*, with two of the campers who are professional musicians playing *rembetika* for everyone for free. We turn off the lights and sit on the sand listening to timeless songs, the sea burnished with moonlight.

All of our friends from Eristos are at the festival of Panayia Kamariani the next night. *Ela Stelio! Pameh!* Let's go! People are pulling me along to dance with them, and we are on our feet for hours, having fun. I show some Italians how to hold their arms for the *sousta*, not crossed but open, just as I was shown three years ago. Suddenly, in mid-flow, there's a power cut. But the music continues. Since there are no amplifiers, people sing along to the songs. The musicians move into the middle of the circle so everyone can hear. Since yesterday was a full moon, there's strong moonlight. It occurs to me that this is how it might have been in the old days. Sons dance with mothers, fathers with daughters.

I now know some of the words to the songs and understand some of the jokes when the singers work in improvised rhymes referring to the men leading the dance – now I have a better idea who people are. Again, I feel happy and at home. I cringe when I think of my first awkward steps when learning to dance, but gradually I know more and aim for better posture and smoother steps, and can enjoy it. I've still only scratched the surface of life on the island, but I feel I know more. I take home a stick of souvlaki for Lisa. Stelios goes back to close the *kantina* then sends me a message saying it's full of people – the after party – so he stays, and I almost wish I was there.

At the *Koupa* a couple of nights later, I realise that knowing more people can be dangerous. When I go to buy a beer at the *kafeneion*, where as usual the older men are 'warming up', Nikos Taxijis along with Stelios' uncle Pantelis and Fotis invite me up to dance with them right there. It's a little embarrassing, but Nikos can be very forceful when it comes to dancing. Then, once the proper dancing in the square begins, Pantelis insists on pulling me to the front of a dance that I don't know well, and it turns out he doesn't know it very well either. I fluff it completely since there's no one to follow, and am sent back to the end of the line again. But, however humiliating it is, I don't mind: it was nice to be asked.

Although I take pains to point out to people that I didn't move to Tilos because of Stelios, and I've sometimes resented being known just as the *kopella*, the girlfriend, Stelios has of course been a major part of my putting down roots here – in more ways than one, thanks to the *horafi*. It's added stress at times, because as the girlfriend of a local, I've been expected to do things in a particular way. But, thanks to him, I've become more connected to the island. And it's been good to help him with his own business.

Gradually the sea daffodils come out on Eristos beach, ragged white wildflowers that emerge from the sand at the end of the summer.

'Khronia polla!' says Stelios, lying down and hugging me when he arrives home towards dawn. 'Do you believe it's two years?'

It's amazing to think of all the things we've done and people we've met this season. I'm incredibly tired, but tanned and toned from dog walking. In the end, I'm glad

I didn't have a job for the past month and have been able to enjoy life more.

I have managed to escape from that full-time job thing. I've left it behind. The years no longer fly by. Like many people in full-time jobs, I used to wonder where the year went. Now, it's hard to believe I've done so much within the space of just twelve months. Life has slowed down at the same time as it's speeded up: I do more and time passes slowly. Breaking the rules of a conventional life is scary at times, but I can't imagine going back; I'd rather scrape together a living in a more fulfilling way if I can. My life has so much freedom. There's so much in the world to see and do and learn and try. It's about learning to live small and think big.

One day, a man I know from the village who works with goats, Antonis, asks if I will help him to find a buyer or new tenant for a house his wife owns in the village, by taking some photos and posting them online. I like having time to help out the people around me like this. His wife takes me to see the place – it's just a little higher up the hillside from the supermarket, above a tiny chapel that I've always thought lovely. The house is basic but functional – the kind of large, practical space I like, with a lot of outdoor areas. She opens up a room downstairs at the front, a self-contained studio, draws back the shutters and there's a view over the chapel right across the valley, to the elephant cave and the hills. I wonder... I wonder if I've found myself an office for my new way of working – my own space to think and work in uninterrupted, with my things spread out around me, a room of my own?

Chapter 31

Small Worlds

In the mornings, I sit and watch the sun creep down the mountains. We have a couple of days of humidity when clouds gather over the bay and the hilltops, and cause the electricity wires to fizz. There are sandy spaces under the trees again, the sea smooth and denim blue. The visitors from northern Europe come back. Most of the dogs that came with campers have gone, and Lisa can return to the beach. She sniffs around to see what's been happening, her fluffy feather boa of a tail waving in the air. Then she sits and stares at the people having lunch at the *kantina*, hoping that by the power of the mind she can remove food from human hands into a canine mouth. It often works, especially with people who have a dog back home that they're missing. She is a very well-loved dog.

Once again, I've seen too little of Anna this summer. She was stuck in London until July, back in the black-pencil-skirt-and-heels routine, watching the Tilos webcam and listening to Greek radio. She did lure me down to Livadia for a few nights out once she arrived, but she's also been away sailing and doing a lot of socialising, and taking the dance classes a lot more seriously than I have.

We resolve to walk to the beach at Tholos in a few weeks
– much more pleasant once the weather cools off – and
in the meantime to go to the last festival of the year
together.

A woman who's been staying on a boat in the bay asks
me about the trail from Eristos to the monastery of Ayios
Panteleimon, a well-known long walk of several hours
across the highest mountain ridge on the island. I tell her
not to attempt it alone in case anything happens, but that
Ian at Ayios Andonis does it regularly and might walk it
with her. He agrees, and I arrange to go along with them
– I am now free to do things like this – but then someone
tells me about an archaeological dig taking place in the
valley below Megalo Horio, and since it's ending the next
day, I decide I must go and investigate.

I'm lucky. When I walk there in the morning, following
a dirt track towards Eristos, I find the archaeologist
standing over a trench dug in the ground. She tells me
they had planned just to fill in the hole today, but decided
to excavate a little more of the wall. 'Palevoumeh akomi,'
we're still battling away at it, says Irini. She's a slight,
delicate-looking woman from Rhodes who wears flip-
flops with cats on them, and a straw hat with a flower
on the side against the sun. Her appearance belies the
difficulty and determination involved in her work. Her
husband, a sculptor, has come along for a break and their
dogs are tied in the shade nearby. Nikos, the farmer who
owns the land and fortunately hadn't ploughed here, is
digging under instructions from Irini. She watches his
work. If she pushes him to keep going when he's tired,

mistakes could be made and they have to work carefully. Good job Lisa isn't here.

To the north, in the gap between the mountains, the island of Nisyros is visible, while in the opposite direction I can see the Harkadio Cave, where evidence of prehistoric man was found. People have been unearthing things in this area since the 1950s. A small trench was dug when an archaeologist came in the 1970s. Last year, they started to excavate properly, then covered the site over to protect it – I saw some of the finds at that temporary exhibition in Athens – and this return visit is Irini's last chance to dig here. 'I'll never see it again. So I want to find as much as I can.'

They have discovered a loose layer of pottery, then a large layer of ash; she will run tests but believes it could be volcanic ash from Santorini, dating back to 1600 BC; this helps to date the findings. She shows me the intact foot of a cooking pot, perfectly conical; cups with a rib design. They found a cache of cups all together – they look like modern teacups with handles – plus storage jars, loom weights, a bronze fishing hook. It all suggests a household, a settlement. There's a brown and red wall of plaster and lime – perhaps wall paintings contemporary with Santorini's Akrotiri and Crete's Knossos. Most of the plain pottery was made here, while the decorative pieces, contemporary with the Minoan culture, were most likely imported from Rhodes and Crete. Perhaps little Tilos could have been part of that sophisticated network.

As they continue to scrape and sift, separating tiny shards of pottery from packed dry earth, occasionally finding something resembling a handle or the side of a jar, dust blows everywhere.

'This wind!' says Irini, exasperated. We stand up and look around, her eyes raised to the terraces on the hillsides. People probably always farmed on those terraces but they would need to find pottery to date them. I hope one day there is a bigger museum here, but I also love living surrounded by the mysteries of the past, some buried but untouched, scattered around.

Ian passes by the dig during the morning on his way to meet the Australian woman on the boat, to take her on the walk. I get a call 10 minutes later from the woman saying she can't make it as they may have to sail that afternoon, but it's too late to relay this to him as he doesn't have a phone; I try leaving a message with Stelios at the *kantina* but it gets somewhat scrambled. When I see Ian later in the village, he explains that he swam out to the boat in rough waves to find out what was happening, and was invited aboard for breakfast. Then he swam back and did the walk on his own.

I travel into the sunset, the huge fiery orb dropping slowly into the sea. Soon, the *Diagoras* is docking at Mandraki. I travelled to Nisyros years ago but this is my first time on our neighbouring island since I came to live here, even though I see its shape on the north horizon most days.

This trip is mainly research for an article, and I have resolved to learn more and make the most of living in such a rich region. Stelios isn't too busy now so Lisa stays at home with him. At the first hotel overlooking the water, Three Brothers, I take a room with a view of the sea over a bamboo garden, with a church to one side and a hillside filled with prickly pear bushes behind. I swing the balcony doors open.

In Mandraki, waves crash up on the rocks and the houses on the edge of the sea. I find the monastery lit up on the clifftop, and a brilliant crescent moon above; wooden balconies almost touch one another across tiny alleys, washing hanging to dry, and groups of women sit chatting on doorsteps, plant pots in every conceivable space. In the square, hidden in the winding alleyways, *rembetika* music plays at the *kafeneion*, and a sign reads *Varda stenahoria* – an old local phrase meaning 'sadness begone'. The owner tells me he's visited England; Liverpool, of course, when he worked on the ships. Two older ladies in almost identical blouses and cardigans sit smiling side by side on a bench, hands crossed in their laps, glasses in front of them of the cloudy local almond cordial, *soumada*. One of them gets up and walks away from the busy cafe to answer her mobile phone, shouting to someone who is clearly hard of hearing: '*Stin Nisyro! Ena nisi! S'ena nisi! Nisi! Neh, ena nisi!* – I'm in Nisyros! An island! On an ISLAND! An ISLAND! Yes, an ISLAND!'

I start the next day at Koklaki beach: black pebbles, rough sea; a view of the green side of Yiali island – half pumice, half obsidian. I learned from posters in the square that turtles are nesting on another beach a few miles around the coast, and decide to walk there, stopping to see things of interest and talk to people. Beyond Palli are volcanic stone walls in dark greys and reds and a road seemingly to nowhere stretching around the island. I swim, read and fall asleep to the sound of sea on an empty stretch of beach. Woken by noise, I see goats reaching for caper bushes on the pumice cliffs above me, dislodging stones. I'm curious to take a peek to see what's over the headland – not expecting to find cows being herded from beach to hillside. At a restaurant that night, fish soup is recommended. 'What fish does it have?' I ask. 'Fish for soup.' Silly question. I also have a salad with Nisyros goats' cheese, which is tasty, hard and crumbly.

By the time the bus has climbed to the rim of the caldera the next morning, I'm already feeling queasy and hoping the brakes are checked regularly. The village of Nikia has stunning views across the blue sea to Tilos on one side, on the other all the way down into the centre of the volcano. After my eyes have been opened by a visit to the volcano museum, no stone is left unexamined as I follow a path through old abandoned settlements: scoria or basalt? I walk down to Stephanos crater, to feel the sulphurous steam rising up from the fumaroles, and listen to the rushing of hydrothermal activity below the yellow crystals, pause to feel a connection with mother earth. Then I continue on a *monopati*, a footpath, up through ancient hillside terraces, until I reach the dirt track and wind my way back around the other side of the island past little chapels and farms, as the sun starts to turn everything silver and gold. Up here somewhere by the defence wall are ancient cemeteries, where people were cremated with vessels of oil, wine, honey, figs and olives.

I leave it very late to buy my ticket home, almost wishing I'll have to stay. But I can come back any time. As we approach Tilos, I meet people who ask me to tell them about the island, and I point out the road that leads up to the monastery, Plaka beach, Skafi beach and the path to my house. When you live on a tiny island, you do have to travel sometimes to experience something different, but I always feel extremely lucky to be going home to Tilos.

Each of the islands is a small world in itself. Just as Nisyros was shaped by volcanic eruptions, the rocky mountains of Tilos are shaped by the old walls of castles, the terraces of ancient farms, the roaming goats that eat the trees. And our lives are shaped by unforeseen events and experiences, by every choice we make and everything we do. If I hadn't gone into that pet shop while I was waiting for the car to be fixed, my life wouldn't be dog-shaped.

My plan is to go back to Tilos for a day, then on to Rhodes where I'll connect with another ferry to Crete to visit the tiny desert island of Chryssi off the south-east coast. But just as I'm about to leave Tilos, Lisa gets something stuck deep in her ear. We find her flapping her head from side to side to dislodge it, but there's nothing visible so it must be deep. I'll have to take her with me, to the vet in Rhodes.

Since none of the taxis at the port in Rhodes will take a dog her size – or maybe they just don't like the look of me – I trudge across the Old Town to the other side, my backpack heavy with clothes, computer and dog supplies. The vet finds a length of dry grass piercing her eardrum and says she could have gone deaf if I hadn't brought her in. He puts her to sleep while he buries his hand in her ear with a long pincer to retrieve it.

The boat to Crete, the *Preveli*, only travels twice a week and I don't have time to take Lisa back to Tilos. So the vet's office manages to book a cab that will take me and a very groggy dog to the port. I have to carry my still-drowsy 20-kilo dog (the vet weighed her for her anaesthetic) on to the ship and up all the steps to the top-deck dogs' accommodation. It's hard to leave her alone there in the cold in the dog cages, with noisy engines all around. There are just two dogs up there, shaking and shivery; I wish I could put her back to sleep.

It's warm and sunny by the time we arrive in Sitia in north-eastern Crete early the next morning. Unfortunately all the other dogs in town are awake and we walk to the palm tree-lined seafront followed by a pack of mean-looking stray canines, while other hounds bark and howl from balconies.

I have three days to take the bus south to Ierapetra on the south coast and a boat to Chryssi, before catching the *Preveli* back. But at the station I discover Lisa can't travel on the bus unless I buy her a cage and put her in the hold with the luggage. There are indeed days when Lisa deserves to be locked up in a cage... But not when she's on antibiotics and painkillers for a healing eardrum, having just endured a cold night on a ship. Alternatively, I can catch the *Preveli* straight back that afternoon, another twelve hours on the ship and all for nothing. I wonder if a car is the answer. And I wonder if I'll even find a hotel that will take a dog.

When I walk into the office of Minoan Car Rental, weary from hefting my backpack to the bus station and all around town after a fairly sleepless night, the man smiles at Lisa and she jumps up and puts her front paws on his desk. Out of kindness (and not just to get us out of his office, I'm sure) Michalis not only says he will rent me a car in the coming days, but rings around and finds a hotel that will take us, too. It turns out to be a very smart hotel right in the middle of the beachfront, called the Itanos. The nice young chap at reception feeds Lisa an almond when we check in.

Later I find myself looking at a lovely long stretch of beach on the edge of Sitia and thinking how nice it would be if they hadn't built a road right on top of it. In fact, the roads out of Sitia, this agricultural town, are full of huge, speeding lorries that would squish this Tilos-only driver like a bug at one false move. I cannot bring myself to drive a car on the first day, so instead walk to Petras, a kilometre east. Sitia might not be blessed with tranquil beaches, but it is rather blessed when it comes to ancient sites. Petras, occupied continuously from 2500 to 1400 BC, was used for the production of purple dye from shells and in later times wine and pottery were made here. The ancient warehouse once had massive pillars and storage rooms for rows of huge jars, and it was here they found the best preserved hieroglyphic archive of Minoan Crete

– the inventory tablets and official seals of the palace. Also, cups and bowls that the personnel used for taking snacks to work – their lunchboxes.

Lisa isn't allowed on the town beach, so later we walk across the town and I see people swimming off the rocks near the entrance to the harbour, just below the road; it isn't beautiful but might be a good place to let Lisa go in the sea.

'*Apogoreveteh*! Not allowed!' women at the water's edge shout nastily, waving their arms, as if I'm deliberately breaking the rules and doing something terrible. And yet the town seems full of dogs! Wherever we go, stray dogs follow us or yappy dogs bark from balconies and every walk takes me past barking guard dogs. Thankfully, I manage to find a place to eat that allows me to sit with Lisa, and I drink some good local wine, and eat *makarounes*, soft local pasta with cheese, comforting and delicious. Walking around later, I get lost but discover a fantastic little shop that sells traditional local dairy products: yoghurt, staka (a heavy cream made only in Crete) and xygalo – a light and sour-tasting soft cheese made from goats' or sheeps' milk in the same way it was made in Minoan times.

The next morning, I find myself staring endlessly at the map with all its different roads, and thinking about what do when I rent my genuine Minoan car, and how much traffic there will be. Then I wonder about putting it off for a day. Small islands like Tilos are relaxing, I think, because you can go everywhere on foot if you like, with nature all around you. I chicken out of hiring a car yet again, and Lisa and I head for the hills. Passing the scrappy outskirts of town, with old bits of machinery, run-down or abandoned houses cheek by jowl with expensive new ones in different styles and colours, I see an intriguing sign and turn off to wander the ruins of an ancient city. Then, to escape the fast traffic and barking guard dogs at the roadside, we head into the hinterland where there is birdsong and olive trees.

I have no idea where I am going, but at noon we reach a village with an old Turkish fountain gushing with spring water. We continue up along paths through the woods, and two hours later we're at a little church high on a hillside in the middle of nowhere. Tired and hungry but exhilarated, I take off my shoes, lie down and listen to the only sounds: rushing water and the squawk of birds of prey circling above. Inside the church are beautiful, delicate paintings on wood. Far below is the coast. I don't have a good enough map to know exactly where we are, but I'm very happy to be up in the rugged hills, pleased to have ended up here.

The research trip is doomed: I haven't figured out what I'd do with Lisa since the island is a nature reserve and dogs aren't allowed. I go to see Michalis and tell him I'm terrified of driving one of his cars to Ierapetra, and he tells me he would therefore prefer I didn't, and everyone is happy. I don't really need to go just to write a paragraph about it. I decide I've done my best, ask a few locals about Chryssi, and make the most of Sitia instead, spending hours the next day at one of the best archaeological museums I've ever seen. I eat more delicious food washed down with local wine. It's been an adventure.

When Lisa and I catch the *Preveli* back to Rhodes, we sit in sunshine together all the way, munching on food from Sitia. I read a book and Lisa sprawls out across the deck, where everyone who passes must pay her some attention. She certainly leads me a merry dance sometimes, but she's worth it.

Back home, I enjoy some September days when I can hand Lisa over to Stelios, lie on the sand and fall asleep listening to the waves: such a simple pleasure.

Chapter 32

Tilos Devil

There are days when the sea is steely grey-blue, and olives are blackening on the trees. Now the *kantina* is closed, Stelios is free to come with Lisa and me on walks through the countryside, exploring, and he often takes her out in the evening on his own, visiting his friends. Back when I was wondering whether we should bring Lisa home, I truly believed that Tilos would be a perfect place to have a dog. It's not so simple, however.

Like many dogs, Lisa likes to chase things for fun, but as she grows up, we learn she can sometimes catch them. She can't do any harm to an adult goat, but Stelios and I let her off the lead on the path to Skafi once and see her catch a very young kid. Something instinctual takes over – she is half hunting dog, after all. She grabs it in her teeth and tosses it around like a rag. Whenever we try to catch her, she dodges away. The kid later dies, Menelaos tells us. He doesn't blame us, but Lisa has to be kept on the lead and cannot be allowed to run free. The countryside is full of goats that wander freely, but most belong to someone, and she could spot one on a hillside and be after it in no time. Sometimes I wish one of the goats with the massive horns would give her a fright by coming for her, but instead they always run.

Another farmer in the village shouts at me for walking Lisa past their sheep, because it scares them. On the other hand, I've been reprimanded for keeping Lisa on her lead. Some people insist I do one thing, others insist the opposite. I've been chastised for leaving her in the car for an hour, even with water and the windows open in the winter. Just as when I was pregnant, people don't hesitate to tell me what to do.

I don't mind people having an opinion but I get sick of people being negative and treating me as if I couldn't possibly have a clue. One day over the summer, when I allowed Lisa to sniff the grass in front of a seafront restaurant in the summer, the owner shouted at me, thinking I was letting my dog pee there. Another day I lost it when a woman started telling me what I needed to do, and I snapped back, 'It's my dog.' It started a big feud. Her boyfriend complained that the frappés I made were undrinkable. We never speak to one another again. It's not good to have enemies in such a tiny community. So much for my efforts to stay on good terms with people.

Still, there are plenty of people who love her. When Eleftheria brings her son Kyriakos to the house so he can practise his English, Lisa leaps up on them, attacking them with love as Stelios calls it. Kyriakos and I come up with a nickname for her: the Tilos Devil.

When Stelios and I have to go away for a few days, we leave Lisa with Nikos Taxijis and Toula. Their old dog Aris loves her, and although they generally keep him tied up, they have a large garden and orchard for the dogs to roam around in. They've always loved Lisa and want us to let her have pups so they can have one.

This is another seahorse moment, a point of cultural difference. Many local people firmly believe that a female dog should not be neutered, or at the very least should always be allowed to give birth to a first litter of pups, otherwise she will have psychological problems. On the other hand, I tend to think keeping a dog tethered somewhere remote for its whole life as a guard dog, as some locals do, would give it psychological problems. I ask what I would do with all the pups, knowing I wouldn't feel comfortable giving them to people who would keep them as guard dogs – that's not much of a life. Menelaos says it's OK, he'll kill them for me. 'No!' I say, laughing.

Lisa is a Greek dog, and lives on a Greek island, so perhaps she should live by the local rules, but I don't think they are always right. One day, someone convinces Stelios that Lisa is a boy, even though I'm pretty sure the pet shop and the vet knew she was a girl, and she does pee like a girl. I figure Tilos locals must know a thing or two about animals so I look at some rather unsavoury pictures online. She's a girl. Stelios still goes round telling everyone she's a boy until my next trip to the vet.

Unfortunately, as we're returning to Tilos after our days away, we hear that Lisa and the other dog have been showing off to one another, racing around the house during the night – it's been pandemonium. Aris has never escaped from his enclosure before now, but together they've been digging their way to freedom and roaming the valley. And although Lisa never touched our chickens, a couple of theirs have been killed. It's a shock. Suddenly, the little bars of chocolate we brought for Toula as a gift for looking after Lisa seem rather inadequate.

It's a good job she's adorable.

The blue sea at Eristos glitters, and the sand is now completely empty, flattened by the first rains of winter. The *kantina* is moved off Eristos beach in preparation for storms. We have the island to ourselves and can relax and breathe normally again. It's warm enough to sunbathe some days; other days it's cool enough to walk to the mountaintops comfortably. Under a perfectly blue sky, I again try the path to the Italian house with Lisa. The sea squills are already blossoming – tall stalks rising from the ground, with clusters of white flowers at the top. Soon Megalo Horio seems far, far below. And this time, at last, I make it to the peak. Beside the empty house, the ground is covered with small mauve colchicums and wild crocus with yellow centres and saffron and white filaments.

I'm never happier than on a new path, alone, discovering. Now that she's strong enough, I walk one day with Lisa to Louboudi, a pretty cove over a steep scrub-covered hill from Skafi; there's much scrambling to get there, and when we arrive there's a dead goat in the water which I know Lisa would love to investigate, so we turn straight back again, and in trying to find the proper path I find myself precariously clinging to the edge of a cliff.

But down below, there are white caves and deep-blue sea with rocks clearly visible underwater, and the view is worth it. It's also good to walk with Anna's company to one of our favourite beaches, Tholos: up a steep path to the ridge above Livadia then all the way down the other side to a fjord-like inlet with green-grey rock, and water that's almost turquoise.

In the house at the honey factory, surrounded by fields, the smell of straw and herbs after rain is astonishing. At night, the sky is mostly unpolluted by lights. Pavlos and Maria originally encouraged me to switch on the electric garden lights in the evening – a seahorse moment, because for me the view of the sky full of stars from the dark surrounds of the house has been breathtaking and unforgettable. I've loved living here. But the house has been feeling small for a while, and with winter coming the three of us will be indoors more, making it feel even smaller. Stelios still wants to finish off his house at the *horafi*, but I'm not sure about living there, and it wouldn't really be any bigger, and would cost a lot – money we don't have. Renting seems to him like throwing money away, but I think it's easier for now.

When I saw that house in the village, I thought about just renting the office space, but then I considered how I sometimes felt cut off from village life down here, retreating to my own private world, especially in the dark of winter. I was concerned about losing my identity, people not knowing who I was. Perhaps it was time to join in the dance a little more. Or at least give it a try. So we arranged to take the village house after closing the *kantina*. It's hard to believe we are leaving the house at the honey factory. I will miss the old place and the family – even though I'll still see them around, Pavlos says it won't be the same.

But I love moving house and am excited when we settle into our bigger place in the centre of the village. Although the front addition is modern, the house has an archway with '1868' carved into the stone and painted over, and the courtyard has a couple of old millstones lying about and is dominated by a lemon tree. I love the fact that my office window overlooks the little whitewashed chapel, the *ekklisaki*. There are frescoes on the inside walls and ceiling, and basil plants in pots outside. Vicky says it is dedicated to Ayios Ioannis Theologos, Saint John the Theologian, whose monastery is in Patmos. She says it's medieval, and the old wall of massive stones it's built on is Hellenistic, from the time of Alexander the Great.

'All these little churches were privately owned. That one was in the family of Stelios' father's uncle, Apostolis Logothetis. He was a teacher, and during the Italian occupation he was persecuted because he taught Greek secretly. It was against the law to teach Greek, or even to speak it on the main street here. Because the Greek language was forbidden, and only Italian language was taught, gradually the parents took their children out of school.'

As I listen to Vicky's stories, Lisa chases a cat, and up the steps walks old Polixeni dressed in black, carrying her walking stick in a jaunty fashion over her shoulder, a bag of vegetables hanging off it. We have the occasional chat, and once when I was feeling down about making a mistake, she said, 'You can't know everything – you're young. When I met my husband I was only nineteen and I learned my work slowly, *siga-siga*.' I walk home past Irini's tiny shop below the *kafeneion*; her daughter, finished with her studies but unable to find work, has returned to Tilos and agreed to start giving me informal Greek lessons. The more I speak the language, the richer life becomes.

In the evenings here I listen to the bells of Rena's sheep as they come running down the mountain, and a woman's voice rounding up animals, shouting *'Elateh elateh, grigora griiigora!'*, come, come, quickly, quickly... In the mornings, I hear cockerels crowing down in the valley. One morning, I'm pondering the strange things I hear shouted across the rooftops and alleys of the village sometimes ('The mulberries are at the house!' – it sounds like secret code) when my phone rings and it's Stelios.

'Jennifer, have you spoken to Dimitri lately? People are looking for him – he hasn't shown up for work.'

Although he's been away for the summer as usual and we're no longer in touch regularly, my old friend Dimitris, the high school headmaster, did come up to talk to me on the beach when he got back in early September; then I saw him at the last *paniyiri* of the year at the church of Zambika several days later, but not since then. He's so steady and reliable, it's strange for him not to be at the school, where he should have been at the rehearsal for 'Ochi' Day.

'Let me know if you hear from him,' says Stelios.

He calls again an hour or two later. What he tells me doesn't seem real. There's been an accident.

Chapter 33

Life on a Greek Island

Someone spotted something unusual on the high mountain road to the monastery. A water pipe running along the roadside was broken. Debris was strewn down the steep cliff. Dimitris' car plunged 300 metres down.

He and a German woman called Uta – apparently she had recently become his girlfriend – were thrown from the vehicle during impact. Tilos doesn't have emergency services, so the island is supposed to wait for a helicopter from Rhodes, but ordinary young men immediately ignore the rules and without a thought for their own safety they brave the treacherous slopes, hoping for signs of life. But they both died, probably the evening before.

For the men who went down there, how will they ever forget what they saw? Once again, I'm reminded of the intensity of life in a small community. The mayor must keep calling Rhodes to convince them to send a helicopter, so that the local men don't risk their own lives further to retrieve the bodies.

I find myself walking along the road towards where it happened but stop, not knowing if it's appropriate. I am walking again, in a daze, when I see a truck driving to

Livadia in the late afternoon as the sun goes down; in case I didn't quite believe what had happened, seeing two wooden coffins in the back makes it feel real enough. I keep walking to the port and in the evening, under a sky full of bright stars, the Milky Way clearly visible, I see Dimitris leave the island for the last time. A small boat has come specially, and I watch its red light disappear into darkness.

For a while, the whole island is in shock, especially the children he taught. Two days later, it's his name day. It being a Saturday, he would undoubtedly have been out in the sea somewhere, fishing for octopus. I walk up the road towards the monastery to see with my own eyes, finally, where it happened and try to understand.

It's a beautiful place. He took me to see the sunset up there once. Perhaps that view he loved was his last. I was up here recently for the baptism of Eleftheria's niece – Kiki got pregnant at the same time as my first pregnancy – and I took photos of the view over the cliffs.

Now I walk down to Plaka, to the little bay on the promontory, and go out with my mask and snorkel. Dimitris took me out snorkelling when I first came to stay in Tilos for a month, introduced me to remote beaches and the underwater life of the island. I see anemones with wavy orange hair, a small eel's ribbon-body curling around a rock, and a slender fikopsaro, its tail fine and silver like a needle. He once said he'd always be there for me, and perhaps in this way he will be.

A week or so later, I see a woman on the deck of the ship crying and know it must be Dimitris' sister. When I introduce myself she greets me warmly and takes me to see his mother and meet his daughter. I've met Dimitris' mother before – we went to the Zambika festival together a few years ago when I was here on holiday. They have come to gather his possessions from his flat.

They ask me what I think happened and I confess I don't understand it. Although that road to the monastery scared me at times, he drove it regularly to fill his water bottles from the spring. He was extremely careful in everything he did, and didn't drink; he knew the road well, and it wasn't a particularly narrow or tricky section. The post-mortem found no evidence of a heart attack. It remains a mystery.

Clearing the flat is a terrible thing for the family to have to do, and in some ways it helps to have company. They also love Lisa – a dog can bring joy even in adversity, as I have learned this year. So, day after day, I drive down to Livadia with her to keep them company, and they invite me to visit them in northern Greece whenever I want.

Dimitris was a hoarder, and his apartment is full of things he diligently stored in case of emergencies. His family, understandably, find it very difficult to throw anything away, so my car is stuffed with things to take home, from fishing and diving equipment to cleaning products and plastic bags. I can't believe I'm doing this: there is something darkly absurd about it all. For years to come, I will think of Dimitris fondly whenever I open my cupboards... It may seem mundane but I think my old friend would have approved.

My smart new office is equipped with desk, computer, printer, stationery, books, and a bathroom with a baby goat inside. Seriously. So I haven't left strange goat incidents behind.

I can't remember how Lisa got free, but she did, and the next thing I knew, she was at the top of the village and had cornered a black baby goat in a field. She didn't want to harm it, just bark at it. And she wouldn't let me near her. I tried to lure her away with every trick up my sleeve, but nothing was as much fun as the goat game. And then I thought of something: I picked up the baby goat and carried it back to the house. Lisa followed me and we slammed the gate closed. We had Lisa… but we also had a baby goat.

Just then, Menelaos came by, perhaps having heard the commotion, so I showed him the goat and explained. He said he thought its mother had died, and that we could keep it. I had bucolic visions of drinking our own goat's milk until Stelios pointed out it was a male. Still, wouldn't it be nice to have a goat, an orphan goat? But how would we feed it? Menelaos says we should feed it warm milk mixed with water.

Proving how much I know about raising goats, I put the milk in a saucer as if feeding a cat. Unsurprisingly, it doesn't know what to do with that: it's only weeks old, and we'll have to feed it using a rubber teat, like the thing on the end of a baby's bottle. Rena in the shop has one. So we warm the milk and soon I'm sitting on my office chair, holding a tiny goat while Stelios tries to get it to drink milk, and Lisa looks on in amazement and adoration, trying to lick the goat as if it's her baby. I notice the goat is absolutely covered in ticks and fleas, but it's still a beautiful moment.

As soon as the goat can, it retreats to the bathroom and hides behind the toilet, not terribly impressed with its new family. And there it stays for the night. I hope it will survive.

In the morning, I'm woken by the kid *me-e-e-h*-ing at the top of its lungs. How can such a tiny creature make so much noise? I dash downstairs, afraid the whole village will complain. How to get it to be quiet?

Then I hear another goat calling from the top of the village. I'm sure they're *me-e-e-h*-ing to one another. What if...? What if Menelaos was mistaken about its mother dying? I grab the goat, fleas and all, and carry it up to the field where I found it, to where a mother goat stands, demanding I return her boy. I set him down and he bounds across the field to be reunited with mother in a glorious moment worthy of Hollywood. There's certainly plenty of Greek drama in Megalo Horio.

Walking through this peaceful village on a November day with a blue sky above, sunlight spilling over stony grey ridges and the gentle arches of the church roof, pink bougainvillaea flowers spilling into blue and white alleyways and the Greek flag fluttering in the breeze, you might think this little island is a place where not much happens these days. And then 40 refugees, probably from Syria, are dropped by people-smugglers from Turkey on one of the most remote beaches of the island. Being just a few miles from the Turkish coast, we are part of the border of Europe. It has been years since the last boat of illegal immigrants came here, but it won't be long before the next arrives. We are about to be part of something big.

In late November rain, I'm with my mother and my second cousin in Athens. We have the Parthenon practically to ourselves. The massive columns look dramatic under dark storm clouds.

'I can't believe there's nobody here,' says Catherine, as we explore the Ancient Agora, once the heart of the city below the Acropolis. I found us a cheap and comfortable apartment to rent half an hour's walk from here via the ancient stadium and national gardens and Temple of Zeus. The weather is a mix of blue skies and grey, but we can wander the city without crowds or queues and we're grateful for soft drizzle rather than summer heat. We duck into cafes and eat mezes, winter salad and marinated anchovies, and drink cold little carafes of raki. At night the rain has cleared and we sit outside to eat prawns and fennel in ouzo, and tender lamb wrapped in paper with herbs and cheese and baked in the oven.

Mum and Catherine have come to Athens to spend my birthday with me since I have to attend the clinic.

I always thought I'd only want a child if it happened naturally. But back in September, Stelios and I decided to listen to what advice the specialists could give. Neither of us was really convinced by any of the three doctors we saw. One seemed understanding but nutty. Another seemed uncaring and pessimistic. The most arrogant of the three seemed to have the best clinic, but he was strictly an IVF specialist, and when I mentioned alternative treatment he turned defensive and blurted, 'They only believe in such things in Africa and countries like that.' Oh dear. I wasn't convinced that IVF was what we needed, but there was always a chance.

Life is short, my old friend Dimitris inadvertently reminded me, and we don't know what is coming. I've spent the last couple of years going for everything I wanted from life. So I decide simply to go ahead with the IVF treatment in Athens, and not lose any more time deliberating.

I take the metro north into the smart suburbs to the cheery private clinic. A hysteroscopy once again confirms I'm healthy, always good to know. I take out more cash than I've ever seen before, for the drugs to prepare my body. I have blood tests and scans. Stelios comes to Athens to do his bit. I jab myself in the belly a record five times one day but the nurses tell me my body is responding very well and the signs are excellent. I have a nice long sleep while they take out some eggs, and wake up in a warm, cosy room. The doctor is jubilant that lots of healthy eggs are collected, and a greater number than expected fertilise nicely. I'm not surprised – we've never had a problem conceiving.

I go back home to Tilos for an extremely careful December. No mulled wine for me, but I make a simple festive decoration for the fireplace from greenery gathered in the valley, and Stelios buys *melomacarona*, honey cakes, and *kourabiedes*, shortbread dusted in sugar. I spend the cold evenings as I always wanted, reading books in front of the fire – because we have a real fireplace in this house – and sharing the couch with Lisa.

On each side of our home in Megalo Horio are empty houses – many of the old homes have been abandoned over the decades and there are broken walls and overgrown gardens. But one day, I unexpectedly see that the house next door is open. It transpires that a potter from Crete bought it as a ruin 'by accident' twenty years ago when a ferry stranded him here for a few days, and he has gradually brought the house back to life, returning for just a couple of weeks a year. Inside, it's beautiful.

We are invited to dinner. Menelaos the goat farmer, a friend of the man from Crete, brings along his wife and youngest son and grills meat on the open fire for us all, and makes a salad. I pretend to take tiny sips of wine. It would be a very special evening, but I am also a bag of nerves inside as tomorrow I go to Rhodes to see if the treatment has worked. The one person in the room who knows what I am going through and should be sympathetic seems oblivious. I feel very alone. Perhaps I have been pushing Stelios away lately.

The next day in Rhodes, the hours of waiting for the results of the blood test are agonising – I'm still being ultra-cautious and it's hard to find something to do to distract myself when one simple word will make all the difference to our lives, determine our future. I sit in the doctor's office as she finds the paperwork, hoping, hoping, hoping... But no. I'm not pregnant. The IVF hasn't worked. We did better without it. I'm miserable and numb, but I'm not grief-stricken because there was never a baby. At least I tried; otherwise I'd always have wondered. The doctor in Athens, perhaps preoccupied with spending Christmas with his children, has no answer for why it didn't work when all the signs were so good and just suggests we schedule another round.

My usual rule of thumb is to listen to what my body tells me I need – for example, when I need meat or sleep. But perhaps that rule doesn't work in this case. Or maybe my head is telling me to keep trying, but my body's telling me to stop. Too much swimming against the current.

There's a silver lining to every cloud. I will get to spend Christmas on the island for the first time, enjoying the therapeutic effects of walking in the rain, wind and sun, high on hilltops.

Village kids come around to the house on Christmas Eve to sing carols. I learn that Santa comes on New Year's Eve in Greece, not Christmas Eve (well of course, he can't be everywhere at once, can he?). People in Tilos don't celebrate Christmas in a big way, but we arrange to meet Ian and Sibylle and Edward at Kali Kardia. New people have taken over the taverna this year and expanded the menu, turning it into an even more inviting place to eat and drink.

We spend New Year's Eve with the same little international group of friends at Ayios Antonis. Because they have cats we must leave Lisa at home, and she looks betrayed as she stands at the top of the steps with dark sad eyes, so I feed her a treat as we go. As the evening progresses, Stelios keeps looking at the clock, as anything after ten seems late now he's fishing again. So there's no danger of missing midnight

– though we might have otherwise, with no television, no mobile phone reception, no other people about. We all take our champagne glasses outside, stand on the end of the jetty at the end of the island, surrounded by sea and dark hills, and look up at the thousands of bright stars.

At the start of the new year, Lisa is looking glum on the couch. After a flash rainstorm that burned out my computer's power cable in the morning, the clouds have cleared, so I pick up the lead, and she leaps up and is at the gate in seconds, stretching and raring to go.

We head down into Potamia. Every day it seems, more bright flowers are emerging, purple and yellow and white. Living so close to nature, I notice the cycle of the seasons more. It emphasises the sense of continuity, the revolving circle of life that has gone on in similar ways century after century, just as those circular dances go on and on into the night at the summer festivals. Life has a constancy that feels secure. Friends return every year, and we follow paths made by others long ago.

Waving to Menelaos, who is herding his sheep, we make our way past his farm and then down the path towards Skafi, and have almost reached the beach when the rain abruptly starts again. I look back and see the sky full of heavy clouds; we're going to get wet, one way or another. Lisa stops to shake the rain off her wet fur every few minutes. We make it into the shelter of the cave. The bay grows pale as the rain becomes more intense, noisy as heavy drops hit the sea, the horizon hidden in cloud. Lisa stares out with me.

The elemental, physical life on this island makes me more whole, grounds me and inspires me. The island is fluid in its boundaries, as the shoreline and beaches change every year, shaped by the sea and the storms that move the rocks and the sand. The view is ever-changing because of the weather – clouds change the colours, wind changes the sea's mood and its direction determines which islands we can see on the horizon. The island's population is fluid, too, evolving as people come and go and bring new life. Births and deaths. The island evolves with its new roads and the old houses being restored or falling down. *No man is an island, entire of itself... Any man's death diminishes me.*

We also must adapt and change. If what life brings is not what you asked Saint Fanourios for, maybe you were asking for the wrong thing. And breaking out of our own boundaries is how we evolve, even if it is frightening sometimes. Like the community of a small island, sometimes we need to break the rules. Sometimes, things are better when the people take matters into their own hands and create their own rules. *The People's Republic of Tilos... An octopus in my ouzo.*

The rain seems to be clearing. Within minutes the hillsides are bright with sunshine. Lisa chews a stick thoughtfully, then rolls around on the pebbles in sheer pleasure. The horizon becomes a distinct line again, with a half-rainbow appearing above it, and the sea in front of me becomes clear and blue. I strip off wellies, two pairs of socks, jumpers... and as a great rumble and crack of thunder comes, I dive in.

Keh tou khronou. Happy New Year.

Epilogue

This is a love story of sorts, but it's not a conventional one. Real life is complicated. Neat endings to life usually aren't good. Thankfully, our stories go on, with twists and turns.

Will it ruin the ending if I tell you that Stelios and I split up soon after? I believe we'd have been a happy family; it often seemed we were at our best as parents of Lisa, and we were a good team on our various projects. But we weren't always such a happy couple, or maybe we just went through too much, too soon. In all the excitement of what we were doing, I think I had forgotten how important language and communication are. The truth is something of a mystery, but I want this to be a celebration of the time we spent together, muddling along happily as we did through those years.

Looking after Lisa has taught me that being a single mother would probably have been extremely tough in a remote place without friends and family around all the time. Hats off to single parents who manage it.

Whatever happened to the dead seahorse? Well, Lisa ate it, of course.

Life on a Greek island has changed me. It can be challenging at times, but for me it's never, ever been boring. Many things big and small have changed since the end of this story and I'm sure they'll continue to. But my appetite for the wild beauty of Tilos continues unabated. Perhaps you share it. Perhaps I'll see you one day on the footpath.

Na ziseteh! May you live!

Food for a Greek Island

As you've probably gathered, I love food... but usually eat quite simply at home. More often than not, I'll put together a big salad from whatever is fresh, along with some olives and feta cheese, oregano and lashings of olive oil. When they're in season, I'll salt some aubergine then rinse and cook in olive oil a big pan with onion and tomato, green pepper or zucchini. In winter I'll make vegetable soup and bake bread, or put meat and potatoes in the oven to roast for a couple of hours with fresh lemon. And apple or walnut cake is often a good idea.

I like recipes to be simple; I generally leave the more labour-intensive dishes like dolmades and moussaka to the experts, and eat them when I visit my favourite tavernas. But the following recipes are worth the effort when you have time, and are a taste of Greece beyond the more obvious ones that we all know and love.

Beetroot *(Pantzaria)* in Lemon and Garlic

My favourite part of this is the leaves, but they need to be fresh. The best way to get beetroot with fresh leaves attached is to grow your own! It's also important to have good extra virgin olive oil, Greek if possible.

Makes a meze plate for 4 to share

3–4 beetroots (depending on their size)
2 cloves garlic, grated
1 fresh lemon
3 tbsp olive oil

Cut off the beetroot stalks a couple of centimetres above the top of the roots, but leave on the skins. Wash off excess dirt, put them in a large pan and cover with water. Bring to the boil and then reduce the heat and simmer until they are soft. This will usually take 30 to 40 minutes. Remove from the pan and leave for five to ten minutes until cool enough to handle, then peel off the skins – sometimes easier to do under a cold tap.

Thoroughly wash the stalks and leaves, and remove the stalks from the leaves. Discard the dirty water from the pan, pour in a centimetre or so of fresh water – just enough to steam the stalks and leaves. Add the stalks first to boiling water, then a few minutes later add the leaves. Cook until they've just darkened and wilted, then drain.

When they're cool enough to handle, hold them together and chop into bite-sized lengths.

Place in a serving dish and sprinkle with garlic, pour the squeezed lemon juice and olive oil over the top and serve.

To make into more of a meal, you can add walnuts and feta cheese (ideally a creamy feta such as Dodoni).

Chickpea Fritters *(Revithokeftedes)*

Finger food to eat with ouzo. Don't skimp on the flavourings, as chickpeas can be a little bland otherwise. The fritters keep well in the fridge.

Makes 20–24 (serves 8)

250 g chickpeas

1 medium onion

1 clove garlic

Handful fresh parsley and dill

Half a green pepper

1 egg

50 g slice creamy feta

Salt and pepper

Sunflower or other oil for frying

50 g flour

Soak the chickpeas overnight unless using tinned; boil for half an hour until beginning to soften, then drain. Rub to remove some of the skins, and leave to dry on a tea towel. It's possible to soak them in baking soda to help remove the skins, if you like; the skins will start to come off otherwise as you mash them. Mash or smash the chickpeas into a rough paste, leaving some small pieces;

you can do this in a food processor if you have one or with a potato masher, or put them in a clean plastic bag and squash them using a jar or bottle.

Finely chop the onion, garlic, parsley and dill and green pepper, and crumble the cheese. Combine with the chickpea mix and egg, and add plenty of salt and pepper to form a firm dough. Use a little flour if needed to bind. Form the dough into small flattish rounds like falafel, and leave on a plate in the fridge for an hour.

Bring back to room temperature, then while you heat a couple of centimetres of oil in a deep frying pan, dredge the fritters with flour. Fry them a few at a time to cook through (5–10 minutes each) until golden on the outside, and place on kitchen towel to absorb excess oil before serving.

Baked Butter Beans *(Gigantes)*

Cooking butter beans – known as *gigantes* or 'giant beans' – takes a while but is worth it. Perfect for a cold day when the house needs warming up. They make a hearty dinner, taste great the next day, and provide good energy for walking.

Makes about 6–8 servings

500 g dried butter beans

3 tbsp olive oil

1 large or 2 medium onions, chopped

3 cloves garlic, chopped

3 medium-sized carrots, chopped

2–3 large tomatoes, chopped

2 tbsp tomato puree

1 tbsp chopped parsley

1 tbsp wild celery leaf (selino) or 1 chopped stick fresh celery

Salt and pepper to taste

Soak 500 g of dried beans overnight, then the next day drain them, add fresh water, and boil them for an hour or more until al dente, not soft. Don't add salt now as it toughens the beans. Rinse the beans and leave to sit in enough fresh water just to cover them.

In another large pan, fry the onion first. Chop and gradually add the garlic, tomatoes and carrots, then the tomato puree, and simmer for 10 minutes. Then add the beans and water. Cook together for 10 minutes to start the flavours infusing, stir in fresh chopped parsley and celery, and simmer for another 5 minutes. Then tip it all into an oven dish, adding a splash of water if needed to ensure there's juice covering most of the beans, and sprinkle with salt and pepper. Bake in a medium hot oven for 2 hours or more, stirring every 30 minutes or so and adding water if needed, until the beans are soft and splitting open, with crispy bits at the edges of the dish.

Serve with wine and bread.

Prawns and Fennel in Ouzo
(a variation on *Garides Saganaki*)

The tiny, sweet shrimp found around Tilos are eaten whole, shell and all, fried in oil, a simple meze to eat on their own with retsina or ouzo. But this dish is made with larger prawns and can be created anywhere, and can be eaten as a main course. If you can't get ouzo, white wine will do as the fennel gives an aniseed flavour. Some recipes cook the whole thing in one pan, adding the shrimp and ouzo to the sauce.

Makes 4 servings

2–3 tbsp olive oil

1 onion, sliced

1 clove garlic, finely chopped

3 large tomatoes, chopped

½ tsp dried oregano

1 fennel bulb, thinly sliced

500 g medium prawns without shells (defrosted if frozen)

2 tbsp ouzo

Pinch salt

100 g feta cheese (optional)

Black pepper

Heat half the olive oil in a frying pan or saucepan and fry the onion until turning translucent. Add the garlic and fry for a few minutes, then add the chopped tomatoes and oregano, and continue to cook for a few minutes more until the tomatoes are turning soft and juicy. Then add the thinly sliced fennel, and cook for around 10 minutes until soft.

In a separate large frying pan with a lid, heat the rest of the olive oil and then add the prawns. Once they begin to turn pink and cook through, add the ouzo; you can also add a splash of water if needed; when the prawns are opaque and cooked through, add salt and pour the tomato sauce into the pan, and stir to mix, then crumble the feta on the top if using, cover the pan with the lid and simmer for a few minutes.

Grind black pepper over the top and serve with bread.

Beef Stifado

It's the aroma of the sauce that makes this dish. You can use rabbit, but one of the best tavernas on the island does a beef or veal stifado that melts in the mouth. Thanks to my friend Yiannis' grandmother for her help.

Makes 4 servings

100 ml extra virgin olive oil
1 kg stewing beef, cut into large pieces
1 kg shallots
Large glass red wine (or small glass red wine and a large splash each of vinegar and brandy)
2 large tomatoes, chopped
1 tbsp tomato paste
2 bay leaves
Sprig rosemary or tsp oregano
3 allspice berries or 1 tsp cumin
3 cloves
Cinnamon stick
Pinch nutmeg
Salt and pepper

Peel the shallots; placing them in hot water will make it easier. Heat the oil in a large pan or casserole dish (it will need a lid), and sauté the meat slowly until partially cooked. Add the shallots to sauté them until just beginning to soften. The secret is to cook the meat slowly and not to overcook the shallots, so they retain their shape.

Add the wine (and the vinegar and brandy if using) and simmer for a few minutes.

Add the tomato, tomato paste and all the herbs and spices, stirring to blend while it returns to a boil. Then reduce the heat, cover with the lid and simmer for an hour and a half or so. Check from time to time and add water if necessary to stop it from sticking – you're aiming for a thick stew with a little sauce, not a soup – then replace the lid.

You can transfer it if you prefer from the stove to an oven preheated to 170°C, and at the same time roast some potatoes, quartered lengthways and placed in a baking dish with oil, water and lemon, to serve with the stifado. Otherwise, it's traditional to serve it with pasta, orzo or *hilopita*. Add salt to the dish towards the end to taste.

Semolina Halva

This is a dessert that can be eaten warm or cold at any time of day, and keeps well in the fridge. Most recipes are measured in cups as that's the easiest way, and use a combination of honey and sugar.

Makes 8–12 servings

2 cups sugar

5 cups water

Peel of 1 lemon or orange

2 cinnamon sticks

3 cloves

½ cup honey

1 cup olive oil

2 cups dry semolina

⅓ cup sultanas

½ cup walnuts, crushed fine

Into a medium saucepan, add water and sugar and stir as it heats on high. Add the rind of a fresh orange or lemon, cinnamon and cloves and boil for a few minutes. Then stir in the honey until melted. Remove the rind and whole spices with a slatted spoon or fork, and move to a low heat to keep the syrup warm.

In a larger pan heat the olive oil to hot, then stir in the dry semolina little by little with a wooden spoon, keeping it moving as the oil is absorbed. Add the walnuts, then keep stirring on a lower heat as it toasts to a darker, tea-like colour. Remove from the heat to add the sultanas.

Now we add the syrup slowly to the semolina mixture – very carefully, as we're adding syrup to hot oil so it's likely to whoosh and splutter a little! The syrup is absorbed as you stir to combine the two mixtures. Keep stirring it over a low heat for a few minutes to be sure all the syrup is absorbed.

Press the mixture into bowls. You can eat it warm right away, or and leave to cool then set in the fridge. Use small individual bowls, or a large bowl to make one large cake that can be cut into slices; or if you have silicone muffin cups, as I do, those are perfect for making lovely individual servings!

Sprinkle with cinnamon to serve. The sharpness of Greek yoghurt and fruit also accompanies it beautifully. In Crete, it may be served with a shot of raki.

Acknowledgements

This book is for Mum and Dad.

Thank you to all the readers who wrote to say they'd gained pleasure or inspiration from something I'd written – this is your fault for encouraging me.

Thanks to Stelios for allowing me to write about you. Thanks to everyone else who's in the book for the same reason, but especially Anna for also reading the manuscript at an early stage and helping so much. I stole quite a few good lines from you, but you were too kind to say. Thanks to others – you know who you are – for reading and suggestions and encouragement, and as always to my family for love and support.

Thanks to my brilliant agent, Caroline Hardman, and to all at Summersdale Publishers, including Abbie Headon for enthusiasm about the idea and editorial suggestions; to Madeleine Stevens for kind and often inspired editorial direction; to Chris Turton for steering the book through the publishing process and responding calmly to my moments of panic that it was all wrong; to Lizzie Curtin for publicity and the whole sales team for working so zealously to ensure people can actually find the book. I'm very grateful for the opportunity to keep writing. Thanks to Andy Bridge for a fabulous cover.

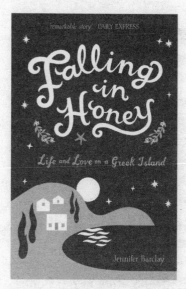

FALLING IN HONEY
Life and Love on a Greek Island

Jennifer Barclay

Paperback

ISBN: 978 1 84953 271 6

£8.99

**I came here looking for some kind of happiness.
I think it might be the cleverest thing I have ever done.**

One heartbroken winter, Jennifer decides to act on her dream of moving to a tiny Greek island – because life is too short not to reach out for what makes us happy.

Funny, romantic and full of surprising twists, *Falling in Honey* is a story about relationships, tzatziki, adventures, swimming, Greek dancing, starfish... and a bumpy but beautiful journey into Mediterranean sunshine.

*'This book will make you laugh and cry again.
I didn't want it to end.'*

Emma Woolf

*'Captures the gentle pace of island life with great charm.
A joy to read.'*

Harry Bucknall

Have you enjoyed this book?

If so, why not write a review on your favourite website?
If you're interested in finding out more about our books,
find us on Facebook at **Summersdale Publishers**
and follow us on Twitter at **@Summersdale**.

Thanks very much for buying this Summersdale book.

www.summersdale.com